ACOUSTIC GUITAR

National Guitar Workshop Method

C000158023

Beginning • Intermediate • Mastering

GREG HORNE

*Alfred, the leader in educational music publishing,
and the National Guitar Workshop,
one of America's finest guitar schools, have joined
forces to bring you the best, most progressive
educational tools possible. We hope you will enjoy
this book and encourage you to look for
other fine products from Alfred and the
National Guitar Workshop.*

CONTENTS

 Contents printed on 100% recycled paper.

 Alfred Music Publishing Co., Inc.
P.O. Box 10003
Van Nuys, CA 91410-0003
alfred.com

ISBN-10: 0-7390-6638-2 (Book & CD)
ISBN-13: 978-0-7390-6638-6 (Book & CD)

Cover photographs
Clockwise from upper left: Photodisc; Karen Miller; Jeff Oshiro; Planet Art.
Series: Karen Miller/Ted Engelbart, Greg McKinney; Photodisc.

ZENITH MUSIC
Stirling Highway
Claremont 6010
Western Australia

BEGINNING ACOUSTIC GUITAR

This book was acquired, edited, and produced
by Workshop Arts, Inc., the publishing arm of
the National Guitar Workshop.
Nathaniel Gunod, acquisitions, managing editor
Timothy Phelps, interior design
Joe Bouchard, music typesetter
CD recorded and mastered by Collin Tilton at Bar None Studio, Cheshire, CT

TABLE OF CONTENTS

ABOUT THE AUTHOR

PHOTO · STUART RABINOWITZ

Greg Horne is a performer, writer, producer and teacher. He holds a Bachelor of Arts in Music from the College of Wooster, and pursued graduate studies at the University of Mississippi's Center for the Study of Southern Culture. Greg has been an instructor at the National Guitar Workshop's summer campuses since 1990, specializing in acoustic and blues courses. He also teaches privately. In 1998, he produced an album of original songs entitled "Floating World." Greg has produced albums for singer-songwriters Deirdre Flint and Jodie Manross. He lives in Knoxville, Tennessee, where he fronts a rock'n'roll band, plays old-time fiddle and writes songs.

00

Track 01

An MP3 CD is included with this book to make learning easier and more enjoyable. The symbol shown at bottom left appears next to every example in the book that features an MP3 track. Use the MP3s to ensure you're capturing the feel of the examples and interpreting the rhythms correctly. The track number below the symbol corresponds directly to the example you want to hear (example numbers are above the icon). All the track numbers are unique to each "book" within this volume, meaning every book has its own Track 1, Track 2, and so on. (For example, *Beginning Acoustic Guitar* starts with Track 1, as does *Intermediate Acoustic Guitar* and *Mastering Acoustic Guitar*.) Track 1 for each book will help you tune your guitar.

To access the MP3s on the CD, place the CD in your computer's CD-ROM drive. In Windows, double-click on My Computer, then right-click on the CD icon labeled "MP3 Files" and select Explore to view the files and copy them to your hard drive. For Mac, double-click on the CD icon on your desktop labeled "MP3 Files" to view the files and copy them to your hard drive.

INTRODUCTION

Welcome to *The Complete Acoustic Guitar Method,* a comprehensive series of books designed specifically for the modern acoustic guitarist. *The Complete Acoustic Guitar Method* consists of three separate volumes now available in this one compilation. Each of the three volumes (*Beginning Acoustic Guitar, Intermediate Acoustic Guitar* and *Mastering Acoustic Guitar*) incorporates rhythm playing, soloing, easy-to-understand music theory and exciting techniques.

This first book, *Beginning Acoustic Guitar,* is designed for the beginning guitarist. By the time you complete this book, you will be able to do the following:

1. Read music in the first position.
2. Play all of the major and minor open chords.
3. Play a variety of strums that sound great for folk, rock and bluegrass styles.
4. Play the two most popular barre chord forms.
5. Play a blues chord progression and improvise a blues solo.
6. Fingerpick in basic arpeggio and alternating bass patterns.

HOW TO USE THIS BOOK:

The individual lessons in this book are grouped by subject into chapters. Once you have covered the basic material in Chapter 1, you can skip around to different chapters in the book. Each chapter is progressive, meaning each lesson builds on the previous ones in that chapter. You may want to work your way through a couple of chapters at a time, alternating lessons for variety.

WHERE TO GO FROM HERE:

This book will give you the foundation of skills needed to study any style of guitar. You can continue in this series, or use this volume to get you ready for other National Guitar Workshop/ Alfred methods. Here are some suggestions, depending on your personal goals.

IF YOUR GOAL IS...

To learn more about rock, jazz, or blues improvisation and chords...

THEN TRY... *The Complete Rock Guitar Method, The Complete Jazz Guitar Method* and/or *The Complete Blues Guitar Method* and some of the 20 different *Stand Alone* play-along CDs.

To learn more about fingerstyle guitar, check out *The Complete Fingerstyle Guitar Method.*

This volume is dedicated to my family and my music teachers. Special thanks to Lou Manzi, David Smolover, Nat Gunod, Jody Fisher and Seth Austen.

CHAPTER 1

Getting Started

This chapter is a review of basic materials. If you already read music and tablature, know how to find any note on the guitar, know some basic chords (such as D, A, G, E and C) and are familiar with basic technique, you can skip this chapter and begin with Chapter 2 which begins on page 16. But before you do, thumb through this chapter and make sure you understand all the material.

LESSON 1: GETTING TO KNOW YOUR TOOLS

TIPS FOR LEFTIES

This series of books is oriented toward right-handed guitar playing. Many left-handed players play guitar right-handed. Others can simply reverse the instructions found in this series.

THE PARTS OF THE GUITAR

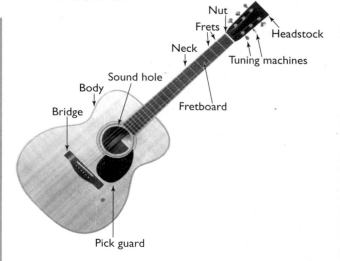

THE NATURAL CURVE

The shoulders, arms, hands and fingers all function best in a relaxed position. Hold your wrist and fingers in a loosely curled position. Any time you flex your wrist or fingers against their natural curve, you put a strain on the ligaments and tendons that control your fingers. This can result in pain and injury.

 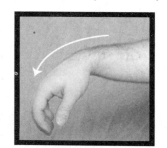

HOLDING THE GUITAR

There are several ways to hold the guitar. They are all governed by the same principle: *relax and follow the natural curves of the body.* Place your guitar so that your back is straight and your hands have easy access to the guitar without stretching or straining. The photos below show some commonly used positions:

Classical   *Folk*   *Standing*

THE LEFT-HAND POSITION

Your left hand should follow a gentle curve through the wrist and fingers. Place your thumb behind the neck, parallel to the frets. Touch the guitar with the pad of your thumb and your fingertips only. Keep your wrist slightly curved and your hand open, as if there was an imaginary golf ball in your palm.

Finger Numbers

Your left-hand fingers are numbered as follows:

Index	=	1st Finger
Middle	=	2nd Finger
Ring	=	3rd Finger
Pinky	=	4th Finger

FRETTING NOTES

To fret a note, press your finger just to the left of the fret you want to play. Do not play on top of the fret. We often think in terms of *position*. A position is one finger per fret over a four-fret span. A position is defined by which fret your 1st finger is on. For example, in 1st position, your 1st finger plays the 1st fret. In 10th position, your 1st finger plays the 10th fret.

THE PICK

Most of this book is oriented toward playing with a *pick* (also known as a *flatpick* or *plectrum*). These are available in a wide variety of shapes and sizes. As you begin, try using a standard, teardrop-shaped pick in a medium or heavy gauge. These allow a great deal of control and more tone from the guitar than the thinner picks. Later, you may want to experiment with different picks. This book may also be studied with the use of a *thumbpick* (see the Appendix on page 92).

Top

Actual size

Point

HOLDING THE PICK

Place your right-hand thumb across the top of the pick, with the point at a 90-degree angle from your thumb. Then, curve your index finger behind the pick of the pick, holding it between your thumb and the side of the first joint of your index finger. Your other fingers can curl into your palm or hang loosely. Just keep them relaxed.

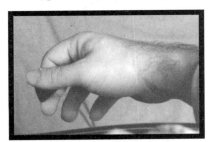

TUNING

The strings can be tuned to a piano, a tuner or to themselves. To tune to a piano, match the strings to the keys as shown. To tune the strings to each other, follow Steps 1 through 6 shown on the right. Play an open string, then play the matching note on the next lower string. Tune the open string up or down until the notes match exactly. Tuning takes practice, and you may want to enlist the help of an experienced player. See page 93 for more information about tuning. When tuning the guitar to itself, start from the lowest sounding strings and work up to the highest.

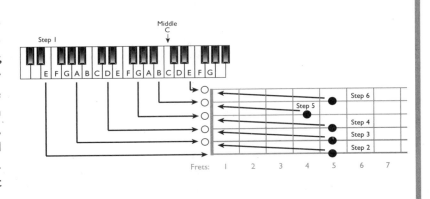

The trick to learning the notes on the fingerboard is understanding the musical alphabet. This is easy. You only need to remember four things:

1. The musical alphabet goes from A to G, then starts over again with A:

> A B C D E F G A B C and so on

This series of seven notes, called *natural notes*, repeats in a continuous cycle.

2. The shortest distance between two notes is a half step.

The closest one note can be to another is the distance of one fret. The distance between two notes that are on adjacent frets is called a *half step*. For example, from the 1st fret to the 2nd fret is a half step. The distance of two frets is called a *whole step*. For example, from the 1st fret to the 3rd fret is a whole step.

> Half step   =   One Fret
> Whole step   =   Two Frets

3. In the musical alphabet, two sets of notes are only one half step apart.

> B to C is a half step
> E to F is a half step

There is no note between B and C, or between E and F. All the other natural notes are separated by one whole step.

4. Special symbols called *accidentals* are used to name the notes between the natural notes. Remember, there are no notes between E and F, or B and C.

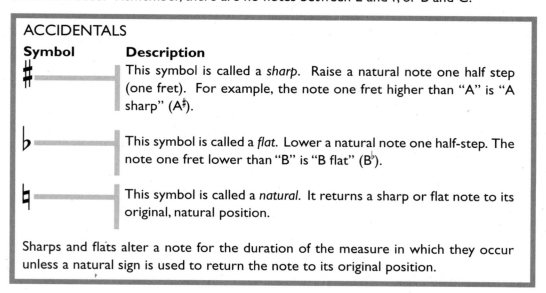

ACCIDENTALS

Symbol	Description
♯	This symbol is called a *sharp*. Raise a natural note one half step (one fret). For example, the note one fret higher than "A" is "A sharp" (A♯).
♭	This symbol is called a *flat*. Lower a natural note one half-step. The note one fret lower than "B" is "B flat" (B♭).
♮	This symbol is called a *natural*. It returns a sharp or flat note to its original, natural position.

Sharps and flats alter a note for the duration of the measure in which they occur unless a natural sign is used to return the note to its original position.

All sharp notes can have a flat name, and all flat notes can have a sharp name. For example, A♯ and B♭ fall on the same fret. Two notes that have different names but have the same sound are called *enharmonic equivalents*.

Practice saying the music alphabet forward and backward. Remember that as you go forward through the alphabet, the notes get higher in pitch. As you go backward, the notes get lower in pitch.

THE STRINGS
Your strings are tuned to the following pitches, low string to high:

Note:	E	A	D	G	B	E
String:	6	5	4	3	2	1

One fun way to remember this is to use the first letter of each word in this sentence:

Eat **A**t **D**ave's, **G**et **B**etter **E**ggs

Start on any open string and follow the alphabet series up the neck. Check your answers on the chart at the bottom of the page.

For example: Going up the 6th or 1st (E) string (either one):

Open	= E	7th fret	=
1st fret	= F	8th fret	=
2nd fret	= F♯ or G♭	9th fret	=
3rd fret	= G	10th fret	=
4th fret	= G♯ or A♭	11th fret	=
5th fret	=	12th fret	=
6th fret	=		

NOTE:

Notice that the 12th fret brings you back to where you started. You have gone an *octave* (distance of twelve half steps)—one cycle through the alphabet! This is why we say the guitar neck "starts over" at the 12th fret.

Here are all the notes on the guitar neck from the open string to the 12th fret:

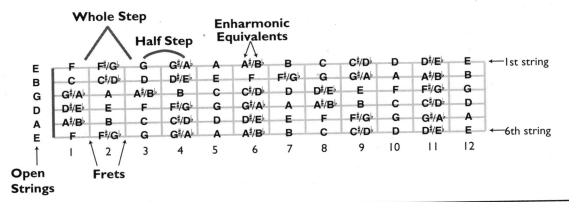

Open Strings   Frets

Now that we've covered the basics, it's time to play a few melodies.

TABLATURE

Tablature, called *TAB* for short, is a system of writing music just for the guitar. It tells you what fret to play and what string to play it on.

When fretting notes, try to get your finger as close to the fret as possible without being on top of it. This will produce clear, ringing notes with a minimum of buzzing or other unwanted noises.

The long, horizontal lines represent the strings. The top line is the 1st string (high E) and the bottom line is the 6th string (low E). Try fingering the notes indicated using any left-hand finger:

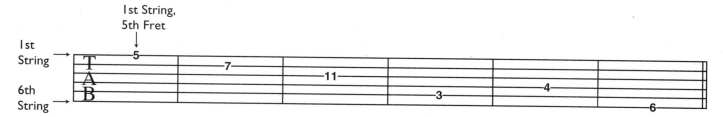

SECRETS OF THE MASTERS
The dots on your guitar neck (if you have any) will help you keep track of the frets. The dots usually come on frets 3, 5, 7, 9 and 12. Look at your guitar and familiarize yourself with where the dots are.

TAB is often attached to written music, so the player will know how long the notes last and what they are. The following examples show TAB and standard music notation. If you do not yet read music, DO NOT PANIC. If you like, you can look ahead to Chapter 2 (page 16) for information about reading standard notation. Or, just play the frets and strings indicated in the TAB in a slow, steady rhythm, giving each note equal length. The numbers under the TAB indicate the left-hand fingers (see page 7).

 COWS THAT BOOGIE ON MY LAWN

Track 2

Left-hand fingers: 3 2 0 2 3 2 0 2 0 3 2 0 3 3 3

If you're looking for a fun challenge, put down that crossword puzzle and instead try to name the notes you are playing from the TAB. Use the musical alphabet from Lesson 2. In *This One's Got Spots*, the note names are given. In *Mary Had a Border Collie*, you're on your own.

THIS ONE'S GOT SPOTS

Track 3

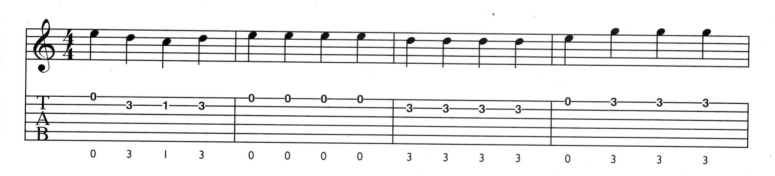

MARY HAD A BORDER COLLIE

Track 4

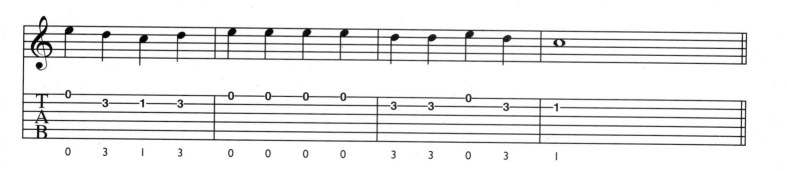

This lesson will get you started playing *chords* that you will use for the rest of your guitar-pickin' life. A chord is three or more notes sounded simultaneously. Each chord is named for the musical alphabet letter that serves as its *root*. The chords in this lesson are known as *open chords* because they use a mixture of *open* (unfingered) strings and fretted notes. They also occur in the first three or four frets of the fretboard.

> **SECRETS OF THE MASTERS:**
> **During this phase of your learning, it is more important to practice often than to practice for long periods. (For more on practicing, see page 94.)**

You will be building new pathways from your brain to your finger muscles. Like mountain trails, these paths need frequent clearing or they grow over and disappear. If you practice for 15-30 minutes every day, you *will* see improvement. On the other hand, if you wait several days between sessions, you will be starting at "ground zero" every time. It make take up to a few weeks before these chords start to feel natural. As you work on them, you may want to begin Chapter 2 to add some variety to your practice.

STRUMMING

One of the most common ways to play a chord is to *strum*. To strum, a pick, a single finger or all the fingers are moved rapidly across the strings, sounding them nearly simultaneously. A downstrum, indicated ⊓, is toward the floor. An upstrum, indicated V, is toward the ceiling.

GUITAR CHORD DIAGRAMS

Guitar chords are most often depicted in *chord diagrams*. A chord diagram is like a picture of the fretboard that shows which strings, fingers and frets you will use to make your chord.

Note that a circle (○) over a string means to strum that string open as part of your chord. An "✕" over a string means to omit that string from the strum. Watch carefully for these symbols and make sure to follow them.

Here is a sample chord diagram and a photograph for comparison:

"D" Chord

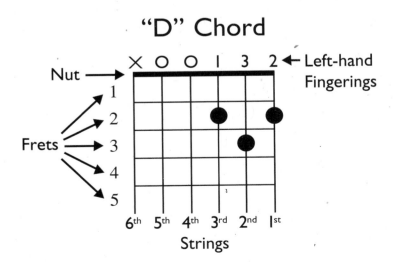

Here are your first three chords:

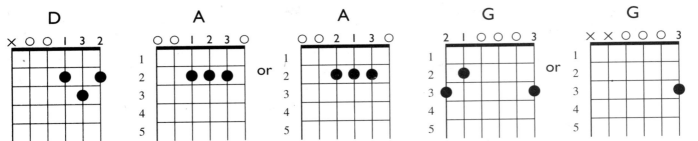

You may find that your fingers are too big to finger the A chord as shown. Try switching your 1st and 2nd fingerings so that the 1st finger is on the 3rd string, and the 2nd finger is on the 4th string. Some folks find that the G chord feels like too big a stretch at first. If that describes you, leave off the 2nd and 1st fingers, use the 3rd finger on the 1st string only, and strum just the upper four strings. When you are feeling a bit more limber, you can try the full chord form again.

Before you rush into trying to play your first song with chords, make sure that each chord is as clean and clear as it can be. While holding a chord with your left hand, pluck each string individually from the lowest string to the highest string. You may have to scoot your fingers around slightly to keep them from bumping into the adjacent strings or getting too far from or too close to the frets. Keep your fingers curved and your thumb behind the neck.

Once the chords are familiar, try strumming through *Canadian Campfire Song*. Use down strokes in time to a slow, even beat. It will help if you tap your foot and count the *beats* aloud. A beat is the basic unit of musical time. When you tap your foot, you are tapping the beats.

Canadian Campfire Song is written in *slash notation*. Each slash / indicates one beat. The song is divided into groups of four beats called *measures*. *Bar lines* separate the measures. Change chords as indicated. For example, in the first measure, start with a D chord and change to an A chord on the third beat. Count slowly enough to allow for changing chords without stopping the beat.

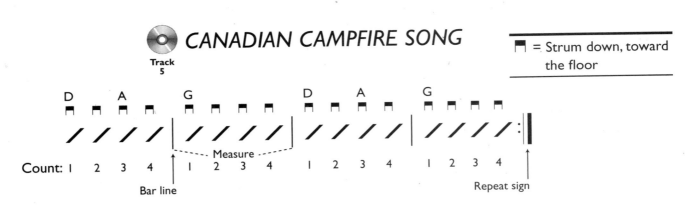

The repeat sign tells you to repeat the song from the beginning. Since this is a short sequence of chords, you may want to repeat it many times.

Remember, there is no need for physical pain and distress when learning the guitar. If your knuckles are turning white and there are shooting pains through your hands, you may be pressing too hard. Take it easy and your strength and accuracy (and calluses) will build in a short time.

LESSON 5: CHANGING CHORDS

Now that you've tried a few chords, here are some techniques to help your fingers learn to get to them faster:

FOUR-STEP FRETTING EXERCISE

This exercise is based on a classical guitar warm-up. Follow the steps slowly and steadily. Once you are familiar with the four steps, try them to the beat of a *metronome* set between 40 and 60 beats per minute. A metronome is an adjustable device used for determining the exact *tempo* (speed) of a piece. It is a great practice tool. (For more on metronomes, see page 93.)

1. Set .... Place your fingers lightly on the strings in the shape of the chord.

2. Press .... Press the fingers down on the frets simultaneously and strum the chord.

3. Set .... Relax pressure, without lifting fingers off strings.

4. Release .... Lift fingers off strings about ⅛ inch, holding fingers in the shape of the chord.

Repeat this process several times.

This exercise is a great way to help your fingers learn the different chords faster. Try it every time you practice and with every new chord you learn. Another benefit is that you will learn to use only the minimum amount of pressure you need to play the chord; it doesn't take as much as you may think!

SWITCHING CHORDS

The secret to good chord switching is learning to move your fingers simultaneously from one chord to another. The exercise you just learned will help your fingers get used to acting together to press down a chord.

Moving your fingers precisely in different directions at the same time is no easy trick. In order to get the hang of it, it is helpful to look at the switching process with a magnifying glass. Each chord switch is like a tiny dance step for your fingers. Learn the first few steps very carefully and with some concentration, and the whole dance will get easier and easier.

For example, look at the switch from D to A.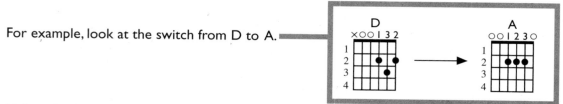

Make a D chord with your left hand. Now look at your hand and imagine where the fingers will need to go to make the A chord:

- The 1st finger moves from the 3rd to the 4th string, staying on the same fret (the 2nd fret).
- The 2nd finger jumps from the 1st to the 3rd string, also remaining on the 2nd fret.
- The 3rd finger slides from the 3rd to the 2nd fret on the 2nd string. It doesn't even have to lift up from the string!

Now try to move from D to A using the four-step exercise.

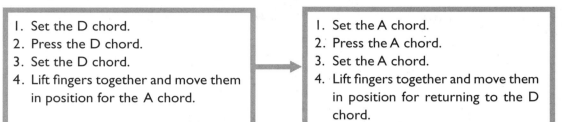

1. Set the D chord. 2. Press the D chord. 3. Set the D chord. 4. Lift fingers together and move them in position for the A chord.

1. Set the A chord. 2. Press the A chord. 3. Set the A chord. 4. Lift fingers together and move them in position for returning to the D chord.

Though this process may seem a little intense, it is actually a short-cut to switching chords cleanly and quickly. A little patience, persistence and focus in the beginning will pay off! Use this technique with each new chord combination you encounter. Try it a few times with D, A and G, then go back to *Canadian Campfire Song* and behold the magic.

LESSON 6: MORE CHORDS—E AND C

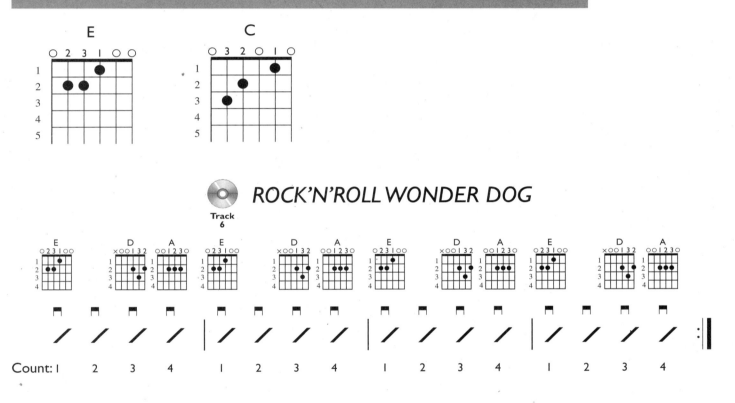

E   C

ROCK'N'ROLL WONDER DOG

Track 6

YOU MOVE MY BOOGIE MACHINE

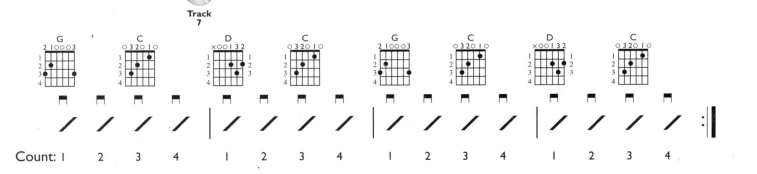

Track 7

CHAPTER 2

Reading Music

HOW TO USE THIS CHAPTER

This chapter will provide a quick introduction to reading music in the first position of the guitar neck (the first four frets and open strings). You may want to work through this chapter at the same time you are learning to play and strum the chords in Chapter 3 (page 28). This will add variety to your practice. Most of the examples in this chapter do not have tablature. Tablature is used throughout the rest of the book. You do not have to master reading music in order to work on the other chapters, since TAB is always available.

WHY READ MUSIC?

Reading music is a rewarding skill that is easier to develop than most people think. It enhances tablature and chord charts by allowing you to read exact rhythms, vocal melodies and music for other instruments. Even the most basic understanding of the notes on the staff (Lesson 1, below) will give you a point of departure for the concepts introduced later in this book.

LESSON 1: THE NOTES AND THE STAFF

We use five horizontal lines as a sort of "playing field" for our notes. This is called the *staff*. The *natural notes* (notes without sharps or flats) are laid out on the lines and spaces of the staff. Lower notes are near the bottom of the staff, higher notes are near the top. A *clef* sign at the beginning of the staff indicates which notes are represented by which lines and spaces. When the *G clef* sits on the second line from the bottom of the staff it is called *treble clef*. The line it encircles is called G.

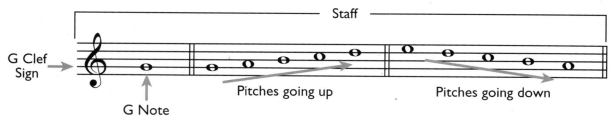

Now that you know the second line from the bottom is G, all the other notes can be related to that line. For example, the space under it is F, the note before G in the musical alphabet. The space above the G line is A, the next note in the musical alphabet.

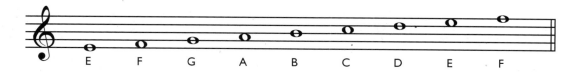

LEARNING THE NOTES ON THE STAFF

There are several memory devices you can use to quickly learn all the notes on the staff. One is to separate the notes on the lines and the notes in the spaces. The notes on the lines give you the first letter of each word of this sentence: "Every Good Beginner Does Fine." The notes in the spaces themselves spell the word "FACE."

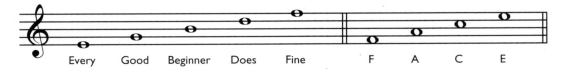

| Every | Good | Beginner | Does | Fine | | F | A | C | E |

LESSON 2: THE NOTES ON THE 1ST STRING

Reading notes on the staff is easier when you learn a few at a time. Each of the following lessons will add a few new notes. The first three are on the 1st string. Here's where they are on the staff and on the guitar:

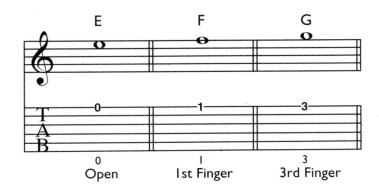

Here are some practice examples using E, F and G. First, make sure you can name all the notes easily. Then, try to play them in a slow, steady rhythm. Using your pick, play each note with a downward stroke. Use just the very tip of the pick, and don't hit the string too hard.

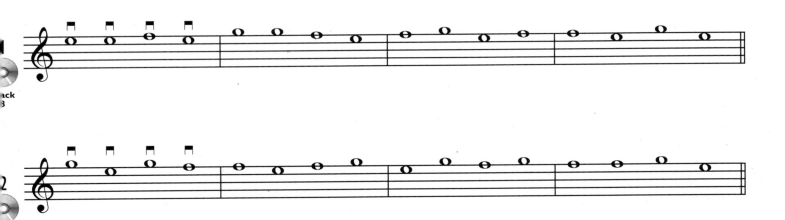

The first three notes on the second string are B, C and D.

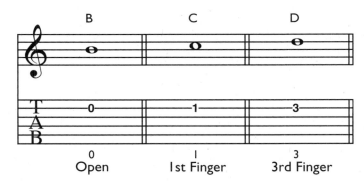

Try these playing examples. As in Lesson 2, pick all the notes with downstrokes. To speed along your learning, say the notes aloud before you play each line. Don't forget E, F and G! They return in these examples.

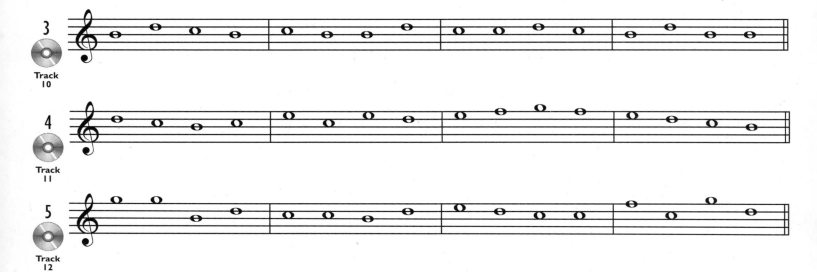

LESSON 4: TIME

The first part of this is a quick review of material you learned in Chapter 1. Read it anyway, as there are important new details.

GET THE BEAT
The *beat* is the steady, even pulse that remains constant throughout a passage of music. It is what the listener's foot taps along to.

THE MEASURE
Musicians count beats and divide them into small groups. As you know, a group of beats is called a measure. Measures can consist of any number of beats. One very common measure is a group of four. Measures are marked on the staff using bar lines. For this reason, measures are sometimes called *bars*. A double bar indicates the end of a passage of music or short example.

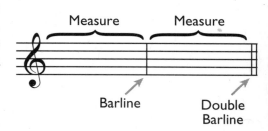

SIGNS OF THE TIMES

The *time signature* tells you how many beats are in a measure and which type of note gets one beat. It is found at the beginning of the piece. The upper number indicates the number of beats per measure. The lower number shows what type of note is one beat.

Time Signature

The time signature reads like a fraction, so ⁴⁄₄ could be read as "four quarters." This would mean that every measure has the equivalent of four quarter notes ♩, with each quarter note equaling one beat. Read on to learn about the different types of notes.

THE LONG AND SHORT OF IT

The *value* of a note is its duration (in beats). The appearance of a note tells us its value. Here are three note values and their durations:

Whole Note

The *whole note* lasts for four beats. Try playing these and counting aloud. Remember to pick the note at the same time you say "one" and let it ring all the way through "two, three, four." Keep the beat steady and even. Tap your foot while you count!

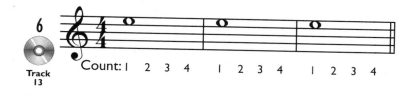

Track 13

Count: 1 2 3 4   1 2 3 4   1 2 3 4

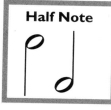
Half Note

The *half note* lasts for two beats. In a measure of four beats, the half notes start on beats "1" and "3." Notice that notes with stems sometimes have the stems going up and sometimes have the stems going down. Normally, notes on or above the middle line have their stems going down, and notes below the middle line have their stems going up.

Track 14

Count: 1 2 3 4   1 2 3 4   1 2 3 4

Quarter Note

The *quarter note* lasts for one beat. Play along with your counting.

Track 15

Count: 1 2 3 4   1 2 3 4   1 2 3 4

Now add D, E, F, G and A to your inventory of notes.

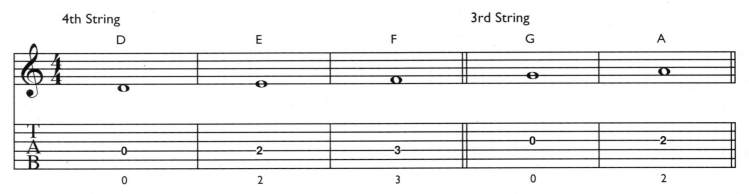

As you play these examples, remember the following:

1. Tap your foot in a slow, steady beat.
2. Count aloud.
3. Do not rush through the tunes. Give each note its full length.
4. Play each note with a downstroke of the pick.
5. Have fun. It's music!

9
Track 16

10
Track 17

Silence is as important a part of music as sound. The symbols that represent silence are called *rests,* and just like notes, they are measured into wholes, halves and quarters.

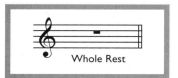

A *whole rest* is four beats of silence. It is a small rectangle that hangs like a full suitcase from the fourth line of the staff.

A *half rest* is two beats of silence. It is a small rectangle that sits like a hat on the third line of the staff.

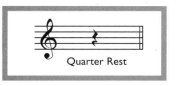

A *quarter rest* is one beat of silence. It looks a bit like a bird flying sideways.

SECRETS OF THE MASTERS
Rests must be "played" with the same precision and importance as pitches! To play a rest, you must stop the string or strings from ringing by using your pick or lifting up a fretted note with your left-hand finger to stop the sound.

The following examples use some of the notes and rests you've learned. Enjoy playing them.

The beat can be divided into smaller pieces to allow for faster notes. A quarter note can be divided into two *eighth notes*. Each eighth note lasts half of a beat. Eighth notes can appear alone (with *flags*) or connected in groups (with *beams*). The stems follow the same rules as for other notes: notes on or above the middle line of the staff have their stems going down, and notes below the middle line have their stems going up. An eighth rest looks like a slash with a small flag waving from it and it lasts for half a beat.

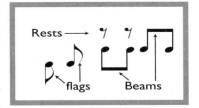

We can organize our note and rest values into a "tree" to help visualize the relationships.

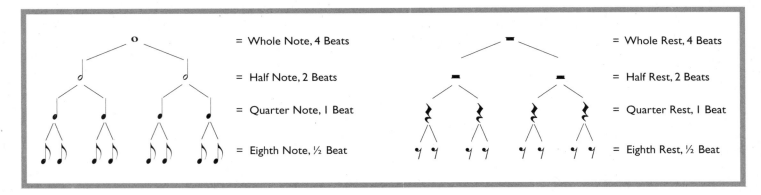

COUNTING EIGHTH NOTES

Eighth notes are counted by dividing the beats (counted "1, 2, 3, 4") into "1-&, 2-&, 3-&, 4-&." Tap on the numbered beats as before. Let's call these "on-beats" ⬛ (sometimes called *downbeats*). Move your foot up on the "&s" ("ands"). These are called "off-beats" ▬ (sometimes called *upbeats*). Try clapping or playing this example on one note while you count and tap.

13

| Count: | 1 | & | 2 | & | 3 | & | 4 | & | 1 | & | 2 | & | 3 | & | 4 | & | 1 | & | 2 | & | 3 | & | 4 | & |

Tap:

WHAT GOES DOWN MUST COME UP

To play eighth notes, use a downstroke of the pick (⊓) for the down-beat, and an upstroke (V) for the up-beat. As you play example 14, try to make the upstrokes sound identical in tone and quality to your downstrokes. Notice that your pick moves exactly the same as your tapping foot: down-up, down-up, down-up.

14

Track 20

SECRETS OF THE MASTERS
Play as steadily as a Swiss watch! By using a consistant down-up motion, you will have an easier time keeping the beat and playing smooth, graceful lines at any speed. Make a lifetime commitment to even down-up picking!

GOING DOWN LOW

In order to add the notes on the 5th and 6th strings, extra lines must be added to the staff. These are called *ledger lines*. As with the normal staff, a note may appear directly on a ledger line or in the space just below it. Here are the notes on the 5th and 6th strings.

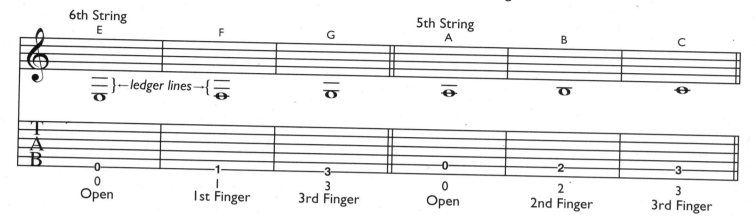

Examples 15, 16 and 17 will help you get used to reading notes with the ledger lines. Try to say the names of the notes aloud as you play them.

Notes on the 5th String

Notes on the 6th String

Notes on the 5th and 6th Strings

THE EIGHTH REST

For every note value, there is also a rest. You have learned quarter, half and whole rests. Remember that an eighth rest looks like a slash with a small flag waving from it and it lasts for half a beat. Unlike eighth notes, eighth rests are not beamed together in groups. They always appear individually.

DOTTED NOTES

A dot placed after a note head increases its duration by half the value of the note. For example, a half note equals two beats. Half of that value is one beat so if we dot a half note, it equals three beats ($2 + 1 = 3$).

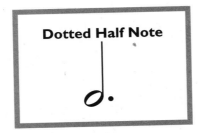

Dotted Half Note

The same logic applies to other note values. For example, a quarter note equals one beat. Half of that value is half a beat so a dotted quarter note equals one and one half beats ($1 + \frac{1}{2} = 1\frac{1}{2}$).

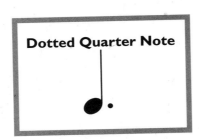

Dotted Quarter Note

Example 18 will give you some practice reading notes with dotted rhythms and eighth rests. To help you with the new rhythms, the counting is shown below the music. The numbers in parentheses are rests.

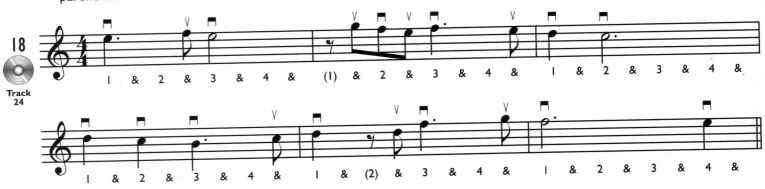

LESSON 10: ADDING SHARPS AND FLATS

ACCIDENTALS DO HAPPEN

Once you have become familiar with reading the natural notes, adding the accidentals (sharps and flats, see page 8) is simple. Here's a quick review:

> ♯ = Raises a natural note one half-step.
>
> ♭ = Lowers a natural note one half-step.
>
> ♮ = Cancels a sharp or flat, play the natural note.

In written music, a sharp or a flat will appear just before the note it affects.

> **IMPORTANT NOTE:**
>
> When a sharp or a flat appears on a note, that note remains affected by the sharp or flat until the end of the measure. In other words, a sharp or flat can be canceled only by a natural or a bar line. Remember: a sharp raises a note by one fret; a flat lowers a note by one fret.

Example 19 introduces some of the sharps and flats in the first position. Tablature has been included to help you find these new notes.

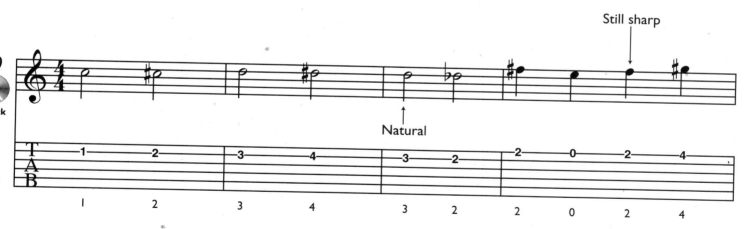

LESSON 11: READING KEY SIGNATURES

Most pieces of music have a *key*. A key is the *tonal center*—the note the piece revolves around. For example, in the key of C, the note C is the *tonic* or *keynote*. It's like home base for the key. Most pieces of music haveWhen you learn about the *major scale* (page 46), you'll discover how a key is really composed of a whole set of notes from a scale and the relationships between them.

A *key signature* appears just after the clef sign at the beginning of each line of music. It is a set of sharps or flats (never both) that are always found in the scale of that particular key. The key signature is a form of shorthand that helps prevent the music from getting too cluttered with accidentals.

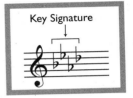

Reading a key signature is very simple. Look just to the right of the clef sign. Any sharps or flats that appear will affect that pitch throughout the entire piece of music.

For example, the key signature in the example on the right has an F♯ ("F sharp") and a C♯ ("C sharp"). This means that *all* of the F notes and *all* of the C notes will be sharped in this piece, unless otherwise marked.

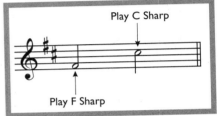

IMPORTANT NOTE:
Accidentals in key signatures affect the note in every octave, not just the line or space on which the accidental appears.

To learn which key signatures go with which keys, check out the *circle of 5ths* on page 47.

Try these examples. Tablature has been included to help you find the new notes. In the first example, the pitches affected by the key signature have been circled. Circle the affected notes in the second example.

LESSON 12: 1ST AND 2ND ENDINGS

1st and 2nd endings are used to add variety to a repeated passage of music. The first time through, play the 1st ending, then repeat the passage. On the repeat, skip over the 1st ending and play the 2nd ending instead. The piece may end at this point or it may continue on to a new section. The piece below, *Line Dancing on Mars*, follows this form:

1. Play up to and including the 1st ending.
2. Go back to the beginning and play up to the 1st ending, *skip* it and play the 2nd ending instead.
3. Continue on in the piece and play the new section, starting at the right-facing repeat sign after the 2nd ending.
4. Repeat the new section.

Line Dancing on Mars uses many of the elements you have learned in this chapter, including accidentals, rests, dotted rhythms and notes on each string. In addition, it includes 1st and 2nd endings. There is no TAB here so that you can practice your note reading. Have fun!

 LINE DANCING ON MARS

Track 28

CHAPTER 3

More New Chords

LESSON 1: MINOR CHORDS

The chords you have already learned are called "major" chords. You will learn the theory behind what makes them "major" in Chapter 5 of this book. Major chords tend to have a bright sound and are sometimes associated with a happy or hopeful emotion. In this section, you will learn the "minor" versions of some of these chords. Minor chords have a darker quality that can have a sad, melancholy or even sinister emotion. Of course, these associations are highly subjective. As with diet plans and stock investments, results may vary from one listener to another.

Minor chords are often abbreviated with "min" or a small "m." In this book, for example, an A Minor chord is marked *Amin*. Here are your first three minor chords:

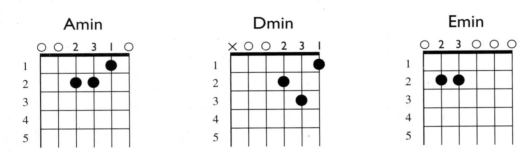

min = minor

Use downstrokes to strum the following progressions.

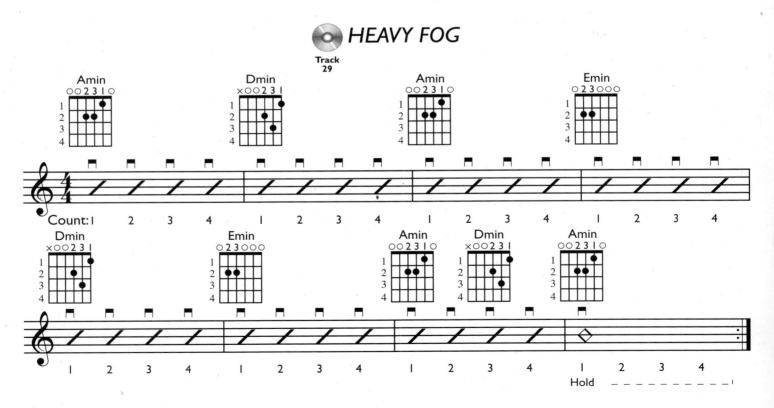

HEAVY FOG

Track 29

◇ = Whole note in rhythmic notation. Strum the chord once and hold it for four beats.

Minor chords can be mixed with major chords to give a more complete harmony and sense of movement to a song.

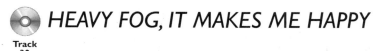

HEAVY FOG, IT MAKES ME HAPPY

Track 30

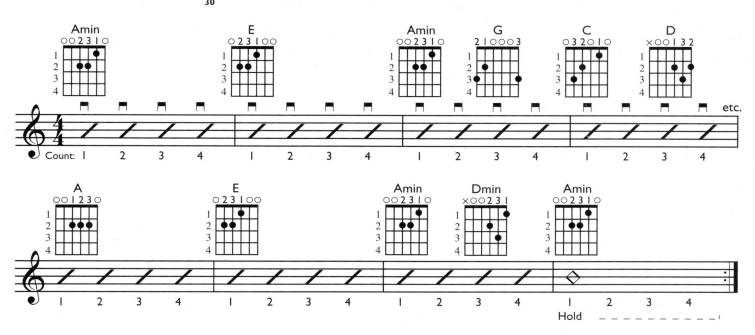

LESSON 2: THE BLUEGRASS G CHORD AND A C CHORD TO MATCH

BLUEGRASS G

Here's a new fingering for the G Major chord (page 13) you will definitely want to try. This fingering creates a new sound by putting the notes of the chord in a slightly different order. This version of the G chord has a big, bright sound. It is very common in bluegrass music. The early bluegrass guitar players often played in the key of G and used this voicing to cut through the sonic mayhem of banjos and fiddles. It has become a standard voicing used in rock, country and contemporary folk styles.

BLUEGRASS C

Try this new way of playing a C chord. It goes well with the bluegrass G chord because the G note on the 1st string is in both chords. This G note is called a *common tone* between the two chords.

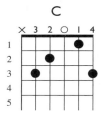

Try playing *The One-Human Garage Band*. To make it more fun, try strumming these chords with a firm snap of the wrist. This will make the chords louder and more percussive, and possibly frighten your pets. Remember that the two dots at the end mean repeat.

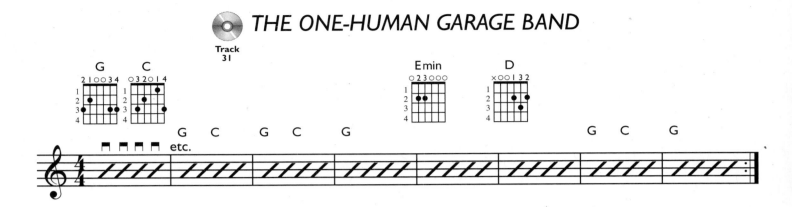

LESSON 3: THE ART OF STRUMMING

Once you are comfortable with at least a few of your basic chords, you can shift your attention from your left hand to your right hand and begin refining your strumming technique.

Here are some things to keep in mind when working on your strumming:

1. Keep your wrist loose and your arm relaxed.
2. Resist the urge to "tighten up" your muscles as you build up speed.
3. Work on developing a steady, even beat. You may want to try using a metronome (see the Appendix, page 93).

> **SECRETS OF THE MASTERS:**
> *To become a truly good rhythm guitarist you must develop an internal sense of rhythm that is steady and predictable. The best way to do this is to tap your foot on the beats and count aloud. Practice slowly and synchronize the movements of your hand with the tapping and counting.*

Rhythmic Notation
In the following examples, a new kind of notation is being introduced. This is a common way to show strumming rhythms when a specific rhythm is called for. The note values are indicated with slashes instead of circles for eighth notes and quarter notes, and with diamond-shaped heads for half notes and whole notes instead of open circles.

Whole   Half   Quarter   Eighths

Practice your strumming with the following rhythms:

Strum #1: Try this strum with a G chord using a steady down-up motion.

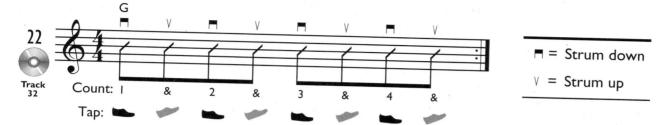

■ = Strum down

V = Strum up

Strum # 2: Here's one that mixes together quarter notes and eighth notes.

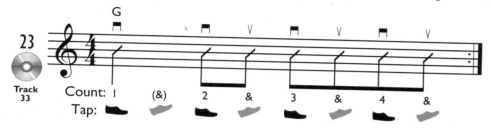

Strum # 3: Here's one that works well for folk songs and group singing. Also, try this with some of the progressions in earlier lessons.

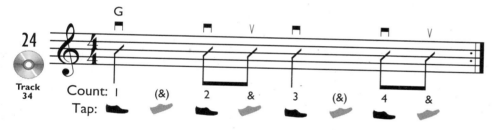

Train of Dreams is based on the folk song, *Midnight Special*. Play it with Strum # 3 (example 24). Remember to keep the beat steady! Use the bluegrass forms of G and C you learned on page 29. You may have to practice a bit to master switching between them.

TRAIN OF DREAMS

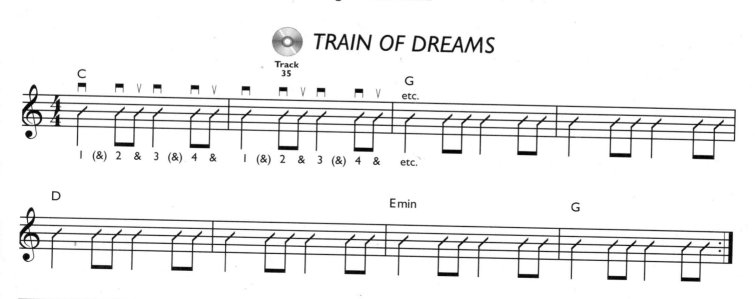

In the old days, the guitarist often had to serve the dual role of bass player and timekeeper. The roots of country, bluegrass and old-time guitar playing come from this style. The bass note of the chord is struck firmly, then the rest of the chord is strummed. What you get is the famous "boom-chick, boom-chick" rhythm.

Each chord has a *root* which the chord is named for. For example, the root of a C chord is "C." The root of an E chord is "E." You will want to play the lowest sounding root in the chord you are playing. Usually, we alternate between the root and another note called the "5th" of the chord. The "5th" is the fifth note above the root. For further explanation of the elements of chords, see Chapter 5 starting on page 45.

To help you, examples 25, 26 and 27 show the "boom-chick, boom-chick" strum written out on each chord you've learned so far. Repeat each one until it feels comfortable and secure. Note that on the C chord, you must move the 3rd finger to the 6th string to reach the alternating bass note.

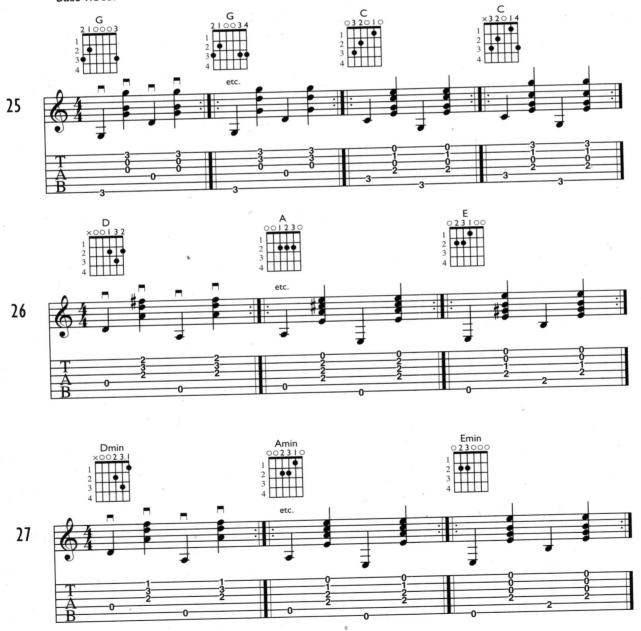

Below are a couple of real live bluegrass tunes for you to try. Use the strum patterns you learned on page 32. Have fun!

BOIL THAT CABBAGE DOWN

Track 36

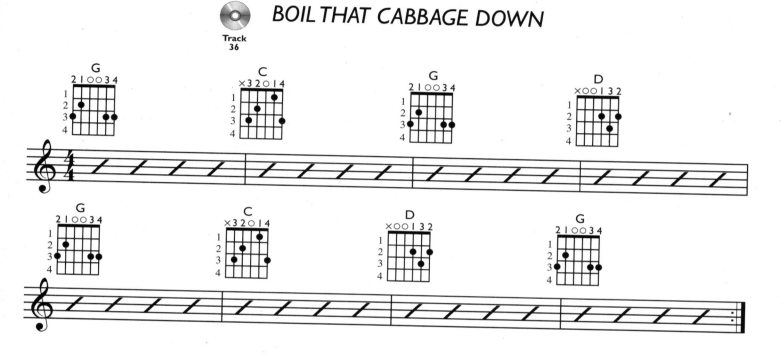

SHADY GROVE

Track 37

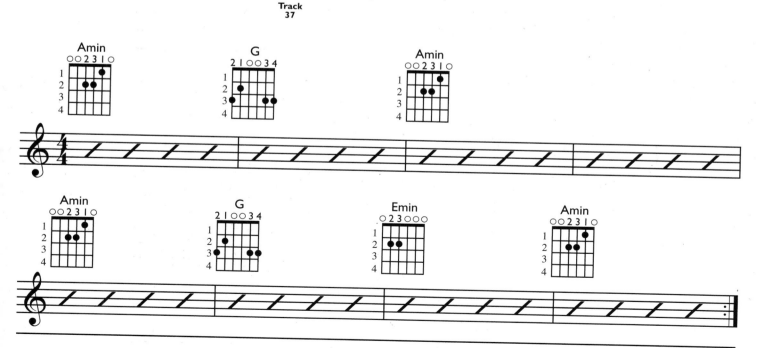

Flatpicking (playing with a pick) melodies is a staple of country, bluegrass and old-time playing. The early and middle twentieth century saw the guitar branching out from its role as a rhythm instrument. Jazz and blues players improvised solos on the guitar, while country and bluegrass pickers began to incorporate the fluid, agile melodies of fiddle tunes into their own playing. Now there are contests devoted solely to flatpicking acoustic guitar!

PRECISION WARM-UPS

The secret to good flatpicking is an absolutely steady down-up picking rhythm and clean, clear notes. Here are some warm-ups designed to help you develop the precision of your picking.

Warm-up #1: Groups of Four

This warm-up has four notes per string, picked down-up-down-up.

Continue this warm-up by repeating it in *second position* (the group of four frets beginning with the 1st finger on the 2nd fret), then third position and so on up the neck.

Warm-up #2: Groups of Three

This warm-up has only three notes per string. This will help you become fluent at beginning with both downstrokes and upstrokes when switching to a new string.

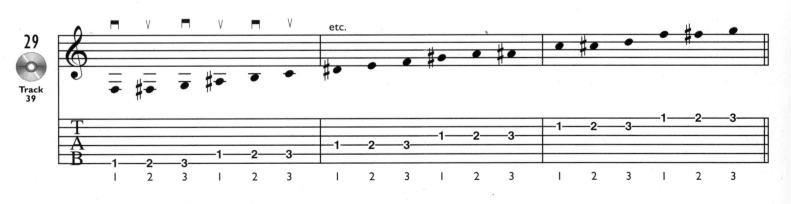

Sail Away Ladies is an old-time tune that can be heard at jam sessions across the country. The melody is shown in music and tab. The chords are indicated above the music. Use the country/bluegrass strum you learned on page 32.

This tune is written in the traditional, two-part fiddle tune form. There are two sections that we call *A* and *B*, respectively. Each section is repeated once and the whole tune is meant to be repeated many times. This is called a *binary form*. The form of the tune looks like this:

A   A   B   B

SAIL AWAY LADIES

Track 40

Syncopation means emphasizing the off-beats in a measure (also known as *upbeats*, page 22). In practice, this means that you will be emphasizing the "&s" of some beats, not just the numbered parts of the beats (the on-beats or downbeats). The end result is a rhythm pattern that rocks and rolls with groovy funkulence (if that's not a word, it should be).

TIES ONE ON FOR FUNK

In order to show syncopation in written music, dotted rhythms (see page 24) and *ties* are often used. A tie is a small curved line that connects two notes of the same pitch to create one longer note. Play the first note and hold it for its full duration plus the duration of the note to which it is tied.

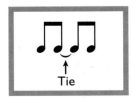

Notice that in the counting below the staff, the tied note is in parentheses.

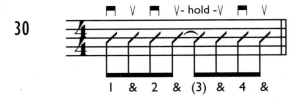

SYNCOPATED STRUM—IF YOU'RE ONLY GOING TO LEARN ONE STRUM...

...then this is it. Your newest strum is not just "Strum #4," it is The Universal Folk-Rock-Alternative-Swing-Funk-Campfire Strum. It is the Swiss Army knife of strum patterns. This is a good one at any speed, fast or slow. Note the tie that connects the "&" of beat 2 to beat 3. Be sure to tap your foot and count aloud. It's a good idea to tap your foot loud enough to hear an audible "thump" on beat 3, where the strings are not being struck. This will help keep you from speeding up every time you go from beat 2 to beat 3.

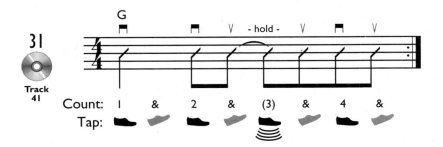

If you find this rhythm to be a little confusing, break it down into one or two beat segments:

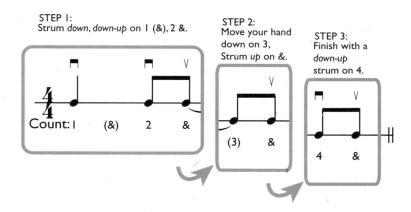

The trick is to consciously move your hand down on beat 3 without hitting the strings. This keeps your hand movement regular and places your hand in the right place to strum up on the "&" of beat 3. Go slowly and keep a steady beat!

This strum has become a staple rhythm in acoustic (and electric) music. It can be heard on songs by R.E.M., The Wallflowers, Joni Mitchell, The Ramones, Steve Earle, Lucinda Williams, Lou Reed and countless others.

Below are a few chord progressions to try. Be patient when trying to switch chords while playing this strumming rhythm. Play slowly, keep your foot tapping and count aloud. Once it begins to feel natural, you can speed up. Try this strum on other chord progressions you come across in this book and in any other songbooks you may have.

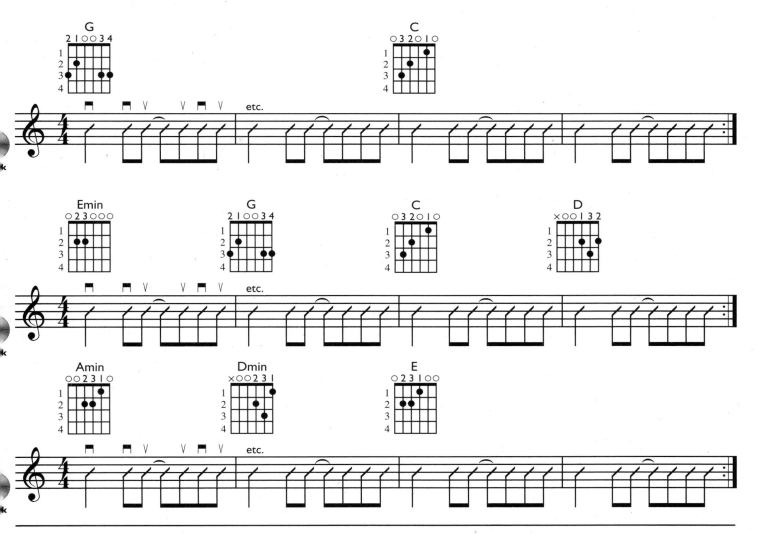

Waltz time is another name for $\frac{3}{4}$ time. This means there are three quarter notes in every measure. First, familiarize yourself with the feel of three beats per measure by counting and tapping your foot for a few bars:

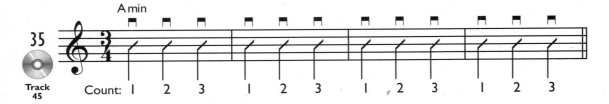

There are a variety of ways to strum in $\frac{3}{4}$ time.

Waltz Strum #1:

Waltz Strum #2:

Waltz Strum #3:

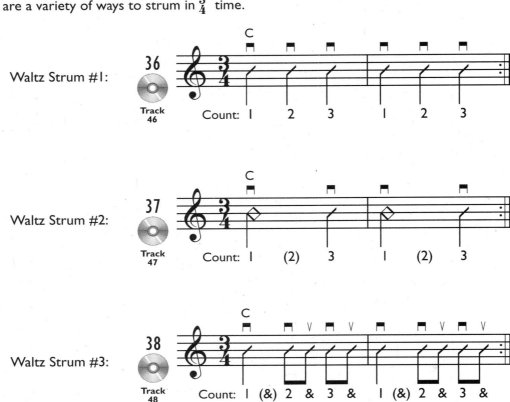

Waltz Strum #4: Country/Bluegrass (also known as "Oom-Pah-Pah"):

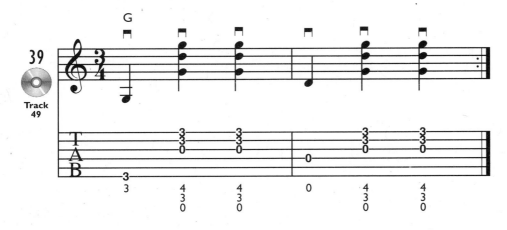

The gentle roll of waltz time can be particularly beautiful and lyrical. One of the most famous songs in $\frac{3}{4}$ is the traditional tune, *Amazing Grace*. Try the *Amazing Grace* melody. Then try the same chords with any of the waltz strums on page 38.

Note that the melody begins on beat 3. This is called a *pickup*. A pickup is a note or groups of notes that occur before the first full measure of a piece. Strictly speaking, where there is a pickup, there should be an *incomplete measure* at the end of the tune that balances out the incomplete pickup measure. In pop, rock, folk and other non-classical styles, this rule is not striclty adhered to.

Also notice the ties in the second and third lines. Play the first note, then hold it all the way to the end of the tied note. Do not strike the tied note. To review ties, see page 36.

AMAZING GRACE

Track 50

CHAPTER 4

Basic Fingerpicking

LESSON 1: THE RIGHT-HAND POSITION

Learning to fingerpick (playing *fingerstyle*) is a great way to overcome "the blahs" in your playing and try something new. Even a few basic patterns can provide textures that you can use for the rest of your life. Players such as Jewel, Steve Earle, John Prine and Tracy Chapman have used very basic fingerpicking to add a high level of impact to their songs. Others, such as Martin Simpson, Rory Block and Leo Kottke, have taken fingerstyle guitar to dazzling levels of complexity and expressiveness. If you find yourself drawn to the techniques touched on in this chapter, check out the *The Complete Fingerstyle Guitar Method*, also published by the National Guitar Workshop and Alfred.

RIGHT-HAND FINGERS

The most common method for naming the fingers of the right hand comes from the classical guitar tradition which uses the Spanish names for the fingers (**p**ulgar = thumb, **i**ndice = index, **m**edio = middle, **a**nular = ring). All you have to memorize is the first letter of each.

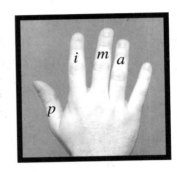

HOME POSITION

Contemporary acoustic and folk fingerstyle playing is based on a basic "home position" that will allow you to play patterns and figures without turning your hand into a pretzel.

p   plays the 4th, 5th and 6th strings
i   plays the 3rd string
m   plays the 2nd string
a   plays the 1st string

THE RIGHT HAND WRIST

To achieve the best technical fluency possible (to maximize tone and minimize stress), it is helpful to understand some basic terms regarding the wrist:

ARCH
(up-and-down motion)

ROTATION
(side-to-side motion)

TILT
(Left-to-right motion from the elbow)

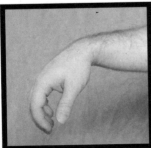
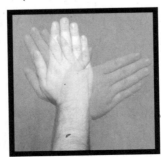
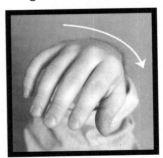

Your wrist should have a slight arch, little or no rotation and perhaps a slight tilt in towards your thumb. Keep your fingers relaxed and avoid tension in your forearm. If you feel tension or tightness, stop and "shake it out."

A good way to start fingerpicking is to learn a few repetitive patterns. These can be used with any chords you know. By placing your fingers in "home position," you can concentrate on which finger to play without worrying about which string to play.

If you find yourself getting tripped up, remove your hand from the guitar. Hold it up in the air and practice moving the fingers to the pattern while saying the right-hand pattern aloud a few times (for example: *p-i-m-a*, *p-i-m-a*, etc.). Then try it on the guitar again.

These patterns are called *arpeggios*. An arpeggio is the notes of a chord sounded one at a time. They can be played in an ascending, descending or more complex pattern. The patterns below are shown with C, G and D chords to help you practice moving the thumb to different root notes. Try them with all of your chords and with different songs and progressions!

ARPEGGIO PATTERN #1 — *p i m a*

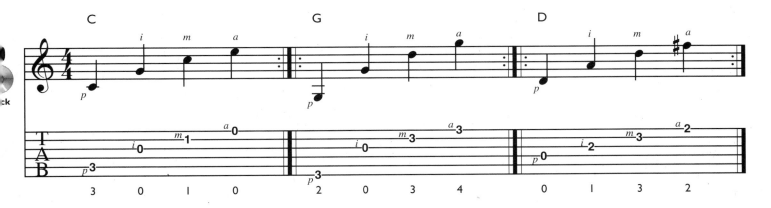

ARPEGGIO PATTERN #2 — *p a m i*

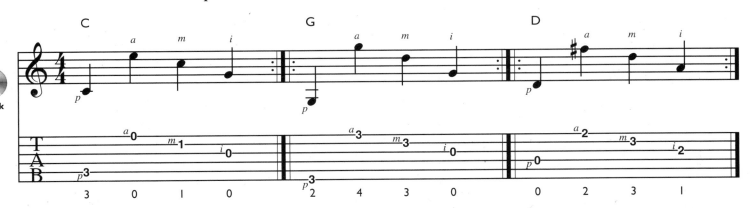

Alternating bass fingerpicking is a style that has roots in ragtime and blues piano playing from around the beginning of the 20th century. The thumb (*p*) plays the *bass* (the lowest note in the chord) and alternates between the root of the chord and the 4th string, while the fingers play with or between the thumb notes. On the D chord, *p* alternates between the 5th string (the 5th of the chord) and the root on the 4th string. Alternating bass is one of the most familiar and recognizable sounds in fingerstyle guitar, from blues and folk to pop, country and rock. It is also much easier to do than it sounds!

Below are a few very useful patterns to try. Practice them slowly at first. Played this way, they have an intimate sound that is good for ballads. Later on, as you gain confidence and speed up, they take on a rolling, syncopated quality. Also try making up your own patterns. Try different fingers in the spaces between the thumb notes.

ALTERNATING BASS PATTERN #1 — *p m p i*

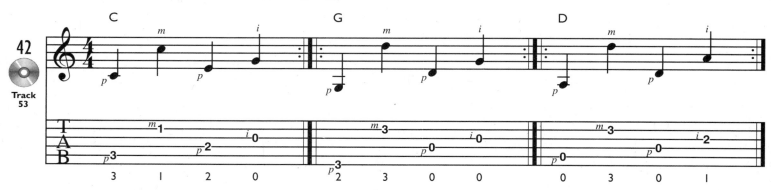

ALTERNATING BASS PATTERN #2 — *p a p i*

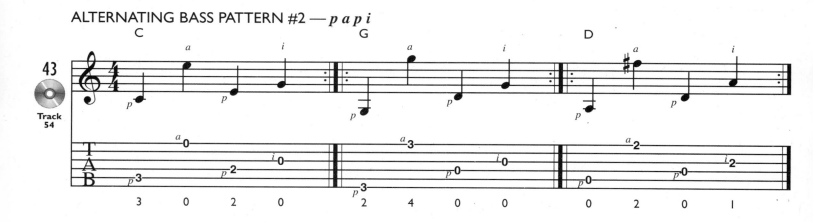

ALTERNATING BASS PATTERN #3 (COMBINATION OF #1 AND #2) — *p m p i p a p i*

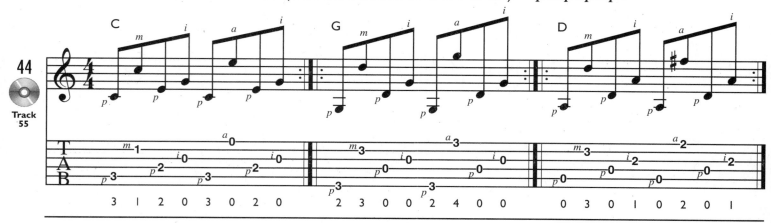

This tune will help you use your fingerpicking patterns in the context of a chord progression. Note that it uses a G/B chord in measures 2 and 9. This is a *slash chord*. This chord symbol is pronounced "G over B." It means that you are playing a G chord but the bass note is B (instead of the more common root G note). This chord allows your bass line to "walk" melodically from C (on the C chord) down to B (on the G chord), and then to A (on the Amin chord).

PRACTICE ROUTINE:

When you are working on putting a new technique to work in a song, try working on one measure at a time.

1. Practice the pattern of the first measure until you are very comfortable with it.
2. Practice measure 2 until you are very comfortable with it.
3. Now put together the two measures. Work on making a smooth transition between the two.
4. Start working on measure three, then add it to the other two. And so on...

CALIFORNIA FLOOD

Track 56

Some fingerstyle patterns work beautifully in $\frac{3}{4}$ time. Here are some patterns to try. Remember that you will only be counting to three! Try some of these patterns with the chords to Amazing Grace on page 39.

WALTZ FINGERPICKING PATTERN #1

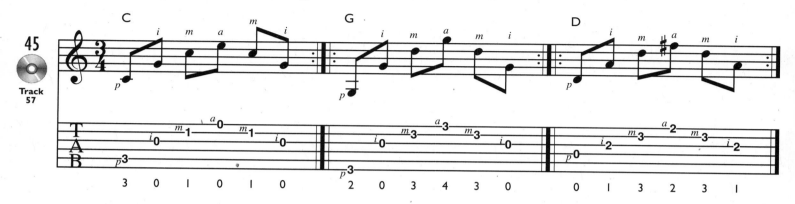

WALTZ FINGERPICKING PATTERN #2

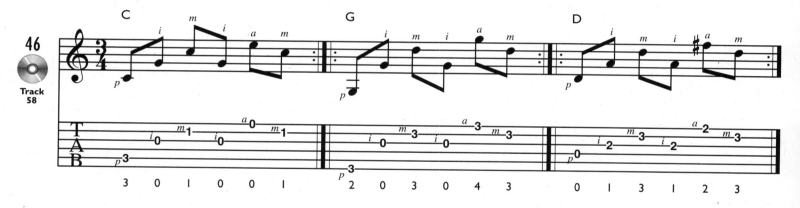

WALTZ FINGERPICKING PATTERN #3

Note that in this pattern, you will play your *a* and *m* fingers simultaneously. Some fingerpickers refer to this as a *pinch*. The technical term for two notes played simultaneously by a single instrument is *double stop*.

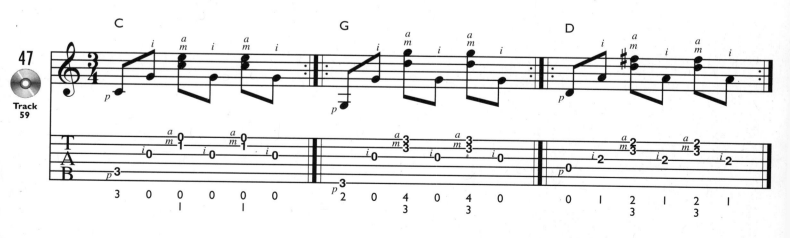

CHAPTER 5

Improvisation

Improvisation is the art of making up new music on the spot. It can be as simple as throwing in a new chord embellishment or strum pattern, or as complex as playing a free-form jazz solo. Improvisation is an important part of modern acoustic guitar playing. For example, many folk and blues players pride themselves on never playing a tune exactly the same way twice. Musicians in all styles use improvisation as a vehicle for expressing the emotions and attitudes of the moment.

> **Why Improvise?**
> - To add a sense of freshness and spontaneity to a performance.
> - To put your own personal expression into a piece of music.
> - To create a dialogue, or musical conversation, with another player.

TOOLS AND TECHNIQUES

There is no single, correct way to go about learning to improvise. You can base improvisation on your experience and knowledge of "what sounds good." On the other hand, you can throw caution to the wind and try to push the boundaries of your mind, ears and instrument. The best improvisers are able to do both.

> **There are some basic tools that can help you begin your journey:**
> - Theory
> - Imitation and analysis of players you admire
> - Playing with other people

A FEW WORDS ABOUT MUSIC THEORY

This chapter will give you some basic theory tools to start you on your way. Theory is the collection of terms and concepts we use to describe musical sounds and how they interact. Some people may fear that learning theory will ruin the spontaneity and creativity of their playing. Not so! Remember, knowledge can't hurt you!

> **What theory can do for you:**
> - Help you make connections between sounds you hear.
> - Broaden your possibilities for musical choices.
> - Help you explain your music to another player.

TAKING THE LEAP

When you combine a growing familiarity with theory, the study of players you admire and the experience of playing with others, you will build a foundation for limitless exploration of improvising. All that remains is to "take the leap into the unknown." When you are learning to improvise, try not to criticize yourself too much. Be fearless, open and have fun. Learn rules and break rules. This is not rocket science, it's music!

Willie Nelson became known as a leader of "outlaw country" in the 1970s. He combines bluegrass, blues and Texas swing with jazz inflections and phrasing.

DOE, A DEER...

A *scale* is an arrangement of notes in a specific order of whole steps and half steps (see page 8). Of all the dozens of scales used in music, the *major scale* has the most instantly recognizable sound. It is the "standard of measurement" that musicians use in order to differentiate between all the other scales. In other words, we define all other scales by noting exactly how they are different from the major scale.

The sound of the major scale is that of the traditional "Do Re Mi Fa Sol La Ti Do" melody (made famous in the musical "The Sound of Music"). It has seven different notes, and uses each letter name from the musical alphabet (page 8) once—though some may be sharped or flatted. The first note, called the *tonic* (or sometimes *key note*) is repeated at the end, for a total of eight notes. The easiest major scale to learn is the C Major Scale, which uses no sharps or flats. Notice that the notes are numbered. These numbers are called *scale degrees*.

THE C MAJOR SCALE

	C	D	E	F	G	A	B	C
Scale degree:	1	2	3	4	5	6	7	8(1)

```
48
T A B
              3       0       2       3       0       3       0       1
```

THE SECRET FORMULA

If you look at the C Major Scale as a series of whole steps and half steps, you will learn the "formula" for all major scales. Say it over and over to yourself and memorize it like you would your own phone number.

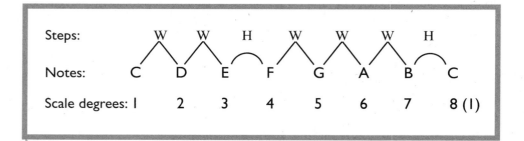

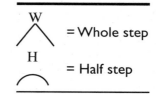

W / H = Whole step

H / = Half step

IMPORTANT NOTE:

The notes of a major scale comprise the notes of a major key. For example, the notes of the C Major scale comprise the key of C Major.

"SPELLING" THE MAJOR SCALE IN ANY KEY—POP QUIZ

With careful use of the formula, you can *spell* (apply the formula of whole steps and half steps) the major scale starting on any note. Just start with the key note (1st scale degree) and then follow the formula, using each letter only once. The D Major scale is shown below. Notice that to make E to F a whole step, as the formula requires, we must raise the F a half step to F♯. Try spelling the A and B♭ Major scales (the correct answers are at the bottom of the page).

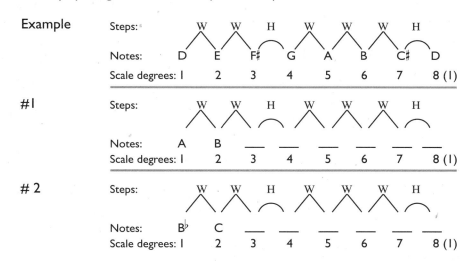

HOT TIPS:
1. Use every letter in the musical alphabet *once*, in alphabetical order.
2. The last note is the same as the first.
3. You will need to use either sharps or flats (never both) to make the notes fit the formula.

Try playing the D Major Scale by going up the 4th string. Playing the scale on a single string makes it easy to see the whole steps and half steps. The half steps are adjacent frets; for the whole steps, skip a fret. When you get comfortable with it, try it backwards!

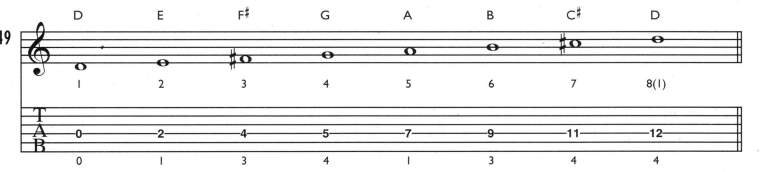

LESSON 2: THE CIRCLE OF 5THS

The *circle of 5ths* is like the "secret agent decoder ring" of music theory. (And you don't have to send in any cereal box tops to get it!) A 5th is the distance between the 1st and 5th degrees of a scale. To make a circle of 5ths, just take the keys and arrange them in a circle so that the next keynote (going clockwise) is the 5th degree of the last scale. For example, the 5th degree of a B Major scale is F♯, so the next key in the circle is F♯.

The circle of 5ths makes it easy to learn the key signatures (page 26) for each key. The "sharp keys" (clockwise on the circle) add one sharp for each new key. The new sharp is always the 7th scale degree of that key. The "flat keys" (counterclockwise) add one new flat for each key. That flat is always the 4th scale degree of the key.

Notice that the keys of G♭ and F♯ are in the same position in the circle. The two scales are played on exactly the same strings and frets and sound exactly the same. Remember when two notes have the same sound but different names, they are *enharmonic equivalents*.

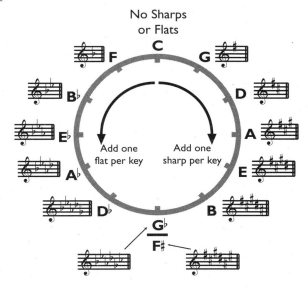

In addition to playing major scales by going up one string, or playing in first position with open strings, we can play them across six strings with no open strings. We can catagorize these types of fingerings according to the finger we begin with. In this lesson, we will look at fingerings beginning with the 1st, 2nd and 4th fingers. There are three common ways of viewing each fingering: with finger numbers, note names or scale degree numbers. Let's look at the A Major scale starting on the 5th fret of the 6th string, with three different fingerings and three different views of each.

THE A MAJOR SCALE, STARTING WITH THE 1ST FINGER

FINGERING

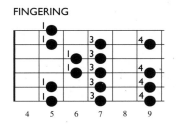

NOTE NAMES

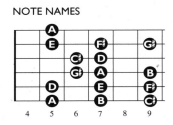

SCALE DEGREES

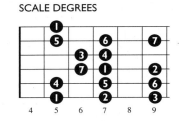

THE A MAJOR SCALE, STARTING WITH THE 2ND FINGER

FINGERING

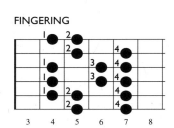

NOTE NAMES

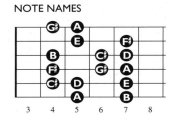

SCALE DEGREES

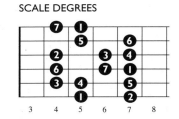

THE A MAJOR SCALE, STARTING WITH THE 4TH FINGER

FINGERING

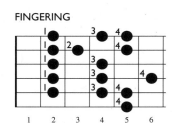

NOTE NAMES

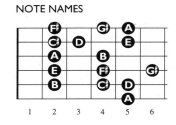

SCALE DEGREES

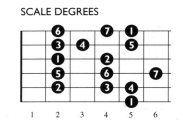

SECRETS OF THE MASTERS:
Since there are no open strings in these fingerings, they are moveable. That means you can move them to any fret to play in any key. For example, the 6th fret of the 6th string is B♭. If you play these fingerings at the 6th fret, you need only change the names of the notes. Everything else—the finger numbers and scale degrees—remains the same.

LESSON 4: THE MAJOR SCALE-DEGREE EXERCISES

Once you are very familiar with playing a scale fingering backward and forward, practice saying the scale degrees aloud while you play them. Then try some of these combinations of scale degrees. You might hear some familiar sounds or melodies!

Using your A Major Scale (any fingering), play the following scale-degree sequences:

A. 1-2-3   **F.** 7-6-4-5
B. 3-2-1-2-3-3-3   **G.** 1-3-5-3-1
C. 1-2-3-4-4-3-2-1   **H.** 2-4-6-4-2
D. 1-2-5   **I.** 5-7-4-6-3-1
E. 5-6-5-1

You can try these exercises in any key. Once your ear gets used to the sound of the new key, the melodies generated by the exercises will sound the same from one key to another (see *Secrets of the Masters* on page 48). Also try naming the pitches you are playing!

LESSON 5: IMPROVISING WITH THE MAJOR SCALE

The first step to improvising with the major scale is to become familiar enough with one of the fingerings that you can play it in your sleep. Then, begin to jump around within the scale, making up new melodies. Play some long notes and short notes, loud ones and soft ones. Don't worry about playing fast! Just try to get clean, clear notes that flow smoothly from one to another.

EAR TRAINING

Ear training is an integral part of learning music. A well-trained ear is what allows an improviser to transfer sounds from the imagination to the instrument. You can do some of this on your own, in the privacy of your own home. Look for opportunities to do this kind of work.

SING, SING, SING

The simple truth: The key to ear training is singing. Using a simple syllable such as "La" or "aaaah," try to *match* (sing) the pitches you are playing on your instrument. When practicing scale exercises, sing the numbers of the scale degrees as you play them. Try to sing a simple melody such as *Mary Had a Little Lamb* and play it by ear on your guitar.

Do a little "ear practice" every day. Also, enlist the help of a teacher if you can.

> **SECRETS OF THE MASTERS:** *A scale is only a bunch of whole steps and half steps! The magic of a scale is unlocked when you begin to explore the infinite melodies that lie within it. Simply learning to fly up and down scale fingerings may be fun for your fingers but it won't be very musically satisfying. Try to use your voice, your ear and your guitar to discover how melodies are put together, where they flow and where they skip around, where they start and where they end.*

An *interval* is the distance between two pitches. You already know three intervals: the whole step (which in interval lingo is a *major 2nd*), the half step (*minor 2nd*) and the 5th (seven half steps). Intervals are best understood relative to a scale. For example, the distance from the 1st degree to the 2nd degree of a scale is an interval of a 2nd; from the 1st degree to the 3rd degree of a scale is an interval of a 3rd, and so on.

INTERVAL QUALITY

Every interval has a *quality*. The quality is the type of sound it makes, such as major or minor. Don't panic! The qualities will be disussed in greater detail in Lesson 7. The major scale generates only major and perfect intervals when measuring up from the tonic (1st degree):

INTERVALS IN THE MAJOR SCALE		
From the 1st Degree to the:	Interval	Abbreviation
1st Degree	Perfect Unison	PU
2nd Degree	Major 2nd	M2
3rd Degree	Major 3rd	M3
4th Degree	Perfect 4th	P4
5th Degree	Perfect 5th	P5
6th Degree	Major 6th	M6
7th Degree	Major 7th	M7
8th Degree	Perfect Octave	P8

Here are the intervals from the major scale in standard notation:

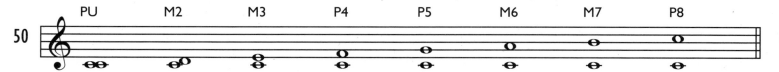

Each interval quality can be measured in half steps. For example, a major 2nd (whole step) equals two half steps. A major 3rd equals four half steps. There are also other kinds of intervals besides major or perfect. If you make a major interval smaller by one half step, it becomes minor. For example, C to E is a major 3rd (four half steps), but C to E♭ is a minor 3rd (three half steps). If you make a perfect interval smaller, it becomes diminished; if you make it bigger, it becomes augmented. Here is a chart showing all the intervals and their measurements in half steps, plus examples measured up from C and up from A.

INTERVALS FROM THE UNISON TO THE OCTAVE				
Interval	Abbreviation	Half Steps	From C	From A
Perfect Unison	PU	0	C	A
Minor 2nd	m2	1	D♭	G♭
Major 2nd	M2	2	D	B
Minor 3rd	m3	3	E♭	C
Major 3rd	M3	4	E	C♯
Perfect 4th	P4	5	F	D
Augment 4th or Tritone	Aug4 or TT	6	F♯	D♯
Diminished 5th or Tritone	dim5 or TT	6	G♭	E♭
Perfect 5th	P5	7	G	E
Minor 6th	m6	8	A♭	F
Major 6th	M6	9	A	F♯
Minor 7th	m7	10	B♭	G
Major 7th	M7	11	B	G♯
Perfect Octave	P8	12	C	A

Here are the intervals from the unison to the octave, measured up from C, in standard notation:

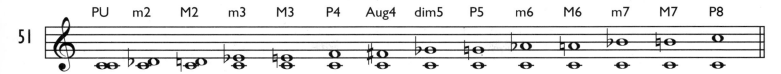

Here are the intervals from the unison to the octave, measured up from A, in standard notation:

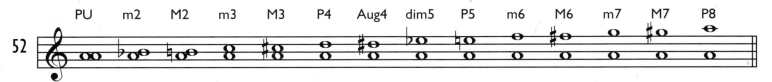

Don't Panic! Lesson 7 will allow you to play, hear and understand the intervals in easy doses.

INTERVAL INVERSION

Each interval can be *inverted*. To invert an interval, we simply take the bottom note and put it on top (or vice versa). For example, if we take C up to E (a major 3rd) and put the C on top so that it is now E up to C (a minor 6th), we have inverted the interval. The numbers of an inverted interval always add up to 9 (a 3rd inverts to a 6th; 3 + 6 = 9). Also, when inverted, major intervals become minor and minor intervals become major. Diminished intervals become augmented and vice versa. Perfect intervals remain perfect (that's what's perfect about 'em).

This table can be read right to left and left to right.

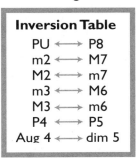

Inversion Table	
PU ⟷ P8	
m2 ⟷ M7	
M2 ⟷ m7	
m3 ⟷ M6	
M3 ⟷ m6	
P4 ⟷ P5	
Aug 4 ⟷ dim 5	

Here are the interval inversions, all beginning with an interval built on C, in standard notation:

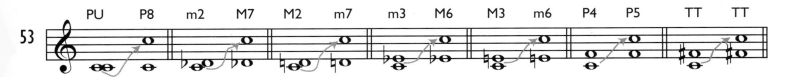

CONSONANCE AND DISSONANCE

Intervals are often described by the qualities of their sound. A *consonant* interval has a harmonious sound that produces a feeling of rest or *resolution*. There is no feeling that further musical movement is required. Consonant intervals include PU, P8, m3, M3, m6, M6 and P5. A *dissonant* interval has a clashing sound that produces an unresolved feeling called *musical tension*. Dissonance asks for musical movement to a point of *resolution*. Dissonant intervals include m2, M2, TT, m7 and M7. A P4 can be considered either a consonance or dissonance, depending on the context.

It is the fluctuation between "tension" and "resolution" that gives music a sense of motion, direction and emotional effect.

Learning intervals on the fingerboard can take a little work but it will help you to thoroughly master the instrument. It is easy if you concentrate on one or two interval types at a time.

To make things consistent in this lesson, each interval fingering is indicated for the same set of pitches (for example, all of the perfect octave fingerings are for A to A). You will be able to hear that each fingering generates the same pitches. Play the notes shown in the fingerings one after another (*melodically*) and simultaneously (*harmonically*), and get used to the sounds of the different intervals.

PERFECT OCTAVES

PERFECT OCTAVE = 12 HALF STEPS
Below are the fingerings for a perfect octave. The frets indicated will sound the notes A and A.

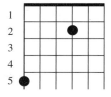

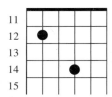

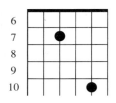

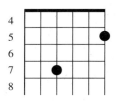

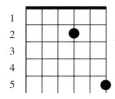

Octaves are one of the best interval shapes to memorize. They are important in blues and funk riffs and in the styles of contemporary players like Ani DiFranco and Dave Matthews. When the two notes are played simultaneously, the octave shape can be moved up or down the neck to create melodies. We call these *parallel octaves*. A master innovator in this style of playing was the jazz guitarist, Wes Montgomery. An octave corresponds to the first two notes of the *Somewhere Over the Rainbow* from "The Wizard of Oz."

Finally, octaves can help you learn the notes on the fingerboard much faster. Every time you learn a note, use the octave shapes to find other locations of the same pitch on the fingerboard.

PERFECT 4THS, PERFECT 5THS AND TRITONES

PERFECT 4TH = 5 HALF STEPS
Below are the fingerings for the interval of a perfect 4th. The frets indicated will sound the notes A and D.

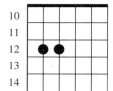

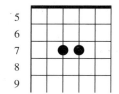

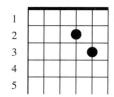

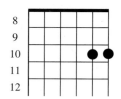

The perfect 4th is the distance between each of the open strings (except between the 3rd and 2nd strings). Perfect intervals have a resonant, "in tune" sound. The perfect 4th interval correspond to the first two notes of the melody to *Here Comes the Bride* (*The Wedding March* by Felix Mendelssohn, 1809-1847). It can be inverted to form a perfect 5th.

PERFECT 5TH = 7 HALF STEPS

Below are the fingerings for the interval of a perfect 5th. The frets indicated will sound the notes D and A.

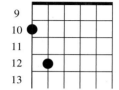 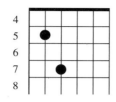 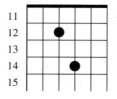 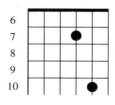 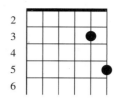

The perfect 5th is also known to guitarists as the *power chord* (page 80). When played on the lower strings, the shape can be moved around to play basic, "stripped down" chord progressions. Power chords are named after the lower note. For example, a perfect 5th with D as the low note is known as a *D Power Chord* or *D5*. The perfect 5th corresponds to the first two notes of a melody from *Also sprach Zarathustra* by Richard Strauss (1864-1949) which was used in the movie, "2001: A Space Odyssey." The perfect 5th can be inverted to form a perfect 4th.

TRITONE = 6 HALF STEPS

Here are the fingerings for the interval of a tritone. The frets indicated sound the notes A to D♯.

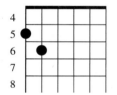 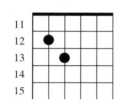 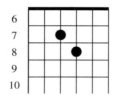 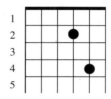 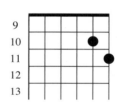

The tritone is a very special interval. It divides the octave equally in half. In other words, the distance from A to D♯ is the same as the distance from D♯ to A (six half steps—three whole steps, hence the name). This means that a tritone inverted is still a tritone.

The tritone is the most unstable-sounding interval, even though it is not necessarily the most dissonant. The tritone carries a lot of tension. Try playing a tritone and then moving each pitch by one half step in opposite directions. Hear the tension resolve!

The tritone is halfway between the perfect 4th and perfect 5th. Therefore, it is also known as an augmented 4th (one half step larger than a perfect 4th) or a diminished 5th (one half step smaller than a perfect 5th), depending on whether the note is sharp or flat.

The first two notes of the melody to *Maria* from the musical play "West Side Story" by Leonard Bernstein are a tritone. The two pitches of the tritone can be alternated to imitate the characteristic sound of European ambulance sirens in World War II movies.

2NDS AND 7THS

MINOR 2ND = 1 HALF STEP

Below are the fingerings for the interval of a minor 2nd or half step. The frets indicated sound the notes A and B♭.

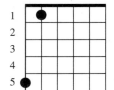 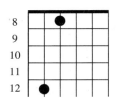 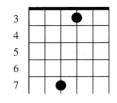 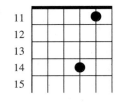 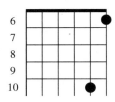

Minor and major 2nds are the building blocks of scales and melodies. Minor 2nds, when played harmonically, are among the most dissonant of intervals. Try moving a minor 2nd shape up and down the neck, playing a melody in parallel minor 2nds. Unless the sound of fingernails on a blackboard bothers you, this can be a cool effect. The minor 2nd corresponds to the first two notes of the theme to the movie "Jaws" by John Williams. The minor 2nd can be inverted to form the major 7th.

MAJOR 7TH = 11 HALF STEPS

Below are the fingerings for the interval of a major 7th. The frets indicated will sound the notes B♭ to A.

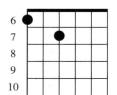 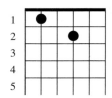 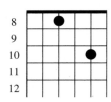 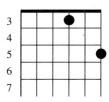

The major 7th is the inversion of the minor 2nd. A major 7th sounds the interval between the first and third note of first two notes of *Bali-Ha'i* from the musical "South Pacific" by Rodgers and Hammerstein. A major 7th can also be thought of as "one half step below an octave." To try this, make an octave shape and move the higher note down one half step. Whammo—major 7th!

MAJOR 2ND = 2 HALF STEPS

Here are the fingerings for the major 2nd (whole step). The frets indicated will sound the notes A to B.

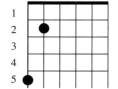 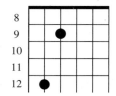 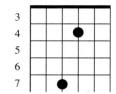 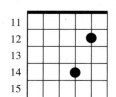 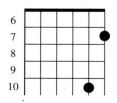

The major 2nd, as mentioned above, figures heavily in constructing scales and melodies. The major 2nd corresponds to the first two notes of *Amazing Grace* (page 39). The major 2nd can be inverted to form the minor 7th.

MINOR 7TH = 10 HALF STEPS

Here are the fingerings for the interval of a minor 7th. The frets indicated will sound the pitches B to A.

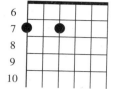 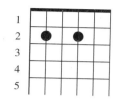 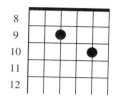 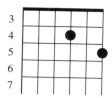

7ths are important intervals in coloring blues and jazz chords and melodies. The minor 7th can also be thought of as "one whole step below the octave." Try making an octave shape and move the higher note down one whole step. The minor 7th corresponds to the first two notes of the song *Somewhere* from Leonard Bernstein's "West Side Story." The minor 7th can be inverted to form the major 2nd.

*While still a teenager, **Ani DiFranco** appeared on the New York folk scene of the late 1980s. A prolific writer and recording artist, DiFranco is a leader in the world of independent music. Her rhythmic, forceful guitar style makes use of alternate tunings, funk rhythms and unusual chord voicings. She uses in-concert improvisations and jam sessions with her band to develop new material.*

3RDS AND 6THS

MINOR 3RD = 3 HALF STEPS

Here are the fingerings for the interval of a minor 3rd. The frets indicated will sound the notes A and C.

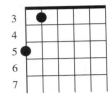 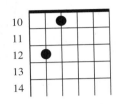 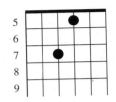 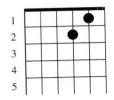 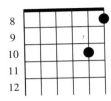

Minor and major 3rds are the building blocks of chords, including all of the chords you now play (see page 58). The minor 3rd corresponds the interval from the second to the third notes of the melody to the famous lullaby by Johannes Brahms (1833-1897), now called *Brahms' Lullaby* ("go to sleeeeeeep, go to sleeeeeeep...."). The minor 3rd can be inverted to form the major 6th.

MAJOR 6TH = 9 HALF STEPS

Below are the fingerings for the interval of a major 6th. The frets indicated will sound the notes C and A.

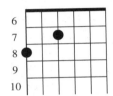 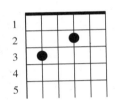 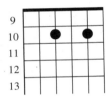 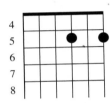

Both 3rds and 6ths are used to create harmonies for melodies. Major and minor 6ths are often used on the higher strings to give a "country harmony" sound that brings to mind the clean, twangy guitar sounds of Nashville. The major 6th corresponds to the first two notes of the melody to *My Bonnie Lies Over the Ocean*. The major 6th can be inverted to form the minor 3rd.

MAJOR 3RD = 4 HALF STEPS

Here are the fingerings for the interval of a major 3rd. The frets indicated will sound the notes A and C#.

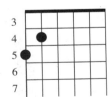 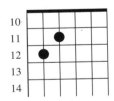 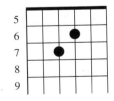 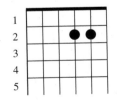 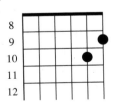

The major 3rd, with the minor 3rd (and their inversions, the 6ths) are crucial to building chords and harmonies. The major 3rd corresponds to the first two notes of the chorus of *Ob-la-di, Ob-la-da* by the Beatles, the guitar riff on *Blister in the Sun* by the Violent Femmes and the guitar riff to *Stir It Up* by Bob Marley. The major 3rd can be inverted to form the minor 6th.

*Known since the 1960s as the arm-swinging, guitar-smashing rock hero of the Who, **Peter Townshend** also developed an acoustic approach to communicate the intensity and emotion of a full-strength rock band. Townshend's style combines flamenco-style strumming, cross rhythms and bluesy leads. His acoustic work is a defining feature of the Who's album, "Tommy," (1969) and of many other recordings.*

MINOR 6TH = 8 HALF STEPS

Here are the fingerings for the interval of a minor 6th. The frets indicated sound the notes C# and A.

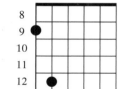
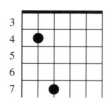
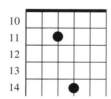
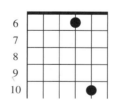
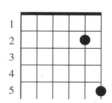

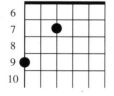
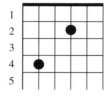
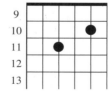
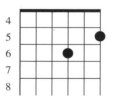

The minor 6th interval, when played melodically (one note at a time), has an unresolved quality that makes it easy to confuse with the tritone. But when the notes are played simultaneously, a very consonant sound emerges. The minor 6th can be inverted to form the major 3rd. The minor 6th corresponds to the first two notes of *Where Do I Begin* by Francis Lai from the movie "Love Story."

LESSON 8: HARMONY AND CHORDS

As you know, a chord is any three or more notes played together. The subject of chords and how they behave is called *harmony*. The most basic kind of chord is called a *triad*. A triad is a three-note chord, generally made by stacking one interval of a 3rd on top of another. All of the chords you have learned so far in this book are triads. Even though you may play all six strings, there are only three different notes; some are just repeated.

Below is a C Major scale that has been *harmonized*. This means that 3rds have been stacked above each note of the scale to form triads. The harmony notes are all within the scale—no sharps or flats have been added or changed. This is called *diatonic harmony*, or harmony within the key. TAB has been included so it will be easy for you to hear what the harmonized scale sounds like. You can also play the same chords any other way that is familiar and comfortable for you. You will find three types of triads—major, minor and diminished, which are all discussed below.

THE HARMONIZED C MAJOR SCALE

dim = Diminished

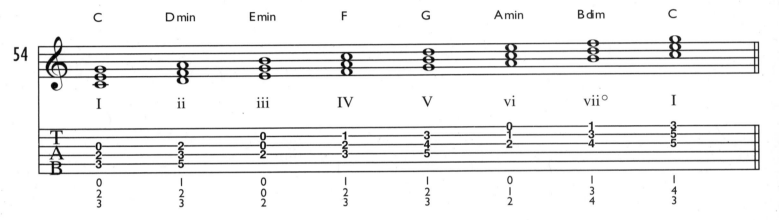

Notice that the chords have been numbered with Roman numerals. This allows for a distinction between scale degrees and chord numbers. The Roman numerals also show the quality of the chord. Check out the chart on the right.

Roman Numeral Review			
I......i* 1	V........ v......5
II..... ii...... 2	VI ..... vi......6
III ... iii 3	VII .... vii....7
IV ... iv 4	

* Lower-case Roman numerals are used for minor and diminished chords.

THREE KINDS OF TRIADS

The three types of triads that result from harmonizing the major scale are all made with different combinations of major and minor 3rds.

- A major triad is a major 3rd with a minor 3rd on top.
- A minor triad is a minor 3rd with a major 3rd on top.
- A diminished triad is a minor 3rd with another minor 3rd on top.

The bottom note of the triad is called the *root*. The middle note, which is a 3rd above the root, is called the *3rd*. The top note, which is a 3rd above the 3rd and a 5th above the root, is called the *5th*.

For easy comparison, example 55 shows all three triad types built on a C root.

5th
3rd
Root

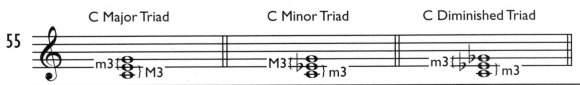

THREE PRIMARY CHORDS

The *primary chords* in every major key are the I, IV and V (one, four and five) chords.

Here is a D Major scale with the roots of the I, IV and V chords circled.

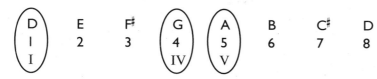

Here is a chord progression using I, IV and V. The key of D Major is indicated. Also try it in G and A. Use any chord fingerings or strum patterns you like.

Key of D Major

Key of G Major
Fill in the blanks. The answers are at the bottom of the page.

Key of A Major
Fill in the blanks. The answers are at the bottom of the page.

THE TRIUMPHANT RETURN OF THE CIRCLE OF 5THS

The circle of 5ths can be used to show basic harmonic movement. Instead of keys, these are major chords. Box or circle any three adjacent chords. The one in the middle is I. The one going clockwise is V. The one going counter-clockwise is IV.

Now that you have experimented a bit with intervals, the major scale and chords, it's time to make the magic happen!

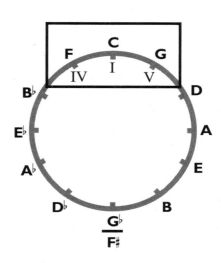

ANSWERS

Key of G: G C D   Key of A: A D E
         I IV V   I IV V

This lesson is going to use a chord progression in the key of A. Roman numerals are provided so that you can try it in other keys. Use any strum rhythm you like. Here is the chord progression:

LAUNCHING THE PLANE SEQUENCE

Improvising a solo melody is a little (very little) like flying a plane. You have to get off the ground, fly around for a while and then come in for a landing. Scale passages are one of many good ways to get going.

One fun thing to do is break the scale into small pieces and then move the pieces up the scale. In other words, we can take a small idea, called a *motive*, then repeat it starting on other scale degrees (either higher or lower). This is called a *sequence*. Imagine yourself walking upstairs. Instead of running straight up, you go up three steps and back one, then up three and back one. If you think of the stairs as notes in a scale, you have performed a sequence.

Here are a couple of sequence patterns for an A Major scale, starting with the 2nd finger on the 6th string (see page 48). Use down-up picking.

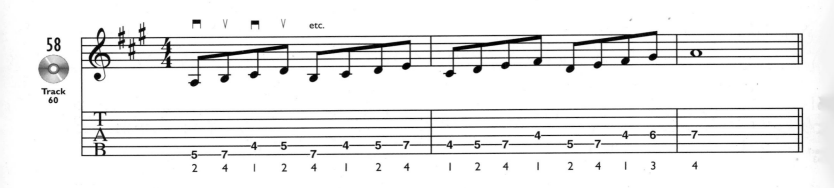

FLYING AROUND—REPETITION

Once you have begun with a sequence, you will want to try different ideas to create the body of your solo. One important concept for building a coherent solo is *repetition*. Repetition can help add a sense of structure to your solo and help it sound organized—like it's more than just a bunch of unrelated notes. Take a small idea and repeat it as the chords change. You will hear the character of the idea change as the harmony moves beneath it.

Here is a repeated idea shown with the chord progression from example 57. Notice the sense of tension and resolution as the chords change under the repeated melody.

LANDING THE PLANE—EMPHASIZE THE TONIC

One way to create a sense of resolution in a solo, or even make a small *phrase* (complete musical thought) within a solo, is to bring it to rest on the tonic (1st degree of the major scale of the key). In this case, that would be an A note. Play a short passage that ends on 1 and allow the note to last for a few beats. This allows some "breathing space" before the start of your next idea.

Here are two phrases that illustrate the technique of coming to rest on the 1st degree. They are shown with the chord progression from example 57.

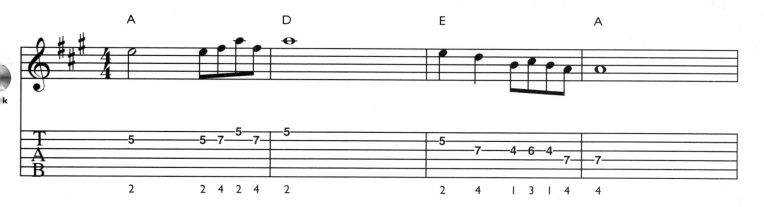

As you continue through this three-book method, you will learn lots of new techniques, scales and chords but these basic improvisational concepts will always hold true. Apply them every chance you get!

CHAPTER 6

The Blues

The blues is so much a part of American music that its influence is felt in nearly every style. Far more than just the feeling of good times that done gone bad,

the blues is:
- **A musical style**
- **A form of poetry**
- **A type of scale**
- **An additude**
- **A specific musical form and chord progression**
- **An incurable, infectious human condition**
that is both miserable and joyful at the same time

LESSON 1: THE TWELVE-BAR BLUES

THE FORM

The *twelve-bar blues* is one of the most basic song *forms*. The form is the organization or structure of a piece. The twelve-bar blues derives its name from the number of measures (also called bars) in the form. Below is a common version of the twelve-bar blues in the key of A. Included are chord symbols and Roman numerals indicating the analysis of the harmony. Try it with either simple downstrokes or a strum pattern from page 31.

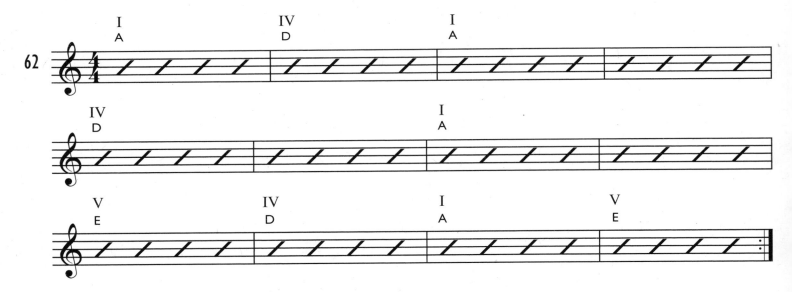

LESSON 2: MEMORIZING THE TWELVE-BAR BLUES

WHY MEMORIZE IT? TO JAM, OF COURSE

There may be times when you want to play with other people who don't know the same songs you do. The twelve-bar blues is widely known by musicians at all levels of experience. A working knowledge of how to play through the progression, as well as improvising on it, can give you an "ace up your sleeve" in those difficult situations when you can't decide what to "jam" on.

BLUES POETRY

The twelve-bar blues is organized in three lines of four measures each. This mirrors the poetic form of many blues lyrics. A common form of blues lyric consists of a statement (line 1), a repetition of the statement (line 2) and a sort of "clincher" (line 3). Check out these common blues verses:

> *My baby just left me, and man I feel so bad*
> *My baby just left me, and man I feel so bad*
> *Since my baby left me, I lost everything I had*

> *I'd rather drink muddy water, sleep in a hollow log*
> *I'd rather drink muddy water, sleep in a hollow log*
> *Than stay in this city, treated like a dirty dog*

PLAY BY NUMBERS

You may have noticed that the blues contains the three primary chords discussed on page 59. These are the I, IV and V (one, four and five) chords. In the key of A, these would be:

$$I = A \qquad IV = D \qquad V = E$$

Try to memorize the progression using these numbers. That way, you will learn its structure without being limited to the key of A. Soon, you will be able play the blues in any key, as long as you know what the I, IV and V chords are for that key. To make it easier, memorize one line at a time.

PLAY IT IN YOUR SLEEP

To get the most out of learning the blues, try to memorize the progression. Be able to play it over and over without losing your place in the form. This will make it much easier to jam with other players. You will be able to enjoy the musical interaction of the moment without worrying about whether you brought your music or whether you are on bar 10 or bar 6.

In addition, you should know that there are many, many variations possible on the twelve-bar blues form. Some have more chords, some have fewer, some have different chords substituted for the common ones. By burning a specific, basic version of the pattern into your brain through repetition and study, you will have an easier time compensating for slight variations from song to song.

THE ALMIGHTY SHUFFLE—SWING EIGHTHS

While the blues progression can be played with any rhythm (from bluegrass to punk to reggae and beyond), the *swing shuffle* is the most recognizable blues rhythm. It is very easy to play and has a propulsive, rocking sound that feels good at any speed.

The first step to learning the shuffle is to learn a new counting rhythm. Until now, you have been counting eighth notes in a steady, even beat like this:

These are known in musical lingo as *straight eighths* because each eighth note is the same length. *Swing eighths* are heard in jazz, blues, rockabilly and folk music. In swing eighths, the on-beat is given longer emphasis while the off-beat ("&") is made shorter.

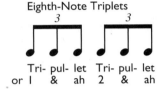

The best way to understand the swing rhythm is to relate the eighths to *eighth-note triplets*. These are groups of three eighth notes that are played in the time of two (one beat). To get the feel, try saying this aloud to a steady beat: "trip-pul-let, trip-pul-let."

In swing eighths, the first two notes of the triplet are tied together.

Swing eighths are usually designated in music in one of two ways:

In this method, we use the latter of the two, *Swing 8ths*. Often, out there in the real world, there is no indication given at all; blues and jazz players just automatically swing the eighths. *And the real kicker is that swing eighths look just like straight eighths!*

PLAYING THE SHUFFLE ON AN A CHORD

One of the most popular blues rhythm figures is called *the shuffle*. We use the swing eighth rhythm with two-note chords. The lower note is the root. The higher note alternates between an interval of a perfect 5th and a major 6th above the root. Here is the way to play it for an A chord:

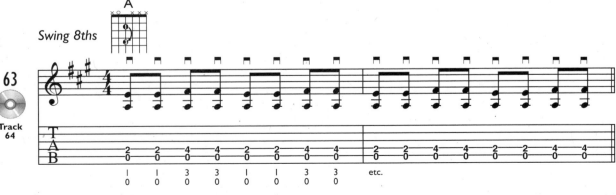

SHUFFLING ON D AND E CHORDS

Here is the shuffle for the D and E chords in a twelve-bar blues. Notice that all you have to do is move the 4th- and 5th-string pattern for the A shuffle on page 64 to the 3rd and 4th strings for the D chord and then down to the 5th and 6th strings for the E chord.

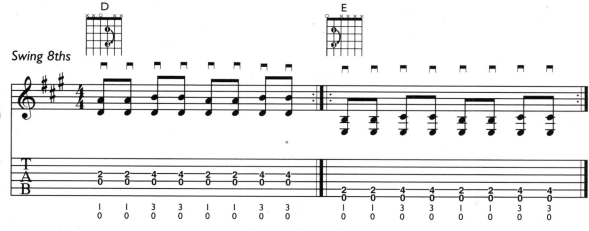

SHUFFLIN' THROUGH THE BLUES IN A

Track 66

Many blues melodies and solos use the notes of the *minor pentatonic scale*. Unlike the major scale (page 46), which has seven different notes, the minor pentatonic scale has only five different notes (*penta* is the Greek word meaning "five"). Pentatonic scales are very common in folk and traditional music from many cultures around the world.

THE MINOR PENTATONIC SCALE IN A

The same five notes are repeated as needed to cross all six strings of the guitar.

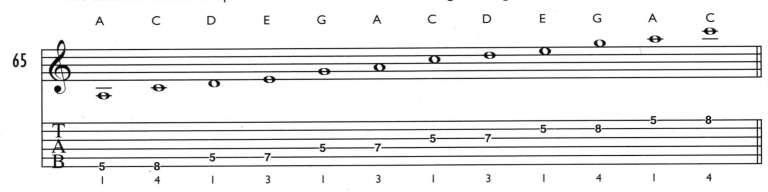

Below is a great fingering for the scale, shown in a single diagram. Play it one note at a time, starting on the 6th string and ascending to the 1st, then descending.

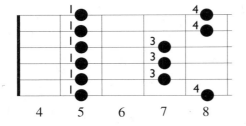

Here are the notes used in the A Minor Pentatonic scale fingering.

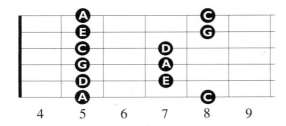

SCALE DEGREES

The minor pentatonic scale can be shown in scale degrees (page 46) just like the major scale. The scale degrees allow you to compare the minor pentatonic scale with the major scale to see which notes are the same and which are different.

A MAJOR SCALE:	1 A	2 B	3 C#	4 D	5 E	6 F#	7 G#
A MINOR PENTATONIC SCALE:	1 A		♭3* C	4 D	5 E		♭7* G

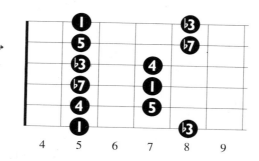

* The flat before the 3 (♭3) and 7(♭7) tells us that these notes are one half step lower than 3 and 7 in the major scale.

The minor pentatonic scale does not use a 2nd or 6th degree. In addition, the 3rd and 7th degrees are one half step lower than they are in the major scale. Musicians refer to these as "flat three" (♭3) and "flat seven" (♭7). These are the famous *blue notes* of the scale.

BLUE NOTES

When a scale has a lowered 3rd degree (flat three), it is said to be a *minor scale*. The cool thing about the blues is that, while the chords are often major, the melody is often minor. This creates a funky, slightly dissonant clash between the chords and the blue notes in the melody and gives the blues its melancholy, expressive sound.

In the old African scales that lie at the core of the blues, the blue notes were actually played somewhere between the blue note and the regular scale note (for example, between C and C# in the key of A). Guitarists often approximate this sound by *bending* the string (actually pushing the string up toward the ceiling or pulling it down toward the floor as explained on page 69) to the blue note, or by *sliding* (gliding along the string to make a sliding sound) from one fret to another. You'll learn these and other techniques later in this method.

LESSON 5: BEGINNING BLUES IMPROVISATION

EXPERIMENTING WITH THE SCALE

The first step to improvising a blues solo is learning to get around in the minor pentatonic scale. Try to make up melodies that use the minor pentatonic scale. Go up a few notes, go down a few notes. Play long and short notes. Skip around. Don't worry about whether it's "right" or "wrong"—just try to stick to the notes in the scale. Above all, have fun and aim for clean, clear tones. Let your ear be your guide. With patience, time and experimentation, you will develop many ideas that you can use in improvising on the blues.

GET IN YOUR LICKS

A *lick* is a small idea or figure that can be used as a building block for a solo. A lick can be repeated, altered or strung together with other licks. This lesson will show you a few ideas for licks that you can incorporate into your improvisations.

EMPHASIZING THE TONAL CENTER

As discussed on page 61, a great way to give a sense of melody and structure to a solo is to emphasize the tonic (1st scale degree). This note is also known as the *tonal center*. Blues players like B.B. King and Eric Clapton often play long, rich notes on the tonal center.

Here are some licks to try. They can be used at any point in the blues chord progression.

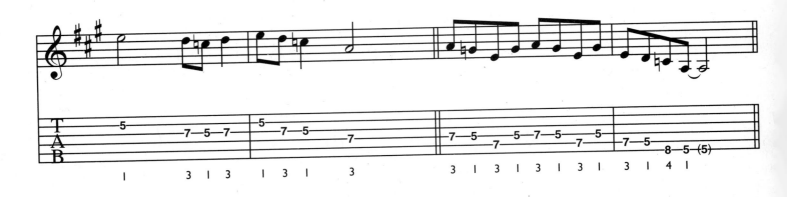

LESSON 6: BENDING

Guitarists often imitate the African vocal sound that is the basis of the blues by *bending* the strings. When we push or pull on a string with the left hand to actually change its shape, we create a smooth, gliding sound that few other instruments can achieve. This allows us to move smoothly into important notes, such as the blue notes discussed on page 67.

Here are a few tips to help you with your bending technique:

1. Try to use the 3rd finger to perform most of your bends, lining up the 1st and 2nd fingers behind it for support. This will get you the maximum leverage (and require the least strength).

2. If necessary, change your hand position so that your thumb hooks over the top of the neck slightly. Use your whole wrist and hand in a "cranking" or "choking" motion to bend the string.

THE ♭5 BLUE NOTE

Hidden inconspicuously between the 4th and 5th degrees of the minor pentatonic scale, the ♭5 is perhaps the most effective blue note. It adds an unmistakeably "bluesy" quality to any melody. It is a great note to approach with a bend. Try it in the key of A. Here's how:

1. Find the 4th degree of an A Minor Pentatonic scale (D) on the 7th fret of the 3rd string. Play this with your 3rd finger and line up your 1st and 2nd fingers behind it.

2. Add your 4th finger to the 8th fret and listen to the sound of that note, E♭, the ♭5. You will need to have this sound in your ear to perfect the bend in the next step.

3. Using your thumb and wrist for leverage, play the note D, then push the string up towards the ceiling. Keep the pressure on the string and listen to the note glide up. Stop pushing when it sounds like the note you played in step 2. This is called a *half-step bend*, because we are bending up to a note one half step higher.

In written music, this is indicated with a *grace* note (a small note) and an arrow pointing up with a "½" above it, to indicate a half-step bend.

Try example 67 using the bend to ♭5. This lick can be repeated all the way through the blues progression. Try it and see how the character of the lick changes depending on which chord is being played. If the strings on your guitar simply won't bend, you can approximate the effect by sliding your finger from the 7th to the 8th fret, keeping the pressure on the string as you go. Don't pluck the second note in the slide.

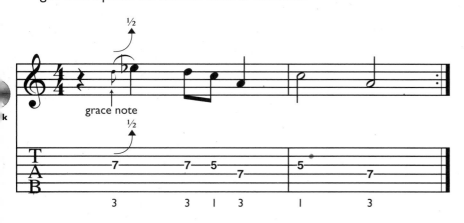

> If you're having trouble bending notes on your acoustic guitar, do not despair. Steel-string acoustics have thicker strings with higher tension than electric guitars. If you're playing a nylon-string guitar (classical guitar), you may find it easy to bend but you may not hear much change in pitch. Nylon strings are very flexible and harder to bend to new notes. Be patient and keep trying!

Up to this point, you have been playing triads, which are three-note chords. To add more harmonic color to the blues (as well as other styles), you can use 7th chords. A 7th chord consists of a triad (root, 3rd and 5th) with the interval of a major or minor 7th added above the root. There are several different types of 7th chords, built with different combinations of intervals.

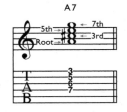

The most common 7th chord in the blues is the *dominant 7th* chord. This is a major triad (such as I, IV or V) with a minor 7th interval added above the root. Remember that a minor 7th interval is ten half steps above the root—or, one whole step below the octave (see pages 50 and 55). The fingering shown here is a bit tough to play but shows the chord tones in a logical, easy to understand way. Below, you'll learn some easy fingerings.

Following are some fingerings for dominant 7th chords you can use in the blues. Note that a dominant 7th chord is indicated with the addition of a "7" to the chord name, such as A7 or D7. Other types of 7th chords will carry different designations. It is also very common to hear 7th chords simply referred to as "7" chords ("seven" chords). This is because there is no "th" in the actual chord names.

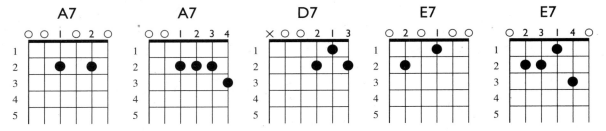

Try these fingerings with the twelve-bar blues. Use downstrokes or make up a strum rhythm.

7 CHORD BLUES

Track 69

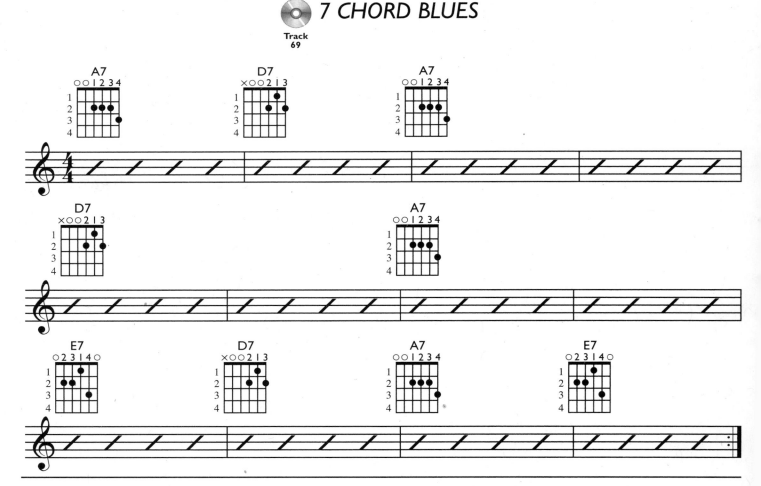

Here are some more fingerings for dominant 7 chords:

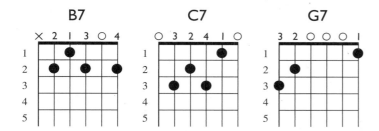

You can use these chords to play the blues in a different key. This is called *transposing* (see page 78). To transpose the blues to the key of E, ask yourself, "What are the I, IV and V chords in the key of E?" (See pages 58 and 59 to review the subject of diatonic harmony.) The correct answers are at the bottom of the page.

<u>I</u>   <u>IV</u>   <u>V</u>

Try playing the twelve-bar blues in E, using dominant 7 chords.

 THE TWELVE-BAR BLUES IN E

Track 70

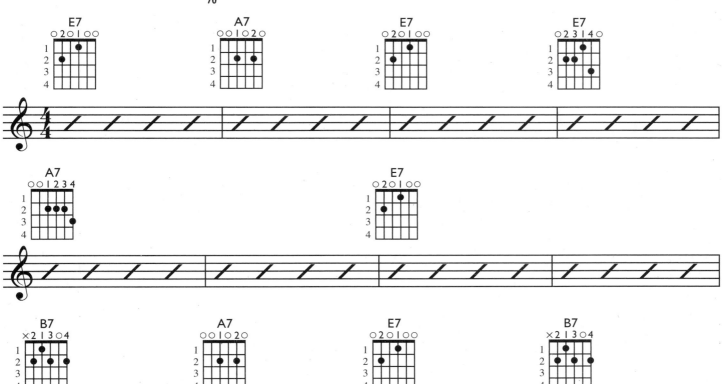

Now, try playing a twelve-bar blues in G using dominant 7 chords. The chords will be G7 (I, shown above), C7 (IV, shown above) and D7 (V, shown on page 70).

Answers:

The I chord is E, the IV chord is A and the V chord is B.

The blues can be played using minor chords, giving it a dark, emotional sound. One of the most famous minor blues songs is B.B. King's *The Thrill Is Gone*. Try playing the blues using triads in the key of A Minor. (See page 28 to review minor chord fingerings.)

A MINOR BLUES

Track 71

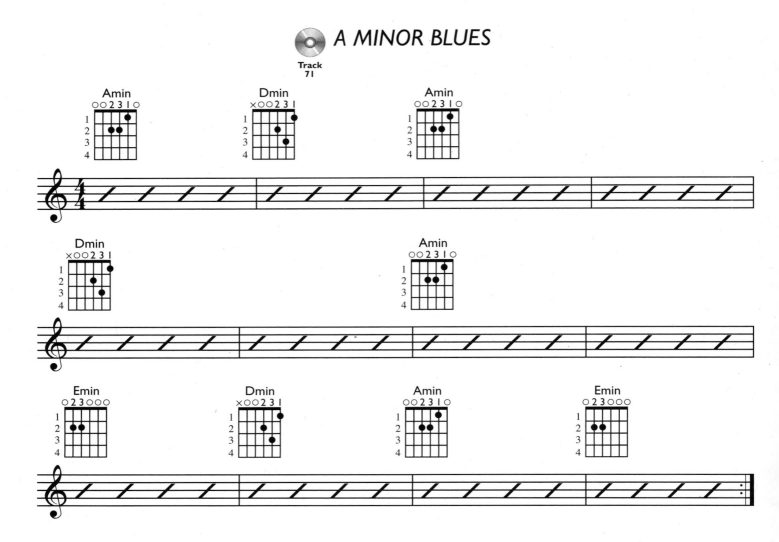

BLUES SOLOING IN A MINOR KEY

One advantage of learning the minor pentatonic scale is that it works for both major and minor blues songs. To improvise over the twelve-bar blues in A Minor, simply use the same A Minor Pentatonic scale you learned on page 66.

Minor 7th chords (min7) are similar to dominant 7ths, except that the triad is minor. Here is an A Minor 7 chord:

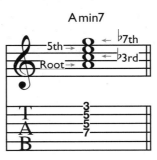

The fingering shown here shows the notes of the chord in an easy-to-understand manner, but is somewhat impractical to play. Below are some easy fingerings for minor 7th chords. You will find that they have more color than simple minor chords, and that they can be easily substituted for them. In other words, when you see Amin in the music, you can choose to play Amin7 instead.

Here are some easy minor 7 fingerings:

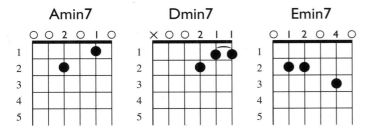

Try using minor seventh chords with the twelve-bar blues progression.

MINOR 7 BLUES

Track 72

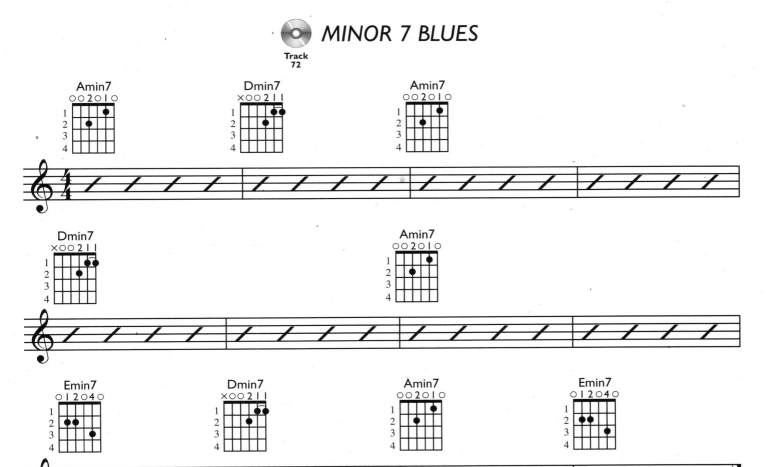

CHAPTER 7

New Techniques

LESSON 1: SWITCHING CHORDS MID-MEASURE

If you have looked at sheet music or songbooks, you have probably noticed that chords don't always change on the first beat of the measure. Even in this book, there have been examples of chords switching on beat 3 (for example, *Heavy Fog* on page 28). If you are doing simple downstrokes or a simple strum, it is fairly easy to adjust. However, if you are playing the syncopated strum from page 36, it can be tricky to know how to switch. Here are three techniques you can try:

TECHNIQUE #1: MIXING STRUMS

The easiest thing to do is to switch to a simpler strum when the chord switching becomes more complex.

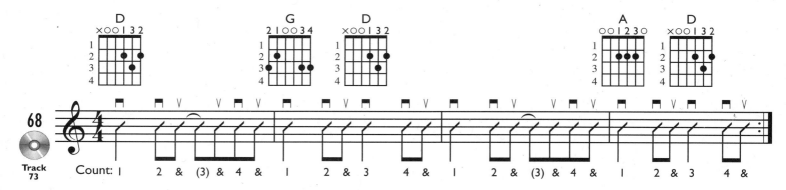

TECHNIQUE #2: SWITCHING ON THE "&" OF BEAT 2

This will cause your chord switch to come a half-beat early. It gives the chord change a funky sense of anticipation.

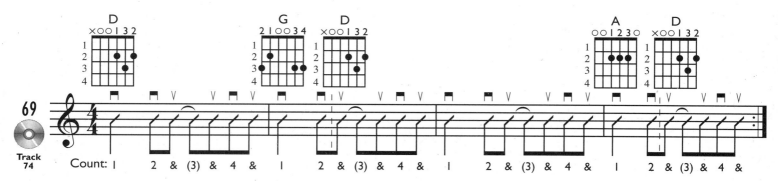

TECHNIQUE #3: SWITCHING ON THE "&" OF BEAT 3

This will cause your chords to change half-a-beat late. This is also funky but in a different way.

Try mixing Techniques #1, #2 and #3 together in the same song.

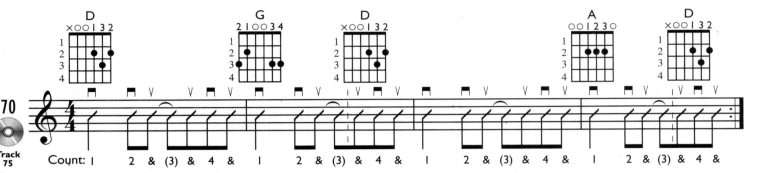

Count: 1   2 & (3) & 4 &   1   2 & (3) & 4 &   1   2 & (3) & 4 &   1   2 & (3) & 4 &

LESSON 2: SPLIT STRUMMING

Many solo acoustic artists use special strumming techniques to create the impression of multiple guitars. One technique is to mentally "split" the strings of the guitar into two groups:

> The *bass* group: Strings 4, 5, 6
> The *treble* group: Strings 1, 2, 3

You can then accent a different group on different parts of the strum. Sometimes, accent the bass group. Then suprise the listener by accenting the treble group instead. This will impart a jangly, dynamic sound to your playing. This technique is heard in the playing of Neil Young, Ani DiFranco, Michael Hedges, Joni Mitchell and many others.

Enjoy playing *I Know How it Feels*, which is in the style of Tom Petty's *You Don't Know How it Feels*. Hit the bass group on beats 1 and 2, then the treble group on beats 3 and 4.

I KNOW HOW IT FEELS

Track 76

> **SECRETS OF THE MASTERS:**
> **Don't try to be too precise with this style! Play it loose and relaxed.**

Another technique that can give the impression of multiple instruments is the *mute stroke*. A mute stroke is a strum (usually a downstroke) that mutes the strings as the pick hits them, creating a percussive sound. Mute strokes can be mixed in with normal downstrokes and upstrokes in a strum pattern.

STEP #1: GETTING THE IDEA

First, place the heel of your right hand (the fleshy part on the "pinky" side) across the strings somewhere between the sound hole and the bridge.

Second, move the pick across the strings while the heel of your hand is muting them. You should hear no notes, just a percussive, clicky, raspy kind of sound.

×   This symbol is generally reserved for percussive, unpitched sounds. The mute stroke is not completely unpitched, but this is still an effective way to notate this kind of sound.

STEP #2: THE MUTE STROKE

Now try to make the same sound in a normal downstroke. Start with your hand off the guitar as if you were going to strum down. Then as you contact the strings, mute them with the heel of your hand. This may take some practice but don't give up!

STEP #3: THE COMBINATION MOVE

Once you've got the downstroke, finger a G chord with your left hand. Play a mute stroke down, then sound the G chord on the upstroke.

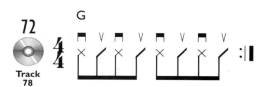

PUTTING IT ALL TOGETHER

Try the following strum pattern with mute strokes. When played properly, it will have the sound of a *backbeat* (stressed notes on beats 2 and 4) and the percussive effect will sound much like a rock drummer.

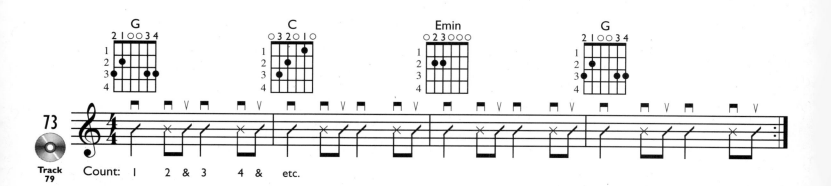

This strum pattern has been very popular with guitarist-singers since the folk revival of the early 1960s. It has been heavily used by Bob Dylan and Indigo Girls.

The strum pattern is based on the country/bluegrass strum but is not as rigid sounding. It combines the "boom-chick" effect with the jangle of the syncopated strum. Before you try this one, review the country/bluegrass strums on page 32.

Try this pattern with the bluegrass G chord (page 29).

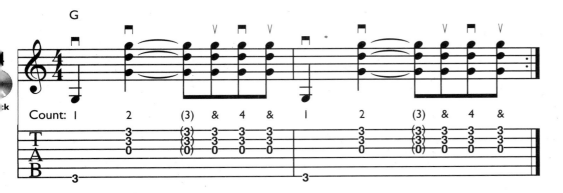

This strum is very versatile in that it can be played fast or slow, with a straight or swing beat. At first, try it slowly with swing (to review eighths check out page 64). Then, as you get the hang of it, try speeding it up with a straight beat.

Try this chord progression with the "other" folk strum.

 ## FLUTTERING IN THE BREEZE

Track 81

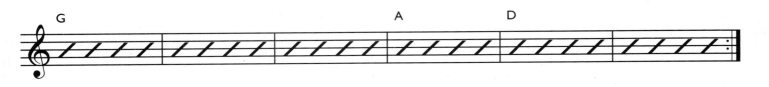

Transposing means changing the key of a song. You have already tried this by learning the same twelve-bar blues progression in both A and E (pages 62 and 71).

WHY TRANSPOSE?

The most common reason for transposing a song to a new key is to better fit the vocal range of a singer. For example, imagine a song in the key of E. If the key of E is too high, you could transpose down to D, or even C. Another reason to transpose is to make a song easier to play on the guitar.

THE SUBSTITUTION METHOD

This method of transposition is the easiest to learn but not the most efficient. First, consider this chord progression in the key of G. Play it with the syncopated strum.

TRANSPOSING TO THE KEY OF D

First, you must know how far the new key is from the original key. The key of D is a perfect 5th (seven half steps) higher than the key of G. To transpose the song, substitute each of the original chords with the chord a perfect 5th higher.

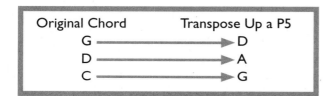

Here is the progression from example 75 transposed up a perfect 5th to D:

TRANSPOSING TO THE KEY OF A

Try using this method yourself. The answers are at the end of the lesson on page 79.

1. How far above G is A?
2. What is the new chord progression?

Transpose example 75 to the key of A (write in your answers):

THE CHORD ANALYSIS METHOD

This method takes more practice and thought at first but eventually, you will be able to transpose songs without having to write the new chords.

Here is your example progression, in the key of D.

TRANSPOSING TO THE KEY OF G

First, analyze the chord progression by chord numbers. Think of the diatonic harmony in D and determine the position of each chord in the key.

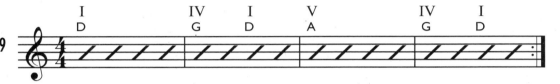

Now you are ready to transpose to any key. Try the key of G.

KEY OF G: I = G   IV = C   V = D

TRANSPOSING TO THE KEY OF A

Try this one yourself. (See the answer at the bottom of this page)

KEY OF A: I =   IV =   V =

ANSWERS TO EXAMPLE 77:

1. The key of A is one whole step higher than the key of G.

ANSWERS TO EXAMPLE 81:

Key of A: I = A   IV = D   V = E

A power chord (first covered on page 53) is a two-note chord that consists of a root and a 5th. Because the power chord has no 3rd, it can be used in place of either a major or a minor chord.

The power chord is a movable shape (it can be played on any fret) that is usually played on the lower strings of the guitar. It is very common in rock, punk, heavy metal and blues guitar. Power chords are especially popular among electric guitar players because of the way they resonate when played with lots of distortion. Many acoustic players who plug in like them for the same reason.

The power chord shape is easy to remember. Play the root (the lower note) with your 1st finger. The 5th (the upper note) is on the next string, two frets up, and is played with the 3rd finger. Try these:

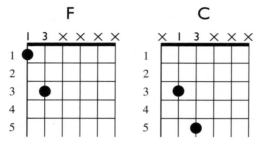

Here is a song using power chords. Play all the eighth notes with downstrokes.

RAGE AGAINST THE GUMBALL MACHINE

Track 82

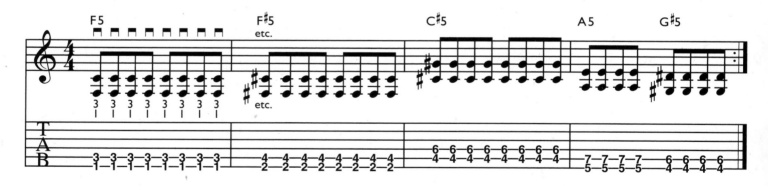

PALM MUTING

Palm muting is commonly used by rock guitarists. It is very similar to the mute stroke on page 76. Use the heel of your right hand to lightly touch the strings just to the left of the bridge.

This effect will "tighten up" the sound of the chords and make them more percussive. If you move too close to the sound hole, you will kill the notes completely. Experiment to find the best position. This effect is also great for the blues shuffle you learned on page 64. Try *Rage Against the Gumball Machine* on page 80 with *palm muting*, and prepare to fend off the groupies!

THREE-NOTE POWER CHORDS

For a thicker, chunkier power chord, you can add an octave above the root. Below are some examples. Try these with *Rage Against the Gumball Machine*.

F

F#

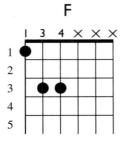

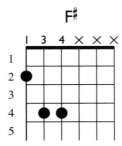

C#

D

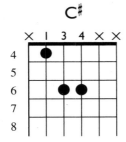

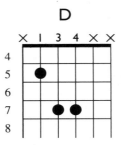

G#

A

B

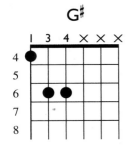

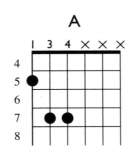

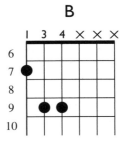

Congratulations! You've made it this far and now you're ready for your biggest challenge yet...

WHAT IS A BARRE CHORD?

A *barre chord* is a chord form that uses no open strings. It can be moved up or down the neck to play any chord.

BARRE CHORDS WITH THE ROOT ON THE 6TH STRING

This barre chord form is also known as the *E-form* barre chord because it is based on the shape of the open E chord (page 15). Simply finger an E chord using the 2nd, 3rd and 4th fingers and leave the 1st finger free to hold the barre. The root is on the 6th string. This barre chord shape is available in both major and minor forms. The minor form is based on the open E Minor chord but is refingered to leave the 1st finger free to barre.

F Major

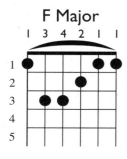

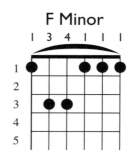

F Minor

⌒ = Barre

BARRE CHORDS WITH THE ROOT ON THE 5TH STRING

These are also known as *A-form* barre chords. Simply finger an A chord using the 2nd, 3rd and 4th fingers and leave the 1st finger free to hold the barre. The root is on the 5th string. Here are the major and minor forms. The minor form is based on the open A Minor form but is refingered to leave the 1st finger free to barre.

B♭ Major

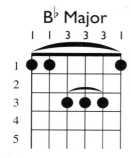

B♭ Minor

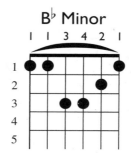

Try these chord progressions with barre chords. Fingerings are provided. Make sure to watch the fret numbers!

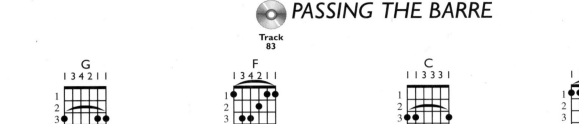

PASSING THE BARRE

Track
83

CAN I BARRE A DOLLAR?

Track
84

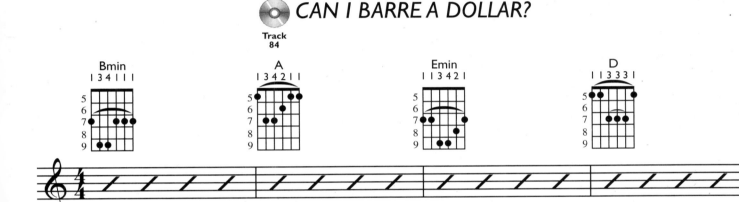

SECRETS OF THE MASTERS: TIPS FOR LEARNING BARRE CHORDS

1. Start with a mini-barre. (No—not the refrigerator in your hotel room.) Master a two-string barre on an easy fret to barre, such as the 5th fret, then a three-string barre, and so on.

2. Be picky and efficient. Don't work on having a beautiful barre sound on a string if another finger is playing above the barre on that string! For example, in an E-form barre, only the 1st, 2nd and 6th strings really need an excellent barre. Other fingers are covering the other strings.

3. Use leverage. Bring your left elbow in slightly toward your body, thus moving your 1st finger further into the strings without actually pressing any harder.

4. Be Patient! Don't worry if you don't get these right away. Work on them a little every day. Try to get each note in the chord to ring clearly. If you have problems in the first few frets, where the string tension is higher, try moving up to the 5th, 6th or 7th frets.

5. Gravity is your friend! Try not to twist your left hand into wild contortions and squeeze all of the blood out of your fingers. Instead, let your left wrist and elbow hang down in a relaxed way. Feel the pull of gravity and let it help your 1st finger "hang" on the fret.

Hammer-ons and *pull-offs* are special techniques that add fluidity and speed to melodic playing. Both techniques allow you to play multiple notes on one string with only one stroke of the pick. In musical terms, this is called a *slur* and is denoted by a curved line connecting notes of different pitches. Be careful not to confuse this with a tie which connects notes of the same pitch.

HAMMER-ON EXERCISE

To play a hammer-on, pick a note and bring a higher-numbered finger down on a higher fret quickly and firmly. You should hear the note change without having to pick again. Here is an exercise for working on hammer-ons with each finger. Try this on each string at different places on the neck.

H = Hammer-on

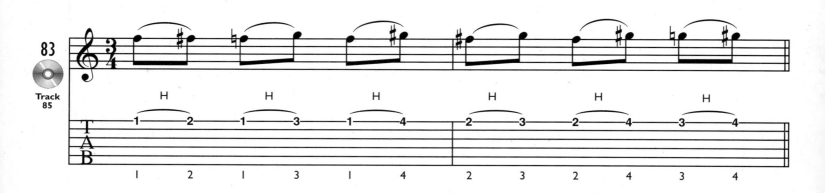

PULL-OFF EXERCISE

To play a pull-off, place two fingers down on two frets and play the note on the higher fret. Then, pull the higher-numbered finger away from the higher fret, making the lower-fret note sound without picking. When pulling-off, don't just lift up your finger; instead, give it a little "snap" by pulling your finger in towards your palm. Example 84 is an exercise for pull-offs. Try it on each string at different places on the neck.

P = Pull-off

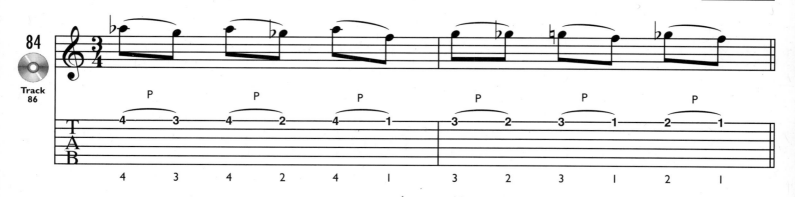

1st and 2nd Endings Review

Often, when we repeat a section, we play the last part of it differently. In the written music, this is shown with *1st* and *2nd endings*.

The first time through, play the music under the bracket with a "1" (the *1st ending*). The second time, skip the 1st ending and play the music under the bracket marked "2" (the *2nd ending*).

Blue Noodles on an E Chord uses hammer-ons and pull-offs surrounding the shape of an E chord. Go slowly and aim for clean notes. Try to make the slurred notes sound at the same volume as the picked notes. Also, try to incorporate slurs into your improvisations.

 ## BLUE NOODLES ON AN E CHORD

Track 87

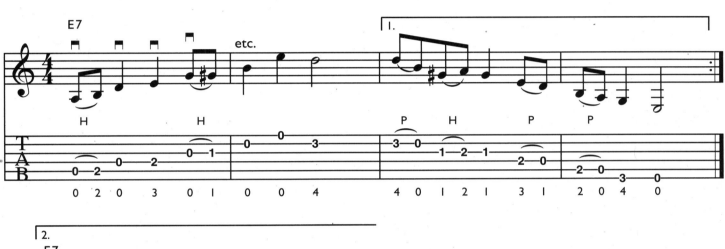

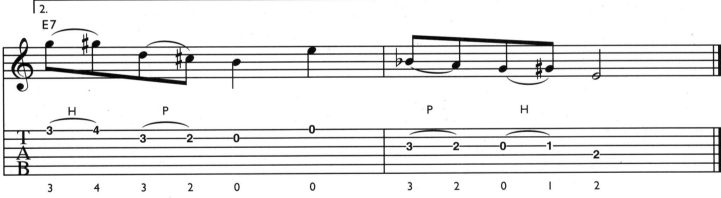

A fun way to spice up your country/bluegrass-style strumming (page 32) is to use short melodies in the bass to connect the roots of the chords. This is called *walking the bass*. Adding simple walks to your bass line helps "lead" the listener's ear to the next chord. This is like using a turn signal on a car to show the person following you where you're going. Here are a few simple walks for the key of G.

WALKING FROM A G CHORD TO A C CHORD

Adding a walk to a chord progression is very simple if you count! The walk in example 85 takes up the last two beats of the second measure. Before you try this, review your chord fingerings and strums from page 32.

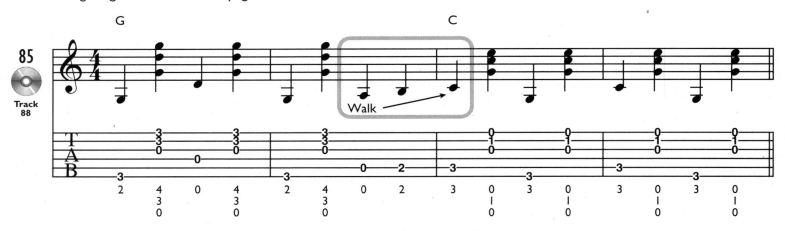

WALKING FROM A G CHORD TO A D CHORD

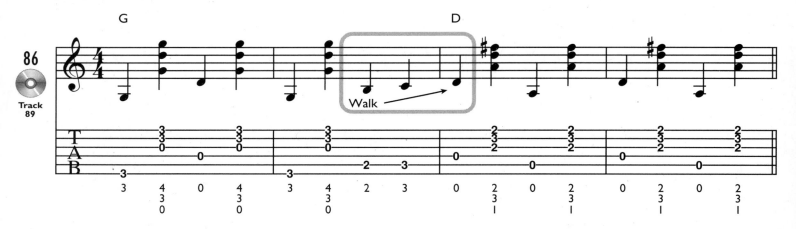

WALKING FROM A D CHORD BACK TO A G CHORD

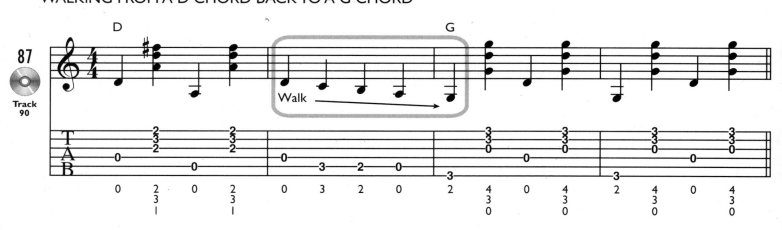

This is the chord progression from an old traditional Appalachian tune called *Free Little Bird*. It allows you to try out your bass walks. Try making up some walks of your own, too. Just make sure you have the correct number of beats in every measure.

FREE LITTLE BIRD

Track 91

CHAPTER 8

Musical Expression and Arranging

LESSON 1: PHRASING AND DYNAMICS

EXPRESSION

Music is not just about keeping time and playing the right notes or chords. In order for music to have an emotional effect, it needs a sense of *expression*. Two very important elements of musical expression are *phrasing* and *dynamics*.

PHRASING

Phrasing is the way that touch, volume and tempo are used to imply a sense of direction, movement and rest in a piece of music. If notes are like words, then phrasing is the way that the words are made to sound like sentences, or complete thoughts.

PHRASING MARKINGS

Written music uses a large number of markings and terms to communicate phrasing and expression to the performer. Many of these terms are Italian. A quick tour of some commonly used terms should give you some ideas for your own music. First, the *phrase mark* is a curved line that loosely connects an entire passage of music. It can be confused with a slur or a tie, but the phrase mark is usually shown above the staff and may have slurs or ties beneath it.

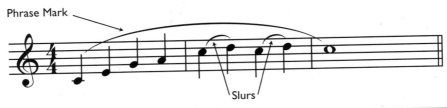

Phrase Mark

OTHER PHRASING AND EXPRESSION TERMS		
TERM	**DEFINITION**	**MARKING**
Legato	Notes are to be played in a smooth, connected fashion.	The word "Legato" marked above the music.
Staccato	Short, detached, unconnected notes.	The word "*Staccato*" marked above the music, or small dots above or below individual note heads.
Accent	A note played louder than the surrounding notes.	This sign > above or below the note head.

DYNAMICS

Dynamics define how loud or soft the notes or passages of music will sound. Dynamic expression and contrast is very important to imparting a sense of emotion in a piece of music.

LOUD			SOFT		
Mark	**Term**	**Definition**	**Mark**	**Term**	**Definition**
mf	*Mezzo Forte*	Medium Loud	*mp*	*Mezzo Piano*	Medium soft
f	*Forte*	Loud	*p*	*Piano*	Soft
ff	*Fortissimo*	Very Loud	*pp*	*Pianissimo*	Very soft
fff	*Fortississimo*	Very, very loud	*ppp*	*Pianississimo*	Very, very soft
⟨	*Crescendo*	Gradually becoming louder	⟩	*Decrescendo*	Gradually becoming softer

THE DYNAMIC SCALE

Arranged from softest to loudest, the dynamic markings look like this:

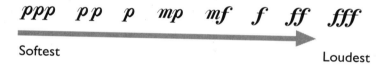

ppp   *pp*   *p*   *mp*   *mf*   *f*   *ff*   *fff*

Softest → Loudest

THE "ARCH"

Many times a phrase or an entire piece of music will lend itself to a dynamic "arch" that begins at a softer dynamic, climaxes at a louder dynamic, then returns to a softer level. This is especially true if the melody moves from low notes up to high notes, then back down. Look for opportunities to place this kind of expression in your music. Also look for spots where a "reverse arch" (loud to soft to loud) might work.

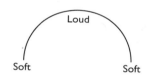

TIPS FOR EXPRESSIVE TECHNIQUE

It takes good control of the pick (or of your fingers) to bring out dynamics and phrasing with your right hand. Here are a few tips:

To play louder
Slightly tighten the grip on your pick. Do not pick "deeper" into the string, or try to use more muscle force. This makes a harsh tone.

To play softer
Slightly loosen the grip on your pick (but don't drop it!).

To play legato
Try to pick notes at the same time as you fret them. Make sure your pick doesn't touch a vibrating string before it's time to pluck again, cutting off the previous note.

To play staccato
You can use your pick to cut off the note by placing it back on the string, or use your left hand to cut off the note by lifting your finger(s) up slightly from the fret(s).

LESSON 2: CREATING AN ARRANGEMENT

An *arrangement* is the musical setting of a song or composition. In simple terms, the song is *what* you play, and the arrangement is *how* you play it. If you've ever heard the same song done by different performers, you have heard the effects of arranging.

LOOKING FOR THE CLUES

When you are trying to build an arrangement of a song or instrumental tune, there are clues within the composition that can give you ideas for the arrangement. The way you interpret these clues will help put your own personality into the arrangement.

LYRICAL CLUES

If the song has words, you can use these to help you build your arrangement concept. For example, if the song has a sad undertone, you might choose a slow tempo and an intimate fingerpicked background. On the other hand, very effective arrangements have been made by contrasting the mood of the lyrics with the mood of the music. Very troubled lyrics can be set to an energetic, dancing background.

MUSICAL FORM

The *musical form* of a piece includes how many sections there are, how long the phrases are, and the order of the sections. For example, you might choose to arrange the *verses* (the parts of the song that tell the story; the lyrics change each time) of a song one way, and give a different style or feel to the *chorus* (the part of the song that expresses the basic idea; it's a refrain wherein the lyrics are always the same).

PRACTICAL CONSIDERATIONS

You may choose to place the song in a new key to better fit your voice. You may also choose your strums, picking patterns and chord fingerings to fit your own playing level.

UNITY AND CONTRAST

Unity and *contrast* are two terms that are used to describe the delicate balance that holds a work of art together and makes it interesting.

Unity is repetition, similarity, the recurrence of ideas.
Contrast is variation, change, alteration or the addition of new ideas.

Here are examples of some key musical elements, and how the concepts of unity and contrast can be applied to them.

MUSICAL ELEMENT	UNITY	CONTRAST
Texture	Using the same strum pattern throughout a song or section of a song.	Mixing strum patterns or mixing melody and chord playing in a song.
Tempo	Maintaining a consistent tempo throughout a song.	Altering the tempo of a section or phrase.
Dynamics	Maintaining a consistent volume or range of volumes throughout a song or section of a song.	Changing the dynamics of different sections of a song or following a dynamic pattern that adds emotional intensity.

EXAMPLE ARRANGEMENT

Try playing *Song of the Elusive Beach Moose* and check out the arrangement tips that have been added for the guitar part.

STEP #1: Play the chord progression of this song using a simple strum such as the syncopated strum.

STEP #2: Try the song using the strums, textures and dynamics as indicated.

SONG OF THE ELUSIVE BEACH MOOSE

Track 92

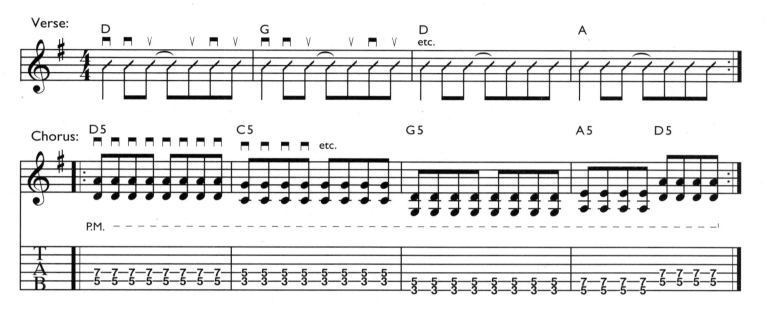

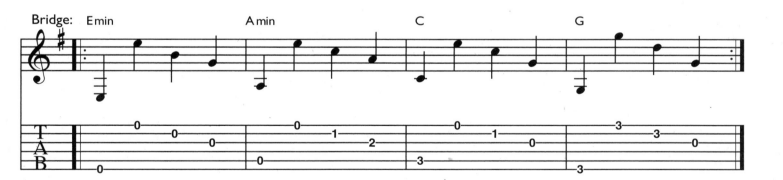

The form of the tune is as follows (each section is eight bars long):
Verse
Chorus
Verse
Chorus
Bridge
Verse
Chorus

APPENDIX

THE WONDERFUL CAPO, THE TERRIBLE CAPO

The capo is a device that clamps onto the guitar neck, fretting all six strings at whatever fret you choose. This fret then becomes like the nut of the guitar, allowing you to play all of your open chords in a higher key. There are many types and they all work (you pay for durability and convenience of design).

Try one and see how the capo can broaden the range of your instrument. The capo can become a bit of a crutch, however. Don't forget to try transposing to new keys without the capo (page 78).

TO FINGERPICK OR NOT TO FINGERPICK

Fingerpicking (discussed in Chapter 4) can be done with bare fingers, fingernails or with *fingerpicks*. Fingerpicks are made of plastic or metal and wrap around the fingers and/or thumb. Once you get used to them, they provide a clear, somewhat louder fingerpicked tone. Another advantage is that you don't have to worry about the condition of your nails because the fingerpicks give the same, consistent tone all the time.

Fingerpicks have many disadvantages, as well. They can compromise your technique, causing you to make special adjustments to your playing in order to get the pick "out of the way" for the next note. In addition, the consistent tone of fingerpicks does not allow for a variety of touches and sounds. Fingerpicks work very well for some players. On the other hand (no pun intended), playing without them affords the widest range of tonal colors, as well as the healthiest technique for the muscles of the hand and forearm. The problem of technical difficulties may be alleviated by checking out some of the new designs in fingerpicks.

One popular compromise is to use just a thumb pick. This allows the player to have clear, loud bass notes and a variety of colors in the touch of the fingers. Also, the thumb pick is popular with players who like to mix strumming and finger picking in the same song.

BUY A METRONOME!

A metronome is an adjustable mechanical device (either wind-up, battery-powered or digital) that generates a beat pulse for you to play along with. You can adjust the pulse from ridiculously slow to very fast. The speed is marked in "beats-per-minute." A metronome speed of 60 is the same as one beat-per-second. The simplest metronomes make a ticking sound, while the more involved ones will make drum sounds and even mark measures of beats for you.

When used regularly (and with a Zen-like patience), the metronome will help you play with a steady rhythm. The only practice technique that is as valuable is to play with another person who has good rhythm—this can be difficult to do on a daily basis.

Don't let the metronome drive you crazy! At first, it may appear to be speeding up and slowing down while you play. Listen carefully—it's probably you. Pick a consistent, slow tempo to work with for the first few days and try the metronome with one favorite song. See how many measures you can play before you and the metronome have a parting of the ways. Gradually increase your endurance before you increase the speed.

HELP WITH TUNING

One particularly tricky challenge for the beginning guitarist is keeping the instrument in tune. Tuning an instrument well takes a great deal of practice and experience. If you find that your chords are just not sounding quite right, consider investing in an electronic tuner.

Electronic tuners come in two basic designs: the guitar-only tuner and the chromatic tuner. The guitar-only tuner has settings for each of the open strings of the guitar. You just select the string, play it into the microphone on the tuner, and the tuner will show you if the note is sharp (too high), flat (too low) or in tune. An advantage of guitar tuners is that they are inexpensive. A disadvantage is that, if one of your strings is way off, the tuner will not know what note you are playing and may direct you to tune too high or low. A chromatic tuner listens to the note you are playing and tells you what note is the closest one, and whether you are sharp or flat from that note. Though a bit more expensive, these are more convenient for tuning a variety of instruments. Just make sure you know which string belongs to which note!

Don't rely completely on electronic tuners. After you've tuned with a tuner, make sure your strings are in tune with each other using the note-matching technique described on page 7. Play a few chords and see if they ring in tune. You may have to go back through the tuning process a few times before the instrument "settles" in tune.

FINGER STRENGTH BUILDERS

There are many gadgets and devices on the market that are designed to build finger strength. Usually these devices are meant to be squeezed with the fingers. While it is conceivable that such items could help build your strength to fret notes, be very careful. In general, devices that force you to squeeze against resistance are actually focusing on the wrong kinds of muscles. Guitar playing requires agility and accuracy more than brute strength. Agility and accuracy are built through practice and technique exercises. "Strength builders," however, can cause strain and inflammation to the muscles of the hand and forearm.

HOW TO PRACTICE

"HOME BASE" TECHNIQUE

It is important from the beginning to play with the best, most relaxed technique you can. Though you will see and learn many variations of technique, this will become the "home base" to which your body will always return. Building these good habits requires two elements:

1. TECHNIQUE EXERCISES

These allow you to concentrate on technique without worrying about keeping your place in the music.

2. MENTAL FOCUS IN PRACTICE

When you work on songs or new skills, be aware of your hand positions, body posture, rhythm and touch.

WHEN TO PRACTICE

When you are first beginning, or when you are learning new skills, it is best to practice often. Five to ten minutes here and there on a new skill will work much better than an hour every three or four days. If you're lucky enough to be able to practice at the same time every day, you will see great improvement. You will also notice that you develop a better ability to focus on guitar playing at that time. If it's not possible to practice at the same time every day, at least try to pick up the instrument for a few minutes every day, and then reinforce with longer sessions every couple of days.

WHAT TO PRACTICE

It is a great idea to have a small number of different "projects" going on in your practice sessions. This keeps you from getting bored or bogged down, and it helps you improve several skills at once. Pick two or three things to work on every day for a week, then adjust your plan for the next week. Some of these projects might include reading music, learning to improvise, playing a new melody or learning a new chord progression. Be sure to spend time on each project every time you play.

ORGANIZING A PRACTICE SESSION

Here's a sample 30-minute practice session you may want to try for a few weeks. If you have more or less time, adjust the time on each item.

1. **Technical Exercises** 5 minutes

   These include finger exercises, counting and foot-tapping practice, warm-ups and scales.

2. **Reading Music/Melody** 10 minutes

   Try reading lots of new material in order to keep your reading skills in shape. If you are not working on reading music, work on melody playing and improvising.

3. **Playing Songs/Chords** 10 minutes

   Spend some time every day working on songs with chords. This may include working on new strums or fingerpicking patterns.

4. **Reviewing Old Material** 5 minutes

   Always save a little time to go back and play songs you are already good at. This keeps them "tuned up" and ready to go for times when you want to play for relaxation or for other people.

WHAT TO LISTEN FOR

Every person who picks up an instrument has his or her own unique taste in music and inspiration for wanting to play. Now that you are delving deeper into the acoustic guitar, go back and listen to some of your favorite music and pay special attention to the guitarists. Notice the role of the guitar in the music—when it is playing and not playing. Pay attention to the touches and tones the player puts into the music. Is the player using a flatpick, or fingerpicking or something else altogether? Try to identify chords and rhythms that you are learning. You'll hear a lot of them!

In addition to listening to your old favorites with "new ears," try out some new music in styles you may have never heard or thought you'd like. Follow the suggestions of other guitarists or musicians. Remember not to limit yourself just to guitar! Every instrument has something exciting to offer the inquisitive musician.

Here are some acoustic guitarists to check out during the beginning phase of your development:

FOLK AND ROCK
Crosby, Stills, Nash and Young
Kurt Cobain (Nirvana)
Bob Dylan
Steve Earle
Melissa Etheridge
Jay Farrar (Son Volt and Uncle Tupelo)
Indigo Girls
Jewel
John Prine
Darius Rucker (Hootie & the Blowfish)
Jeff Tweedy (Wilco and Uncle Tupelo)

BLUES
John Lee Hooker
Mississippi John Hurt
Brownie McGhee

COUNTRY, BLUEGRASS AND OLD-TIME
The Carter Family
Johnny Cash
Lester Flatt (Flatt & Scruggs)
Cary Fridley (Freight Hoppers)
Nancy Griffith
Woody Guthrie

INTERMEDIATE ACOUSTIC GUITAR

This book was acquired, edited, and produced
by Workshop Arts, Inc., the publishing arm of
the National Guitar Workshop.
Nathaniel Gunod, acquisitions, managing editor
Timothy Phelps, interior design
Scott Smallwood and Gary Tomassetti, music typesetters
CD recorded and mastered by Collin Tilton at Bar None Studio, Cheshire, CT

TABLE OF CONTENTS

INTRODUCTION

Welcome to *Intermediate Acoustic Guitar*, the second book of *The Complete Acoustic Guitar Method*! This volume builds on the skills and techniques introduced in *Beginning Acoustic Guitar*. This book is designed for the intermediate player interested in the many styles and techniques of acoustic music, from the funk of Ani DiFranco and Dave Matthews to traditional bluegrass, blues, alternate tunings and harmonic techniques.

This book focuses on playing with a pick, including strumming and melodies. To focus on fingerstyle techniques, check out *The Complete Fingerstyle Guitar Method*, also published by the National Guitar Workshop and Alfred.

WHO SHOULD USE THIS BOOK

This book is written for the intermediate player. You should be familiar with open chords, some barre chords, the twelve-bar blues progression, basic strumming, the major scale and the minor pentatonic scale. All of these are covered in *Beginning Acoustic Guitar*. You do not have to be able to read music to use this book. However, reading music will help you to better understand the scales and chord constructions. Reading music is covered in *Beginning Acoustic Guitar*.

HOW TO USE THIS BOOK

The lessons in this book are organized in three major sections:

       Part One   – Styles and Techniques
       Part Two   – Improvisation
       Part Three – Alternate Tunings

The book is designed so that you can study the major sections in any order, or work through them simultaneously. Many of the chapters are progressive, meaning each lesson builds on the previous ones within that chapter.

This volume is dedicated to Evan Horne and Timothy Berry.

An MP3 CD is included with this book to make learning easier and more enjoyable. The symbol shown at bottom left appears next to every example in the book that features an MP3 track. Use the MP3s to ensure you're capturing the feel of the examples and interpreting the rhythms correctly. The track number below the symbol corresponds directly to the example you want to hear (example numbers are above the icon). All the track numbers are unique to each "book" within this volume, meaning every book has its own Track 1, Track 2, and so on. (For example, *Beginning Acoustic Guitar* starts with Track 1, as does *Intermediate Acoustic Guitar* and *Mastering Acoustic Guitar*.) Track 1 for each book will help you tune your guitar.

To access the MP3s on the CD, place the CD in your computer's CD-ROM drive. In Windows, double-click on My Computer, then right-click on the CD icon labeled "MP3 Files" and select Explore to view the files and copy them to your hard drive. For Mac, double-click on the CD icon on your desktop labeled "MP3 Files" to view the files and copy them to your hard drive.

CHAPTER 1

Reading Music and TAB

LESSON 1: PITCH

This book assumes that you have either completed *Beginning Acoustic Guitar,* or you consider yourself an intermediate player because of what you have learned from a teacher or on your own. While you don't have to read music to use this book, it will definitely help if you can. This section is included as a quick review or introduction to reading. For a more thorough treatment of the subject, refer back to *Beginning Acoustic Guitar.*

STAFF

Music is written on a *staff* containing five lines and four spaces. Notes are written alternately on the lines and spaces in alphabetical order.

CLEF

The *clef* indicates which notes coincide with a particular line or space. Different clefs are used for different instruments. Guitar music is written in *G clef.* The inside curl of the G clef encircles the line which is called "G." When the G clef is placed on the second line, as in guitar music, it is called the *treble clef.*

G clef

Using the G clef, the notes are as follows:*

E   G   B   D   F   F   A   C   E

LEDGER LINES

Ledger lines are used to indicate pitches above and below the staff.

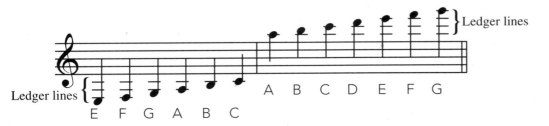

* In standard notation, the guitar sounds an octave lower than written.

The staff is divided by vertical lines called *bar lines*. The space between two bar lines is a *measure*. Each measure (or *bar*) is an equal unit of time. *Double bar lines* mark the end of a section or example.

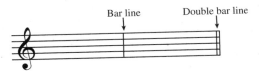

TIME SIGNATURE

Every piece of music has numbers at the beginning that tell you how to count the time.

Examples: $\frac{4}{4}$ $\frac{3}{4}$ $\frac{6}{8}$

The top number represents the number of beats, or counts, per measure.
The bottom number represents the type of note receiving one count.

For example: when the bottom number is 4, the quarter note (see below) gets one count.

when the bottom number is 8, the eighth note (see below) gets one count.

Sometimes a **C** is written in place of $\frac{4}{4}$ time. This is called *common time*.

Joni Mitchell was born in Alberta, Canada. After studying art in Calgary, she moved to Toronto in 1964, where she performed in coffeehouses and folk clubs. Her first album, Joni Mitchell, *was produced by David Crosby and was released in 1969.*

PHOTO COURTESY OF PAUL STARR/REPRISE RECORDS

NOTE AND REST VALUES IN $\frac{4}{4}$ TIME

These symbols indicate rhythm:

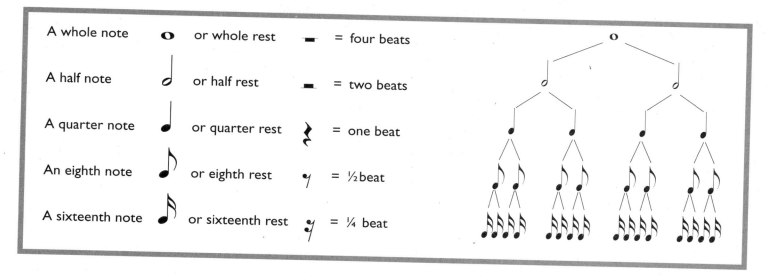

A whole note	𝅝 or whole rest	▬	= four beats
A half note	𝅗𝅥 or half rest	▬	= two beats
A quarter note	𝅘𝅥 or quarter rest	𝄽	= one beat
An eighth note	𝅘𝅥𝅮 or eighth rest	𝄾	= ½ beat
A sixteenth note	𝅘𝅥𝅯 or sixteenth rest	𝄿	= ¼ beat

Notes shorter than a quarter note are usually beamed together in groups:

LESSON 3: TABLATURE

Tablature (TAB) is a graphic representation of the strings of the guitar. The top horizontal line represents the 1st string; the bottom line represents the 6th string. The numbers on the lines indicate which frets to play.

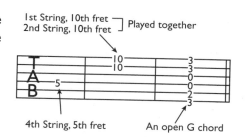

CHAPTER 2

New Colors and Textures

LESSON 1: FLATPICKING ARPEGGIOS

ARPEGGIOS

An *arpeggio* is a "broken chord"—a chord that is played one tone at a time. Mixing arpeggios and strummed chords gives a great variety of textures to your playing.

ALTERNATE PICKING

To play arpeggios with a pick, make sure that you are alternating down (⊓) and up strokes (∨) for the eighth notes. This can be tricky at first, because you will sometimes play down on one string then up on a higher or lower string. Practice these string changes slowly at first.

Example 1 has some arpeggio patterns using a D chord. Once you get the hang of these patterns, try them with other chords. *Be patient* and make sure that you are alternating your picking regularly. This will help you when you try to speed up the patterns.

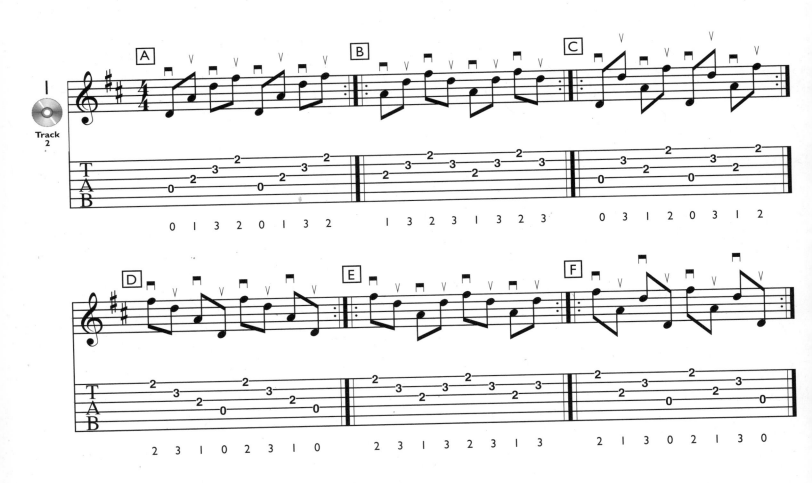

This tune is in the style of the Rolling Stones' arrangement of *Love in Vain* by Robert Johnson. Practice it slowly and try to get clean, clear, sustaining notes. Make sure your alternate picking is exactly right!

This tune also incorporates some hammer-ons. Note that the music tells you to use down-strokes on the hammer-ons. This gives a more authentic sound to this piece. Sometimes it's okay to break the pattern of alternate picking to give a specific emphasis to the sound!

H = Hammer-on

LOVE AND TRAINS

Track 3

Suspended chords can be used as decorations on basic triads, or they can be used by themselves to give a dreamy, unresolved sound.

A suspension is a very old musical device, used by everyone from J. S. Bach to James Taylor. Put simply, a suspension occurs in a passage of harmony where a note from one chord is held, or "suspended," over the next chord. In modern music, a suspension occurs when the 3rd of the triad is replaced by the 2nd or 4th degree of the scale. Thus, we have two types of suspension, the *suspended 2nd (sus2)* and the *suspended 4th (sus4)*.

Example 3 shows the two types of suspensions possible on a simple C Major chord.

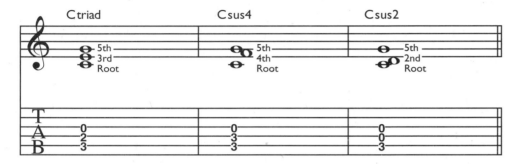

SUSPENDED MAJOR CHORDS

Sus chords can be constructed on any major chord. Simply find the 3rd of the chord, and move it down one whole step to form a sus2 or up one half step to form a sus4. Below are some common sus chord fingerings for some commonly used chords. The unaltered chord is shown first. The chord tones are notated underneath each chord diagram (R=Root, 3=3rd, 5=5th, 2=2nd and 4=4th).

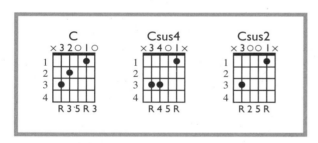

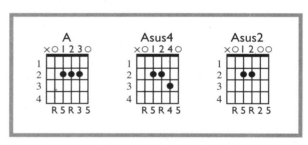

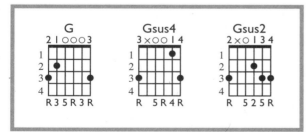

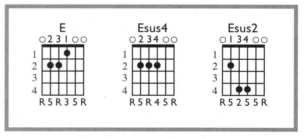

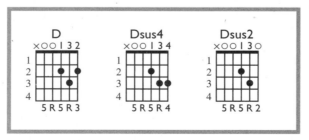

SUSPENDED MINOR CHORDS

Minor triads can also be suspended. Simply move the 3rd of the chord down one half step to form a sus2 or up one whole step to form a sus4. A suspended chord is neither major nor minor, since it has no 3rd. The major or minor sound is only implied when the chord that precedes or follows the sus chord is major or minor. Try the progression of A chords in example 3. Hear how the character of the suspension changes in a major or minor context. Also try suspensions of other minor chords you know.

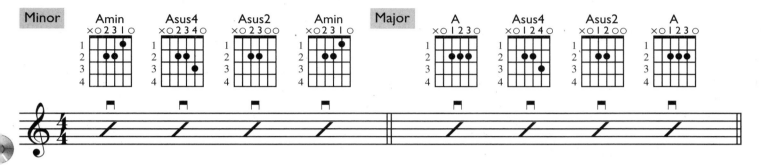

MOVABLE SUSPENDED CHORD FORMS

Here are some voicings for suspensions that can be moved up and down the neck to sound any suspended chord you choose. Simply locate the root of the chord you want on the neck, and form the fingering at that fret.

SUSPENDED CHORD FORMS WITH THE ROOT ON THE 6TH STRING

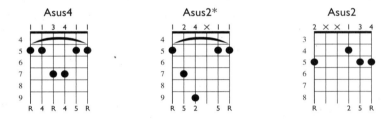

*With this voicing, use your 3rd finger to mute the 3rd string.

SUSPENDED CHORD FORMS WITH THE ROOT ON THE 5TH STRING

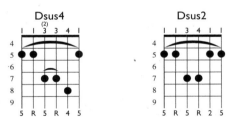

SUSPENDED CHORD FORMS WITH THE ROOT ON THE 4TH STRING

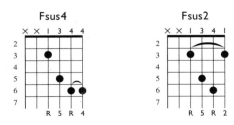

Try this tune using suspended voicings. The strum patterns are indicated.

SUSPENSION BRIDGE

Track 5

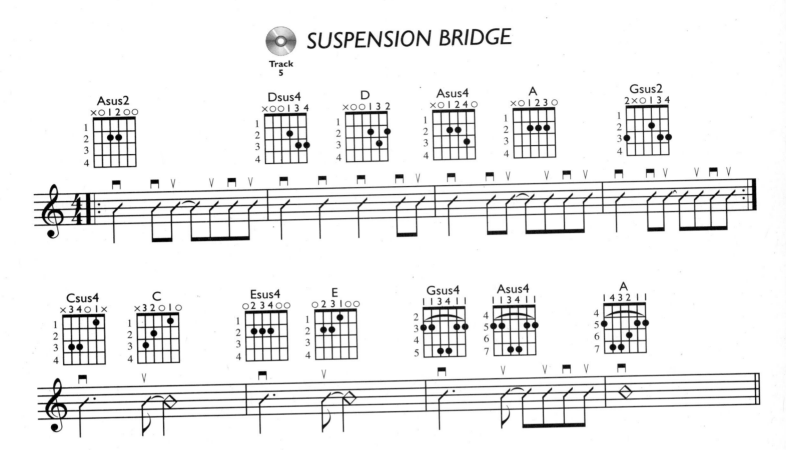

HAMMER-ONS AND PULL-OFFS WITH SUS CHORDS

Suspensions can be particularly effective when they are approached or resolved with slurs (hammer-ons and pull-offs, see page 84, *Beginning Acoustic Guitar*). Try example 5 using a simple downstroke on each chord. Hammer-ons and pull-offs also work great in a fingerpicked passage. Try to make your slurred notes as loud and clear as your picked notes.

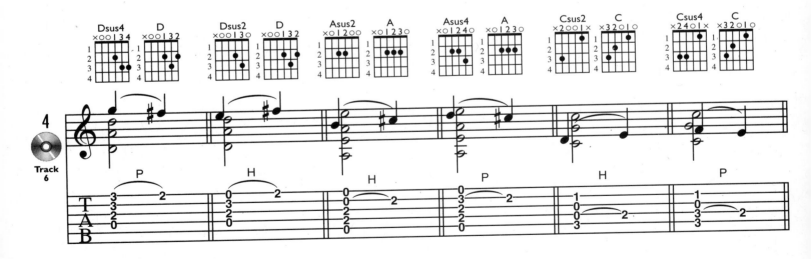

Track 6

Not a Solution, Just a Suspension uses slurs with suspended voicings. It can be played with a pick or fingerstyle. If you are playing with a pick, try to alternate down and up picking in the arpeggio passages. This tune uses suspended chord sounds that can be heard in the playing of James Taylor and David Wilcox.

NOT A SOLUTION, JUST A SUSPENSION

Track 7

Dominant 7 chords were introduced on page 70. To briefly review, every dominant 7 chord has a root, major 3rd, perfect 5th and minor 7th interval. They are commonly called the root, 3, 5 and $\flat$7. You can also think of a dominant 7 as a major triad with an added $\flat$7. The $\flat$7 is a whole step below the root. For example, C7 contains C, E, G and B$\flat$ (B$\flat$ is a whole step below the root tone, C).

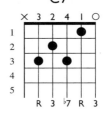

MOVABLE CHORD FORMS

Here are some *movable* chord forms for dominant 7 chords. These will be used to play acoustic funk, swing, and blues music in the next chapter. Movable forms are playable anywhere on the neck because they use no open strings. The chord tones are listed under the diagrams. To find a particular chord on the neck, locate the root in the voicing and place that finger on the appropriate note on the neck for the chord you want. The frets indicated below will sound D7 chords.

MOVEABLE DOMINANT 7 CHORD FORMS

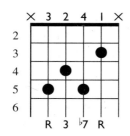 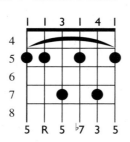 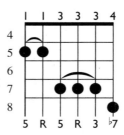 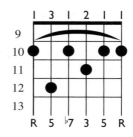 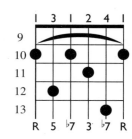

DIATONIC DOMINANT 7

In many cases, especially in the blues, we use dominant 7 on almost every chord in a song. It's a matter of style—the dominant 7 chord is a great "color." But in any given major key, the dominant 7 chord only occurs once naturally (*diatonically*—with no alterations to the scale). This would be a good time to review "Lesson 8: Harmony and Chords" on page 58.

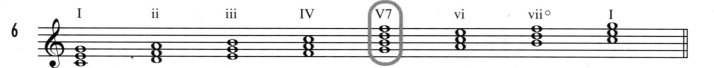

The other 7 chords in major keys will be covered later in this method (they include the *minor 7, major 7* and *minor 7$\flat$5* chords). Rest assured, the only diatonic dominant 7 chord in a major key is on the V. If we play other dominant 7 chords in a song, they are either strictly for color (*nondiatonic*) or they are functioning in a very special way, which is discussed in the next lesson.

Read on...

Roman Numeral Review			
I ...... i* 1	V .... v 5
II ..... ii 2	VI ..... vi 6
III ... iii 3	VII .... vii 7
IV ... iv 4	

* Lower-case Roman numerals are used for minor and diminished chords.

LESSON 4: SECONDARY DOMINANTS

Because the diatonic dominant 7 chord only occurs once in any major key, *every dominant 7 chord can be thought of as V of a chord a perfect 5th below!* Here is a list of dominant 7 chords and the major or minor chords they resolve to:

V7	I or i		V7	I or i
G7	C or C Minor		**D♭7**	A♭ or G♯ Minor
D7	G or G Minor		**A♭7**	D♭ or D♭ Minor
A7	D or D Minor		**E♭7**	A♭ or A♭ Minor
E7	A or A Minor		**B♭7**	E♭ or E♭ Minor
B7	E or E Minor		**F7**	B♭ or B♭ Minor

Sometimes a song will contain dominant 7 chords from outside the key that resolve to diatonic chords in the key. These are called *secondary dominants*. To understand this better, let's review the key of G.

Diatonic Chords in G Major						
I	ii	iii	IV	V	vi	vii°
G	Amin	Bmin	C	D	Emin	F♯dim

Now look at example 7 below. The E7 chord in bar 3 is in the key of G. It is a V7 for Amin (the following chord), which is a perféct 5th below E. Since Amin is the ii chord, E7 is called V/ii (five of two). Here are the other secondary dominants for the key of G.

SECONDARY DOMINANTS FOR THE KEY OF G AND THE CHORDS TO WHICH THEY RESOLVE:

Secondary Dominant	Chord Name	Resolution	Chord Name
V/ii (five of two)	E7	ii (two)	Amin
V/iii	F♯7	iii	Bmin
V/IV	G7	IV	C
V/V	A7	V	D
V/vi	B7	vi	Emin

Example 7 uses secondary dominants to "set up" ii, IV, V and vi in the key of G. Use a country-style strum.

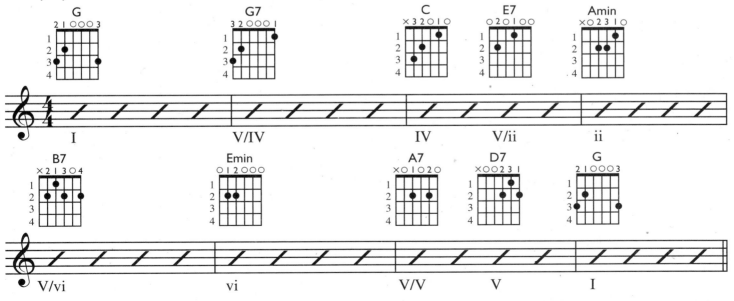

Harmonics are pure, chiming, bell-like tones that sound different from regular open or fretted notes. To play them on the guitar, it is helpful to understand the *overtone series*.

THE OVERTONE SERIES

The overtone series is actually the foundation of both music and the construction of musical instruments. It can be related to the spectrum of colors in light. Just as every beam of light includes a spectrum of different colors, every musical sound includes a spectrum of pitches. The guitar string makes a great musical prism—it is able to break a note into the different pitches that are combined within it. It is easy to see how the overtone series works on a guitar string by using simple geometric divisions of the string length. Look at the low E string:

Open E is the *fundamental* note of the string.

Dividing the string in half, by playing at the 12th fret, gives a note one octave higher (E).

One third of the string length (the 7th or 19th fret) gives a note a 5th higher than the octave (B).

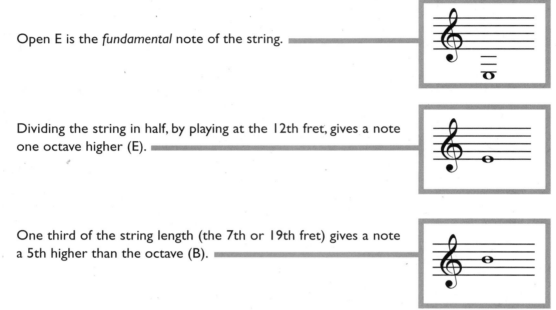

These simple geometric divisions can be carried on to generate all the basic notes of the chromatic scale. They can also be used to find harmonics on the neck of the guitar.

HARMONIC NODES

Certain spots along a string can generate strong harmonic tones. These spots are called *harmonic nodes*. The ones are at the 12th, 7th, 5th and 9th frets (yes, in that order). These nodes divide the string by half, thirds, quarters and fifths, respectively.

To play a harmonic, lightly touch the string (just grazing the surface) directly above the chosen fret. Pick the string firmly and then quickly remove your finger from the string. This allows the harmonic tone to ring clearly. With a little practice, you will get the timing down. Try the node at the 12th fret first (it's the easiest) and then the 7th, 5th and 9th frets.

Touch lightly.

Pick and release.

HARMONICS ON ONE STRING

Try playing the harmonics on the 1st string (E) shown in example 8. Check out the series of notes generated by the harmonics. Harmonics are designated by diamond shaped note heads. In the TAB, diamonds above a fret tell you to play the harmonic node at that fret. The notation *8va* means "sounds an octave higher than written."

◇	=	Harmonic
8va	=	*Ottava alta.* Sounds an octave higher.

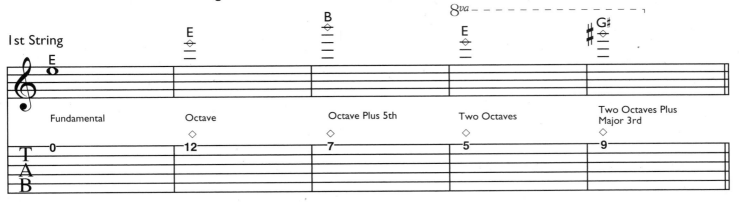

Here are the harmonics generated by the strong nodes on the other open strings. The frets are indicated below the notes.

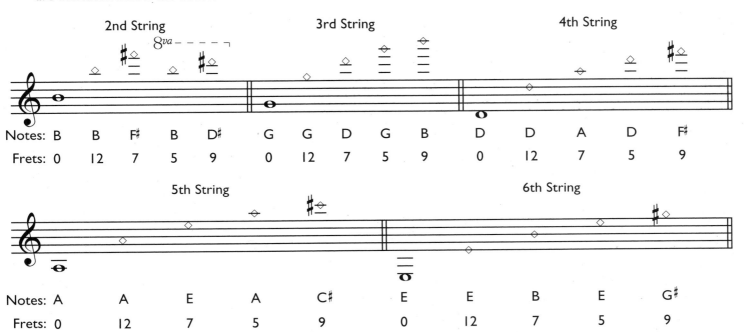

Harmonic notes can be creatively combined to play melodies. Try this tune:

🔘 THE BELLS OF WHIMSY

Track 9

> ### SECRETS OF THE MASTERS
> *With some skill and practice, you can play harmonic tones at almost any point along the string. They're everywhere! They are even between the frets and over the soundhole. Some of them repeat themselves at different points along the neck. This is because of the mathematics. For example, when you perform a harmonic at the 7th fret, you are dividing the string into thirds so there is another node that does the same thing—the 19th fret.*

nut   7th fret   19th fret   bridge

ARTIFICIAL HARMONICS

It is possible to play harmonics on fretted notes as well as open strings. The many techniques for this are called *artificial harmonics*.

PUT DOWN YOUR PICK

To play an artificial harmonic, the left hand frets a note or chord while the right hand touches the harmonic node *and* plucks the string simultaneously. For this reason, it is difficult to play artificial harmonics with a pick. You may want to put your pick down or hold it in the palm of your right hand with fingers you're not using while trying these techniques.

Below are a few different techniques for playing artificial harmonics. They are shown using the harmonic node twelve frets (one octave) **above the fretted note**. Remember that they can also be used at the other harmonic nodes, particularly the strong ones at the 7th, 5th and 9th frets above the fretted note.

Technique #1

Fret the 2nd fret of the 1st string (F♯). Use *i* (right-hand index finger) to lightly touch the node at the 14th fret (one octave above your fretted F♯). While touching the node, put *p* (right-hand thumb) under *i* and pluck the string, then quickly lift *i* from the node. If you get the timing just right, a perfect harmonic will sound!

Technique #2

Fret the 2nd fret of the 1st string (F♯). Again, use *i* to lightly touch the node at the 14th fret. While touching the node, use your *a* (right-hand ring finger) to pluck the string, then quickly lift *i* from the node. This technique also works great if you want to play several strings in succession with a chord. Just "drag" *i* along the harmonic nodes from the high string down to the lower strings.

Technique #3

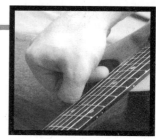

This one is a little trickier but can be very useful. Fret the 2nd fret of the first string (F♯). Use the knuckle of *p* to lightly touch the node at the 14th fret. While touching the node, use your *m* (right-hand middle finger) to pluck the string, then quickly lift *p* from the node. This technique allows you to continue holding your pick, though you won't use it to play the harmonic. This technique also allows you to "dig in" a little for a louder, stronger note.

Try this tune, which uses artificial harmonics, open-string harmonics and regular notes. For the harmonic arpeggios, fret the chords with your left hand and play the harmonics with your right hand, twelve frets above each fretted or open note. You will notice that your right hand is tracing an imaginary outline of the chord tones one octave higher on the neck.

The artificial harmonics are notated in the TAB with diamond shapes above the fret numbers.

CRYSTAL CHORDS

Track 10

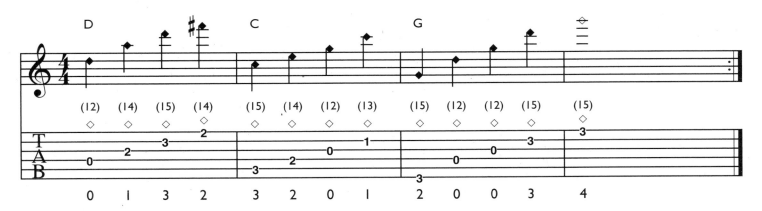

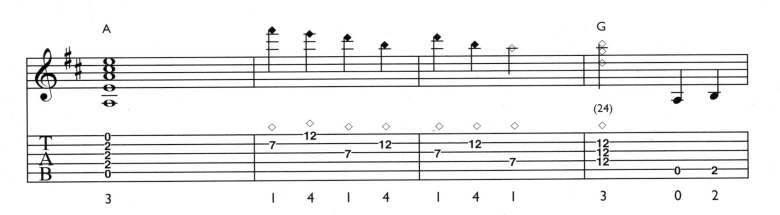

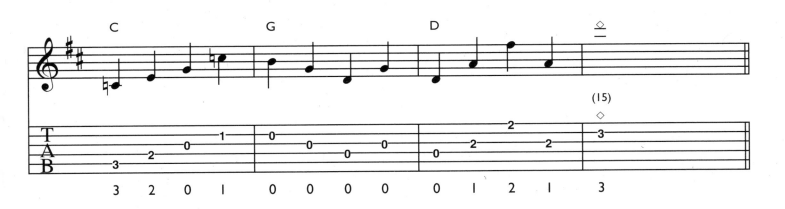

LESSON 6: TUNING WITH HARMONICS

Harmonics can be used to tune your guitar. Tuning with harmonics is very helpful because it allows you to check lower strings against higher strings. For example, using a harmonic, you can match the 6th string to the 1st string. By using these tuning techniques you can help eliminate microscopic tuning differences that can happen as you tune each string to the previous one using fretted notes.

STEP #1: TUNE TO A REFERENCE NOTE (A 440)

To tune with harmonics, you must first tune one string to a reference note from an outside source. This could be a tuner, a keyboard or other instrument, or a tuning fork. The most commonly used tuning fork is *A 440*. 440 *cycles per second* is the speed of the vibrations in the air that cause the musical pitch A to be heard. You can match the A harmonic found at the 5th fret of the 5th string to this pitch.

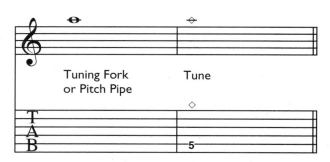

STEP #2: TUNE THE 1ST STRING

Match the open 1st string (E) to the 7th fret harmonic of the 5th string. Remember, the 5th string is your reference tone, so don't change its tuning!

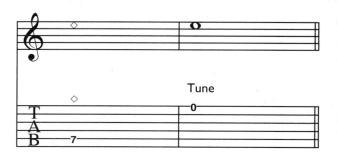

STEP #3: TUNE THE 6TH STRING

Tune the 5th fret harmonic of the 6th string (E) to the 7th fret harmonic of the 5th string. Also, make sure that the open 1st string matches both of these notes exactly.

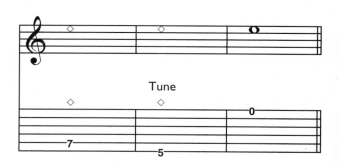

PART ONE—STYLES AND TECHNIQUES

STEP #4: TUNE THE 2ND STRING

Tune the open 2nd string (B) to the 7th fret harmonic of the 6th string. Remember, you've already tuned the 6th string, so don't change its tuning! You can also match the 5th fret harmonic of the 2nd string with the 7th fret harmonic of the 1st string.

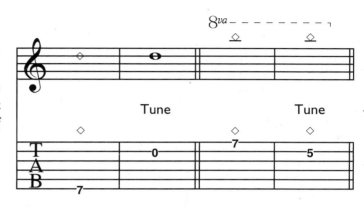

STEP #5: TUNE THE 4TH STRING

Tune the the 7th fret harmonic of the 4th string to the 5th fret harmonic of the 5th string (your original reference string).

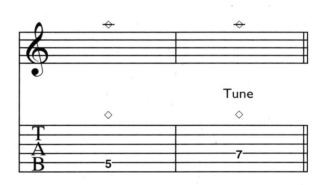

STEP #6: TUNE THE 3RD STRING

Make sure your other strings are in tune, then match the 7th fret harmonic of the 3rd string to the 5th fret harmonic of the 4th string. You can also match the 9th fret harmonic of the 3rd string to the 5th fret harmonic of the 2nd string.

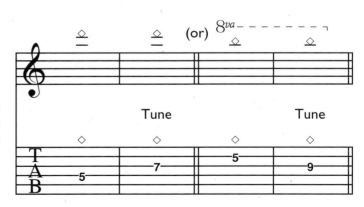

This lesson will help you refine and expand your technique for sliding. This technique, along with bending (page 120), will be used in Chapter 3 of this book to help you build acoustic funk riffs and bass lines.

SINGLE-NOTE SLIDES

Sliding up or down the neck from one note to another can add an expressive touch to a phrase. A little practice can improve your technique. Here are a few tips:

Tip #1 Keep the pressure on the fretboard even and fairly strong. This will prevent the note from "dying" a gasping, muted, pitiful death in mid-slide.

Tip #2 When you look at the fretboard, look at the fret you are sliding *to*—the *target note*—not the one you are sliding from—the *starting note*). This will improve your accuracy.

There are two basic types of slides.

 = Slide

GRACE NOTE SLIDES

A *grace note* is a a quick, decorative note indicated with a small notehead in the music. In this type of slide, the starting note is not distinctly heard. The slide is heard as a swoop up or down to the target note. Try these examples:

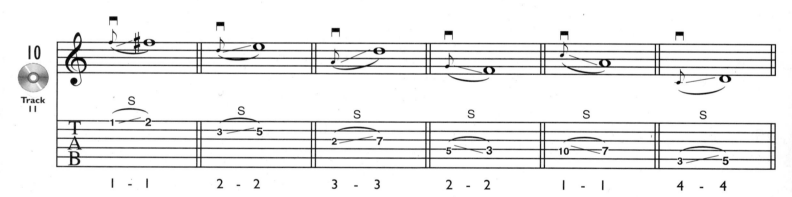

PORTAMENTO SLIDES

A *portamento* is a smooth slide from one note to the next. In this type of slide, the starting note has its own rhythmic value and is heard as a distinct pitch. You then slide to the next note (the target note). A slur notation tells you to slide quickly at the very end of the starting note, avoiding a disruption of the rhythm of the two notes. A jagged diagonal line tells you to slowly drag your finger from the starting note to the target note, making a more pronounced slide effect. Try these examples:

= Slow slide

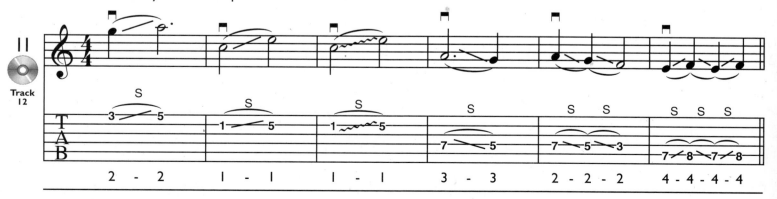

MIXING SLIDES WITH CHORDS

Slides are very effective in little licks played between chords. This example is in the style of the main guitar riff in the Dave Matthews Band song *Ants Marching*.

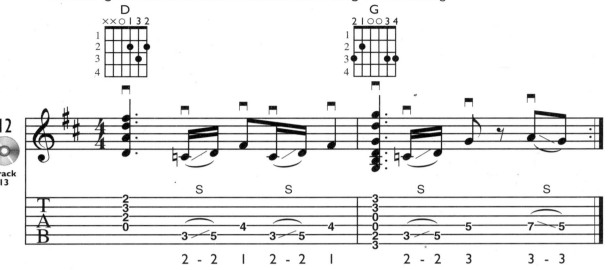

DOUBLE STOP SLIDES

A *double stop* was originally a violin player's term for two notes played at once. A double-stop slide occurs on two strings at once. They may be adjacent strings or nonadjacent strings. Try this example, which uses both grace notes and portamento slides.

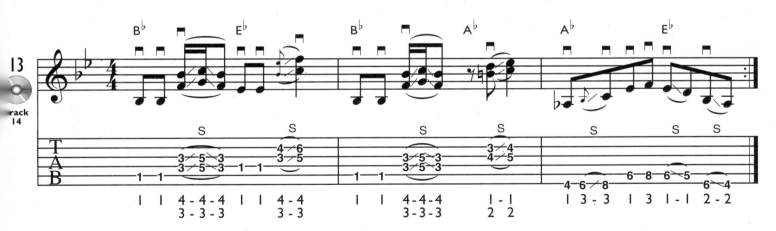

LESSON 8: BENDING STRINGS

This technique was introduced on page 69. While it is true that string bending is harder on acoustic guitars than electric guitars (due to thicker strings and greater tension), there are a few things you can do to improve bending:

1. Use the 3rd finger to perform most of your bends, lining up the 1st and 2nd fingers behind it for support. This will give you the maximum leverage (and require the least strength).

2. If necessary, change your hand position so that your thumb hooks over the top of the neck slightly. Use your whole wrist and hand in a "cranking" or "choking" motion to bend the string.

3. Practice bending notes on the higher strings (3rd, 2nd and 1st) and in the upper positions on the neck (7th fret and above), where the string tension is more flexible.

4. Keep a steady pressure on the string to keep the note from dying!

5. Check the accuracy of your bend by first playing the note you are bending up to with a fretted note (usually a half step or a whole step higher). This will get the correct note "in your ear." Try to match the bend to the sound of the fretted note exactly!

SINGLE-NOTE BENDS

Try the following examples of single-note bends. Line up all three fingers, fretting the actual note with the 3rd finger. To bend the string up, play the fretted note, then push the string up. You can also bend and release: Bend up, then release the string from the bend to its original position and the original note. To bend down, perform a *pre-bend*. Bend the string first, before playing, then play the note and relax the string back down to its original position. Notice that, in the TAB, released notes are shown in parentheses.

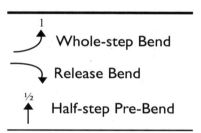

14 / Track 15

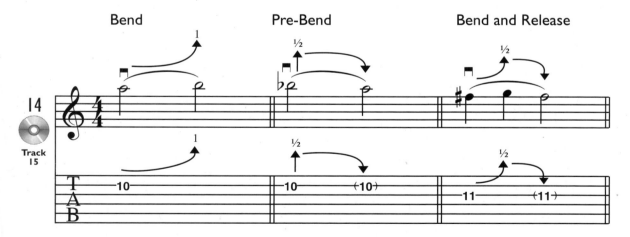

Try this example in the style of Barenaked Ladies' song *One Week*.

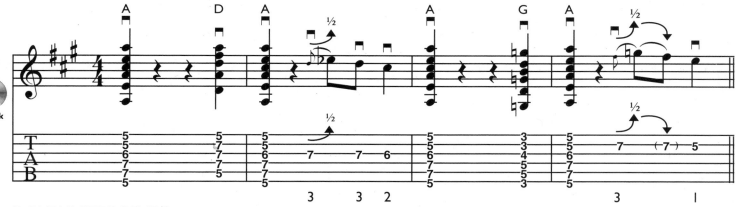

DOUBLE-STOP BENDS

Double-stop bends are a little trickier than single-note bends but well worth trying. Sometimes you will bend one of the two notes, other times you will bend both. If the bend arrow is next to just one note in a double stop, the other note is not bent, as in the first measure of example 16. If the bend arrow is above both notes in the double stop, both notes are bent, as in the third measure of example 16. Make sure to check your bent notes against the fretted versions of the notes to see if you're bending the right amount. A whole step bend will sound like a note two frets higher. A half step bend will sound like a note one fret higher.

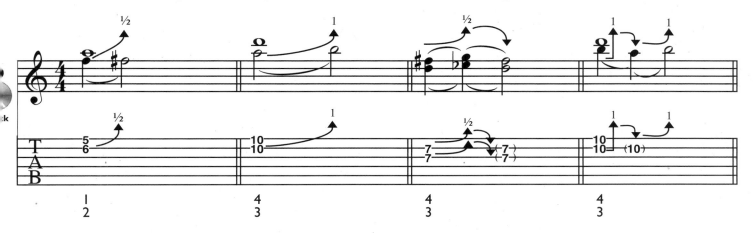

Try this example, which uses double-stop bends and bass-note bends to give a bluesy, countrified sound. Notice how the bending licks imply the harmony of E and B chords without playing full chords.

SWAMP GREASE

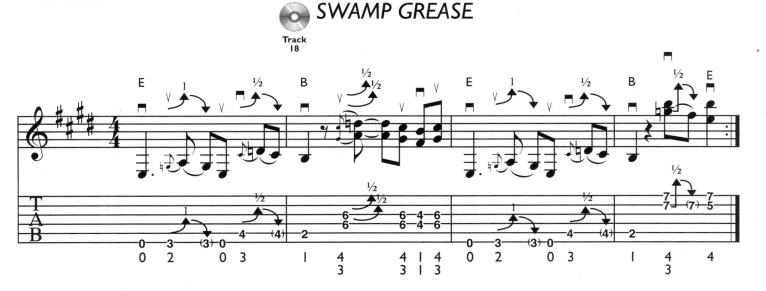

Track
18

CHAPTER 3

New Grooves and Styles

LESSON 1: ACOUSTIC FUNK STRUMMING

USING YOUR GUITAR LIKE A DRUM

The modern acoustic guitar styles of players such as Ani DiFranco, Dave Matthews and Michael Hedges combine traditional folk and rock sounds with a heavy dose of funk. Funk music treats every instrument like a drum, building up layers of rhythm out of repeated, interlocking patterns with percussive effects and rhythmic accents.

SIXTEENTH-NOTE STRUMMING

The foundation of funk strumming technique is the ability to strum and count sixteenth notes. Try this pattern just to get your right hand and foot coordinated. You may have to keep coming back to this exercise until it comes naturally. Notice the down-up strumming style.

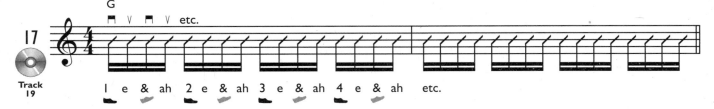

LEFT-HAND MUTING ("SQUEEZING AND SCRATCHING")

The secret of funk strumming is to keep the right hand moving in a steady, down-up sixteenth note rhythm while the left hand controls the rhythmic accents of the chords. This works especially well with barre chords. The left hand presses down to sound the chord ("squeeze") and releases the pressure just enough to create a muted, scratching sound. Make sure you don't lift your left hand all the way off the strings.

First, make an A chord by barring at the 5th fret (E-form, page 82, *Beginning Acoustic Guitar*). Then practice the muted strumming. Try to set the pressure of your left hand so that no open strings or notes are sounding at all, just the "scratch."

✕ = Mute or scratch

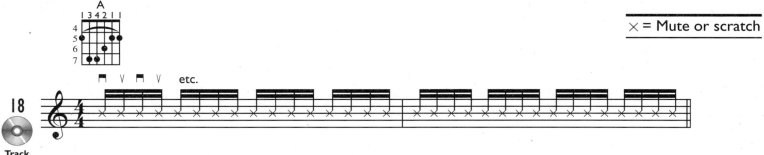

Now try this combination rhythm. Squeeze your left hand down for the first sixteenth note of each beat, then let up the pressure for "e, &, ah."

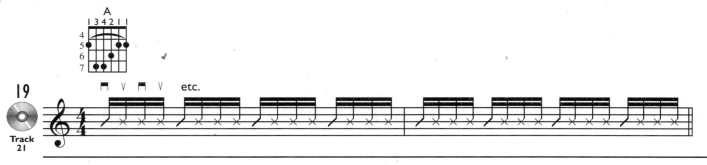

In this rhythm, you squeeze the first two sixteenth notes (1-e) and scratch the second two sixteenth notes (&-a), then reverse the procedure in the second measure.

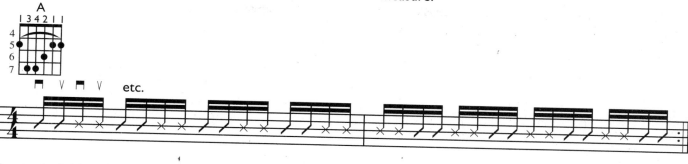

Try the funk-blues progression below. Notice that in the first beat of every bar, you will only strum "1" and "ah." Keep your hand moving in the steady rhythm, even though you won't hit the strings for "e-&."

Tip: try practicing each beat of the strum separately, adding one new group of four sixteenths at a time.

Use dominant 7 bar chords you learned in Chapter One to get the bluesy, funky sound. Try making up many of your own strums, too!

FUNK ON THE CUE-STICK TIP

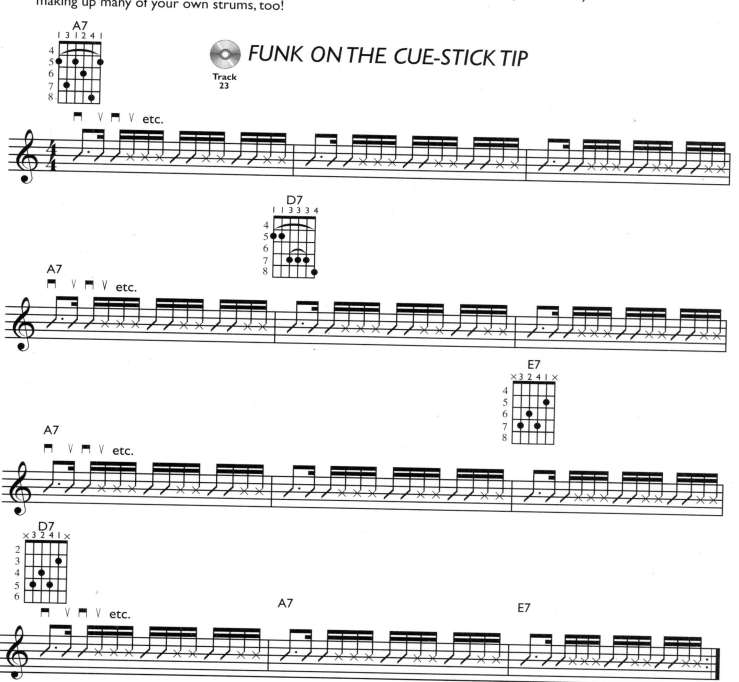

The technique of split strumming allows you to divide the strings of the guitar into two or three "zones" in order to create a more complex sound out of one strumming pattern. Example 21 splits the strings into bass and treble (low- and high-sounding) "zones."

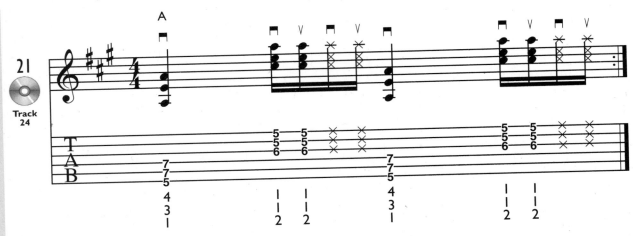

You can combine split strumming with barre chords and funk strumming to create funkilicious booty-shaking grooves! Try these examples.

FUNKILICIOUS BOOTY-SHAKING GROOVE #1

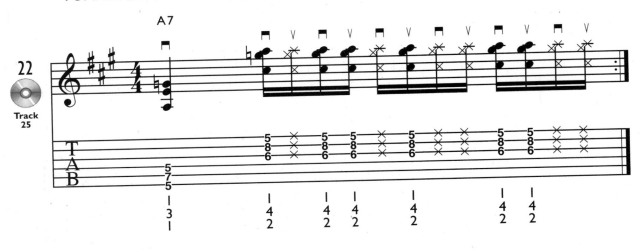

FUNKILICIOUS BOOTY-SHAKING GROOVE #2

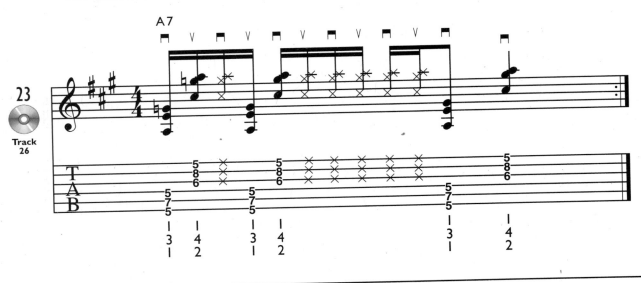

You can play these "squeezing and scratching" rhythms with chords that use open strings. This causes the open strings to keep ringing while the fretted notes provide the percussion and syncopation. Try this progression using open G and C chords.

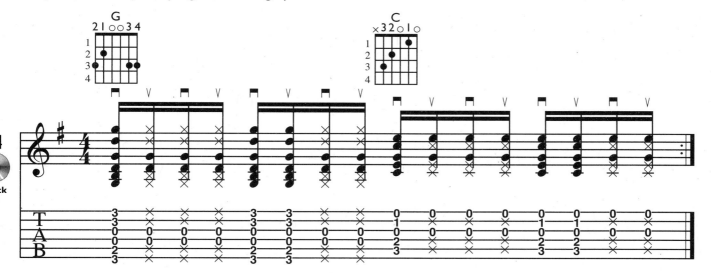

The progression in *Open for Bidness* is in the key of G, using open chords for a contemporary folk sound. Pioneers such as Neil Young, Joni Mitchell and Shawn Colvin have used this style of strumming to imply the sound of a full band with a solo acoustic guitar. Note the use of the Cadd9 chord, which is a C chord with a "D" note added to it. The progression also uses a Dsus2 chord (page 106) and split strumming.

OPEN FOR BIDNESS

Track 28

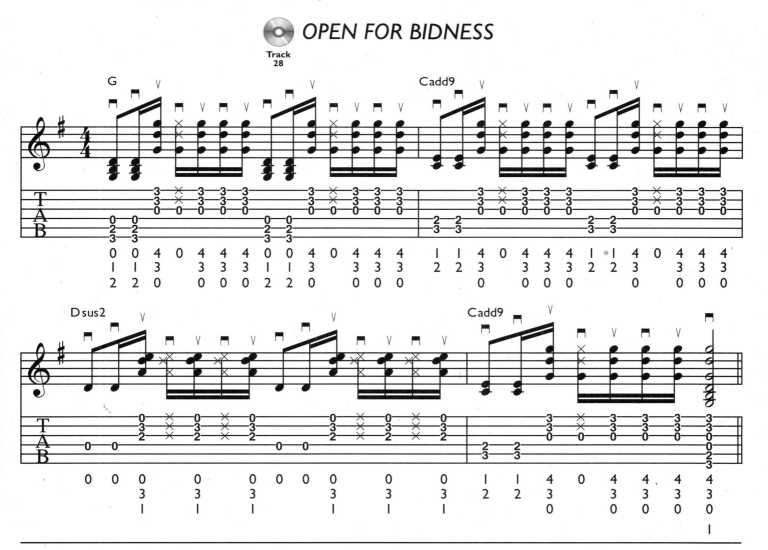

LESSON 4: CREATING A MONSTER FUNK GROOVE

Now it's time to put together what you know about funk to create a monster groove!

Whatchyoo Talkin' 'Bout, Willis? is in the style of the Dave Matthews Band song, *What Would You Say.* Work on it section by section, bar by bar, even beat by beat if you have to. There's a lot going on here! The first section incorporates slides, bends and split strumming. The second section (top of page 127) adds a new twist: a time signature change! The first four bars of the second section are in $\frac{3}{4}$ time, or, three beats to a measure. Count it out.

This piece has a *coda*. A coda is an extra passage of music at the end of a piece. At the end of the second section, you will see this marking: *D.C. al Coda.* This means go back to the beginning and play until you see the special "To Coda" sign: ⊕. When you see it (at the end of the first section), skip ahead in the music and start playing the Coda, which is also marked with the coda sign ⊕. In rock songs, it is sometimes called the *ride-out,* because you can keep jamming on the Coda over and over as you "ride" the song "out."

 WHATCHYOO TALKIN' BOUT?

Track 29

Swing was the popular dance music of the 1930s and '40s. Recently, bands like the Squirrel Nut Zippers, the Cherry Poppin' Daddies and the Brian Setzer Orchestra have created a revival of interest in this music, as well as swing dancing! Traditional swing can be a blast to play on the acoustic guitar, bringing together driving rhythms, cool chords and a hip attitude.

SWING EIGHTHS—HOW TO COUNT 'EM

The swing feel was introduced on page 64. The underlying pulse of swing is a *triplet* feel. Triplets are groups of three notes played in the time of two. An eighth-note triplet is three eighth notes played in the time of two eighth notes—or three notes per beat. To get the feel of them, try saying this aloud to a steady beat: "Trip-Pul-Let, Trip-Pul-Let."

In *swing eighths*, the first two notes of the triplet are tied together and the last note is the "and."

In this book, swing eighths are indicated with a "*Swing 8ths*" marking at the beginning of the piece. When counting swing eighths, you can still count "1-&-2-&" etc., but the on-beat (the first, numbered, part of the beat) will feel longer and the "&" will feel shorter. Try clapping triplets and counting the swing eighths. Feel eighth-note triplets as you clap on the first and the third eighth in each triplet.

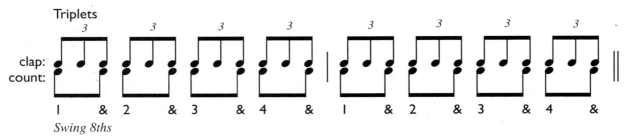

STRUMMING ON DOWNBEATS

The most traditional swing strum is to strum percussive, clipped chords in a quarter-note rhythm. Freddie Green was a master of this style. Try the progression in example 25. Use your left hand to cut the chords short (*staccato*) by slightly releasing pressure on the chord. Staccato notes are notated with a small dot above or below the note head (opposite the stem).

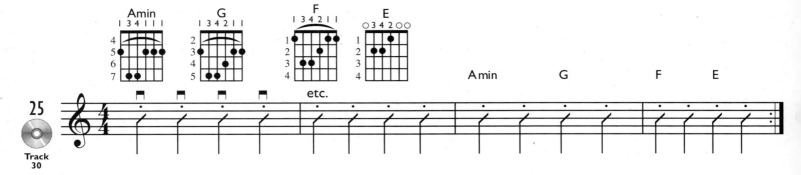

ADDING SOME UPBEATS

Now try the same progression but this time add an upstroke on the last part of beat 2 and beat 4. Your downstrokes should have a crisp snap of the wrist to enhance the percussive effect.

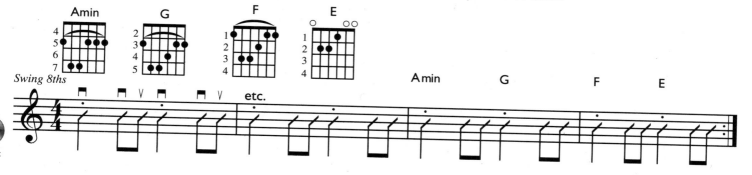

NOW SYNCOPATE AND ANTICIPATE!

The strum in example 27 incorporates syncopation on the chord changes. *Syncopation* means that the accent is shifted to the off-beats, or the upstrokes. In this strum, you will actually change to G, F and E on the off-beats. Changing chords "early" is called *anticipation* and is a fundamental part of the swing guitar style. The dotted lines are there to clarify exactly when the chord is played.

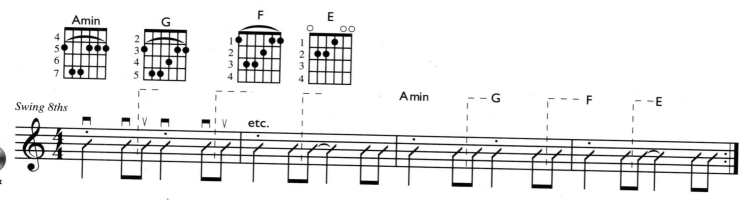

HOT GYPSY RHYTHM GUITAR STRUM

Another approach to swing playing draws inspiration from Gypsy guitarist, Django Reinhardt. Try this heavily syncopated strum on an A Minor barre chord.

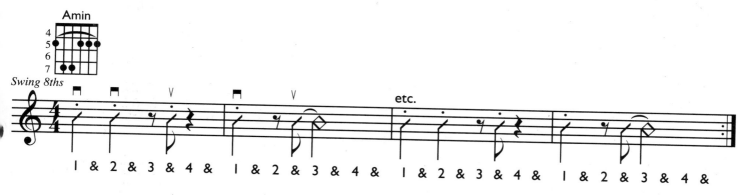

THE 32-BAR SONG FORM

The thirty-two-bar song form is found in countless jazz tunes (known as *standards*). It is an old pop song form in which a melody lasting eight bars (the *A* section of the song) is played twice, then a contrasting section of eight bars (the *B* section) is played, followed by a repeat of the A section. This form is repeated as many times as the players want to go through the song, and is used for the melody as well as improvised solos. In jazz lingo, each repetition of the song is called a *chorus*. Here's what the form looks like for three choruses of a tune:

A A B A — A A B A — A A B A

It does get tricky trying to remember where you are in the form, since the A section can be heard up to three times in a row. With a little practice of some simple tunes, you'll get the feel of it!

Try to memorize the progression in *Still a Minor at 32* and play it several times through without losing track of the B section. It uses the Hot Gypsy strum (page 129) in the A sections and a straight downbeat strum in the B section. You can also improvise with the A Minor Pentatonic scale you learned on page 66 of *Beginning Acoustic Guitar* (and in Chapter 5 of this book).

STILL A MINOR AT 32

Track 34

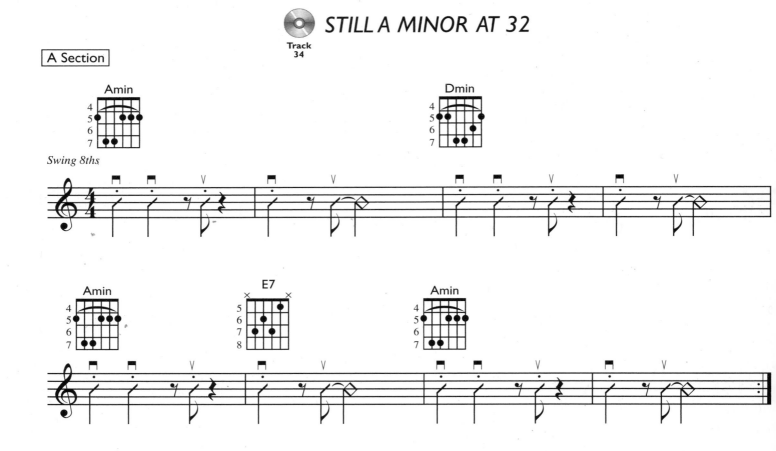

B Section

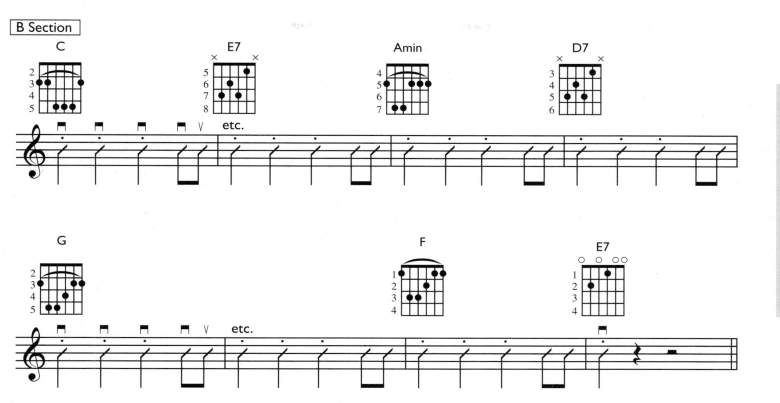

A Section

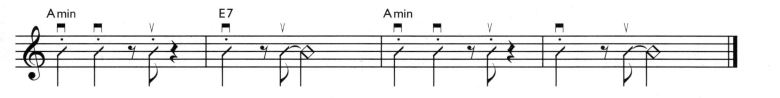

COOL SWING CHORDS

What makes swing guitar so exciting is the driving rhythm combined with interesting jazz chords. Some of the great swing players change chords on every beat! Below are some chords to add to your vocabulary. You can use them in a souped-up version of *Still A Minor at 32* but remember, they are all movable—just locate the root in the form and move it to play in any key, anywhere on the neck!

MINOR 7 CHORDS

Here are two *voicings* (a voicing is an arrangement of pitches) for a *minor 7 chord*. This chord is built with a minor triad with the note a minor 7th above the root added. It can also be thought of as a minor triad with another minor 3rd stacked on top. (This would be a good time to review the section on intervals on pages 50 through 57.)

DOMINANT 9 CHORDS

A *dominant 9 chord* is a dominant 7 chord (page 70) with a *9th* added. The 9th is an octave-plus-a-whole-step above the root.

MAJOR 6 CHORDS

Major 6 chords are very common in swing music. They consist of a major triad with a major 6th above the root added. The major 6th is one whole step above the 5th of the chord.

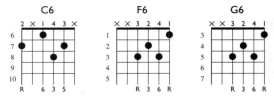

Now try *Still A Minor at 32, Souped-Up Hep-Cat Version*. This tune includes some new strums for you to try. They are variations on the Hot Gypsy Rhythm Guitar Strum you learned on page 129. Notice that the end of each section has a special two-measure strum pattern that adds a sense of closure and punctuation to the section. Try to make up your own strum rhythms, too!

STILL A MINOR AT 32, SOUPED-UP HEP-CAT VERSION

Track 35

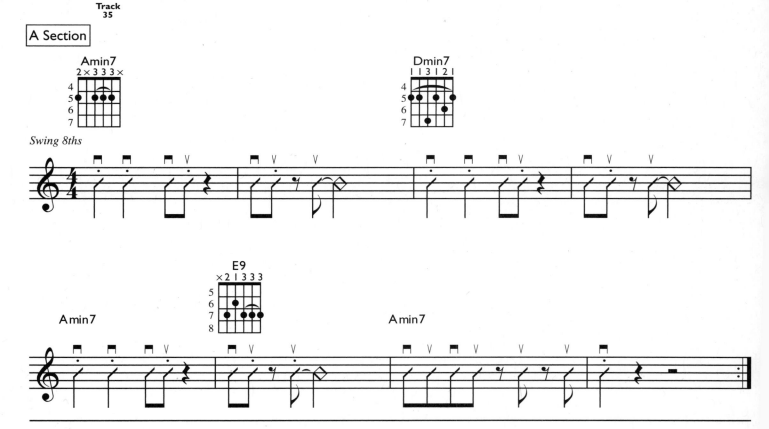

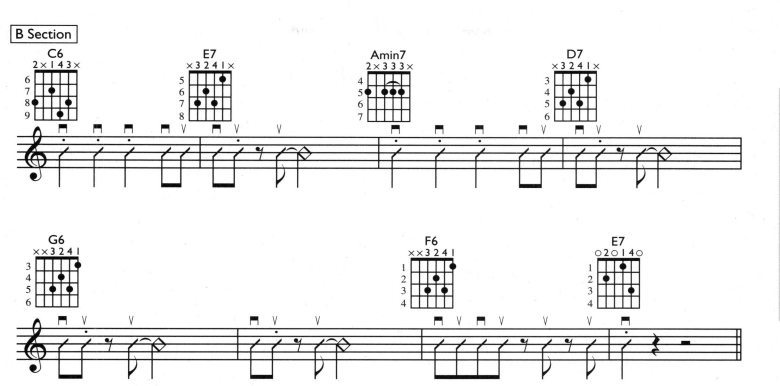

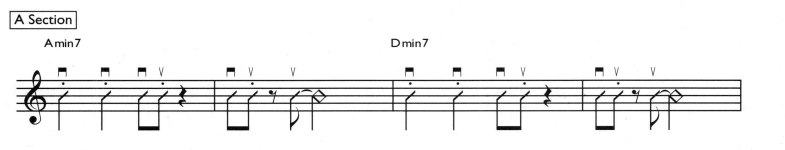

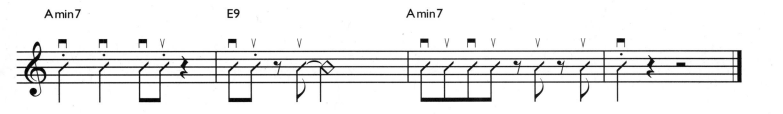

THE GROOVES OF NEW ORLEANS

An important (and fun) skill in rhythm guitar playing is the ability to accent beats in groups of three. This sound is fundamental in rock, funk and blues. In part, this is because of the New Orleans influence. Since the earliest "Dixieland" jazz and right up through modern funk and Zydeco, the foundation beat of New Orleans music is a $\frac{4}{4}$ time signature with triplet accents.

CLAP THE CLAVE

The *clave* (pronounced KLAH-vay) is an important percussion rhythm found in Latin music (music of South America) and played on wooden sticks called—believe it or not—*claves*. It is very similar to the rhythms of New Orleans jazz and funk. Try tapping quarter notes while clapping the clave rhythm.

PLAY THE CLAVE IN SIXTEENTH NOTES

Try strumming the clave rhythm using the "squeeze and scratch" technique you learned in the funk lesson on page 122.

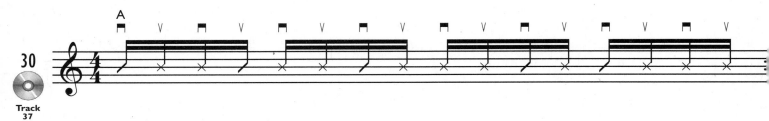

THE BO DIDDLEY BEAT

This is a variation of the clave made famous by Bo Diddley. It has been borrowed by Buddy Holly, The Rolling Stones, The Band, The Grateful Dead and countless others. It looks harder on paper than it is in real life, so just loosen up and go for it! If you're having trouble, break it down one beat at a time.

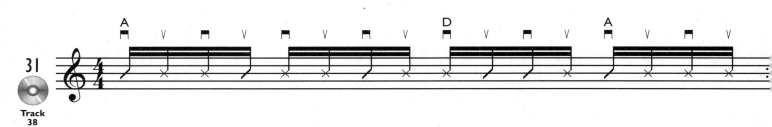

THE RUMBA BASS LINE

The *rumba* bass line is another essential component of the New Orleans sound. It sounds the notes of an ascending triad (root, 3rd, 5th) in a syncopated rhythm.

Elysian Fields Boogaloo incorporates the Bo Diddley strum, the clave strum and the rumba bass line. It even uses a secondary dominant chord (page 111). The F# triad in the rumba section (bars 5 – 8) is the V/V chord (five of five e V of the B chord, which is V in E).

As you learn the piece, keep your foot tapping even quarter notes. This will help you establish a solid rhythm.

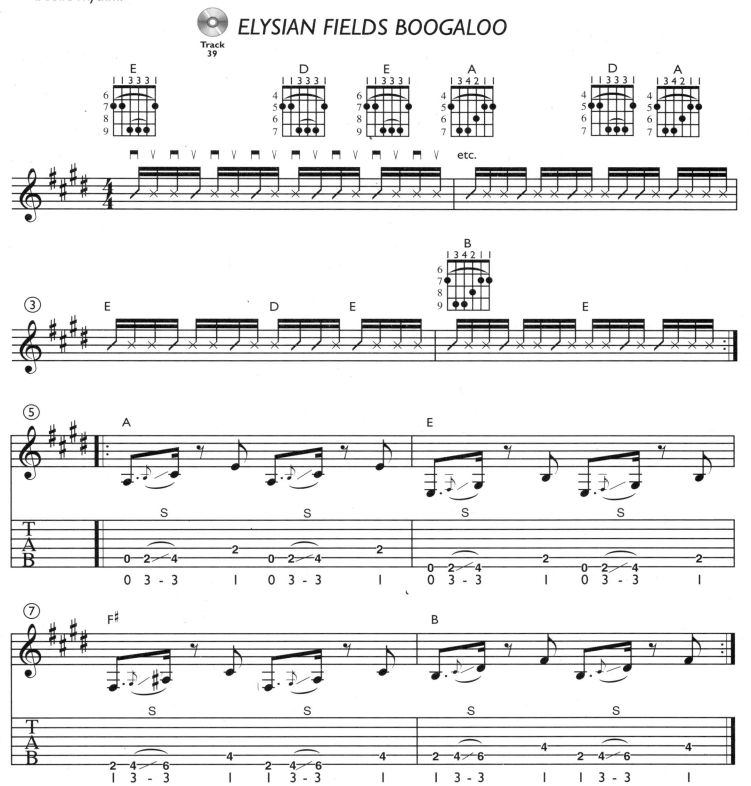

Groups such as Fairport Convention and Steeleye Span combined the traditional music of Ireland, Scotland and England (often referred to as Celtic music) with electric rock 'n' roll in the 1960s and 1970s. Later groups—such as the Bothy Band, Altan and the Tannahill Weavers—put the rhythmic drive of rock into an acoustic format, creating a unique style of rhythm guitar playing. Celtic players make great use of open tunings, open strings and complex syncopation to add excitement to the fiddle tunes and bagpipe tunes they accompany.

WORKING IN $\frac{6}{8}$

Many of the fiddle tunes heard in Celtic traditional music are *jigs*. Jigs are tunes that fall into the $\frac{6}{8}$ time signature, where there are six eighth notes in every measure. Notice that the number six is divisible by three. Any of the time signatures where the number of beats is divisible by three ($\frac{3}{8}, \frac{6}{8}, \frac{9}{8}, \frac{12}{8}$) and has an "8" on the bottom implies that the underlying pulse of the music has the effect of an eighth-note triplet.

In other words, $\frac{6}{8}$ is actually felt as two groups of three. You can count it either "1-2-3-4-5-6" or "1-&-ah, 2-&-ah." Try the counting and tapping exercise in example 32 to get the idea. Stomp your foot loudly to make sure you get the feel of the two big beats that divide up the six small beats.

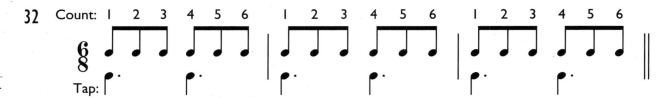

STRUMMING IN $\frac{6}{8}$

It can take a little effort to learn how to strum $\frac{6}{8}$ because your strum only has two parts, "down" and "up." To feel the pulse of $\frac{6}{8}$, you have to accent your strum in groups of three strokes. Your accent beats (1 and 4) will alternate between a downstroke and an upstroke. This will make more sense when you try it.

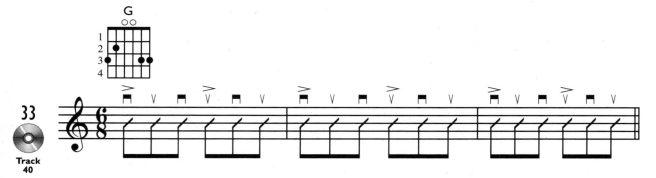

When you are playing this rhythm, make sure to exaggerate the accents. This will help "program" the rhythm into your hands. Keep a very loose wrist, and use a "snap" of your wrist to accent the first beat of each three-note group. Start out slow but keep loose so that you won't freeze up when it's time to speed up!

SYNCOPATING A $\frac{6}{8}$ STRUM

Once you have a very solid foundation in the basic strum, try the syncopation shown in example 34. There are accents on the upstrokes. Alternating this syncopated version with the basic rhythm is an extremely effective combination.

Try the following chord progression. It makes use of chord voicings that contain open strings and fretted notes to produce a thick, ringing sound. It uses the basic strum in the first part, then alternate the basic and syncopated strums in the second part.

Notice that there are some pretty fancy-sounding chord names in this tune. Don't panic. The chord forms are easy and they sound great. The 9s, 11s and 13s referred to are all intervals measured from the root of the chords.

Track 42

THE ROCKY ROAD TO THE FOGGY CLIFFS OF ERIN'S GREEN SHAMROCK SHORE

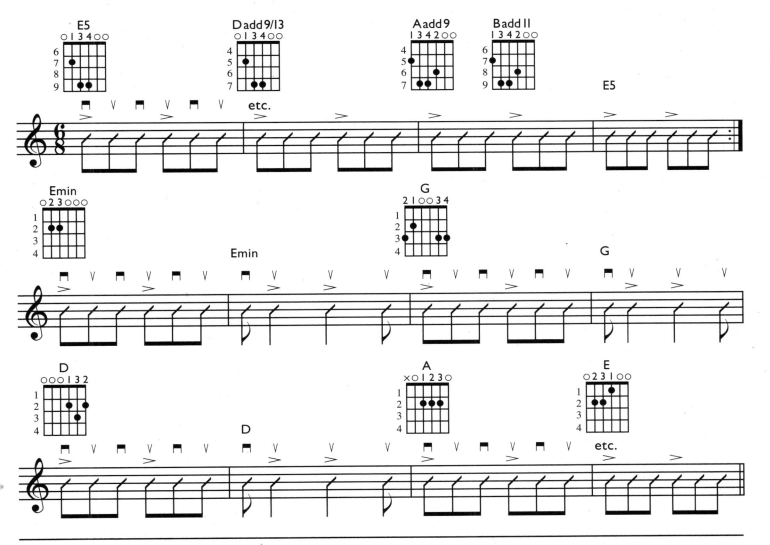

LESSON 8: ONE TUNE IN THREE TRADITIONS—OLD-TIME, BLUEGRASS AND CAJUN

This lesson will examine the traditional folk styles of *old-time*, *bluegrass* and *Cajun* acoustic guitar. The lesson uses the Appalachian song, *Fall on My Knees*—a favorite of North Carolina mountain fiddler, Tommy Jarrell—to illustrate the similarities and differences of these three styles.

OLD-TIME AND "CARTER FAMILY" STYLE

The old-time tradition is one of the oldest American folk styles, and yet is still being revitalized by new players such as Gillian Welch and the Freight Hoppers. This music is rooted in the Southern Appalachian Mountains and has many regional variations in style. The role of the guitar is generally that of a rhythm instrument, with banjos and fiddles taking the melody.

BASIC OLD-TIME STRUMMING

The basic strum in old-time music is the classic "boom-chick" strum. The idea is to hit a clear, strong bass note on the first part of the beat, then play the chord on the higher strings in the second part. Also try this example using the C and G chords. Notice that the first bass note is the root of the chord, while the alternate bass note is the 5th of the chord. The bass notes are circled.

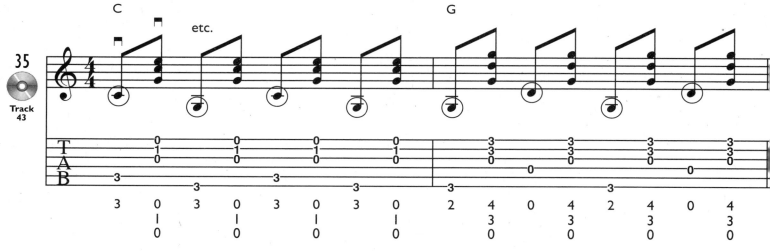

CARTER FAMILY STYLE

The *Carter Family style* is the most recognized guitar style in old-time music. It is based on the playing of Mother Maybelle Carter, who would play the melody of the tune in the bass notes and fill in chords as the rhythm allowed. Many old-time players use a thumbpick to play the bass notes, strumming the chords by brushing the back of the fingernails down on the strings. Other old-time players use a flatpick. In example 36, the melody notes are circled.

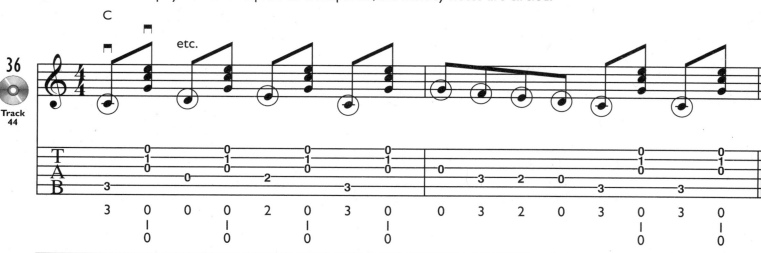

Fall on My Knees is still heard at old-time and bluegrass jam sessions all over the country. It is generally played in the key of D. Old-time guitarists sometimes play D tunes in a C position (using the primary chords of the key of C), using a capo at the 2nd fret to convert the chords from the key of C to the key of D. This version incorporates a Carter Family-style strum in C position.

FALL ON MY KNEES—CARTER FAMILY STYLE

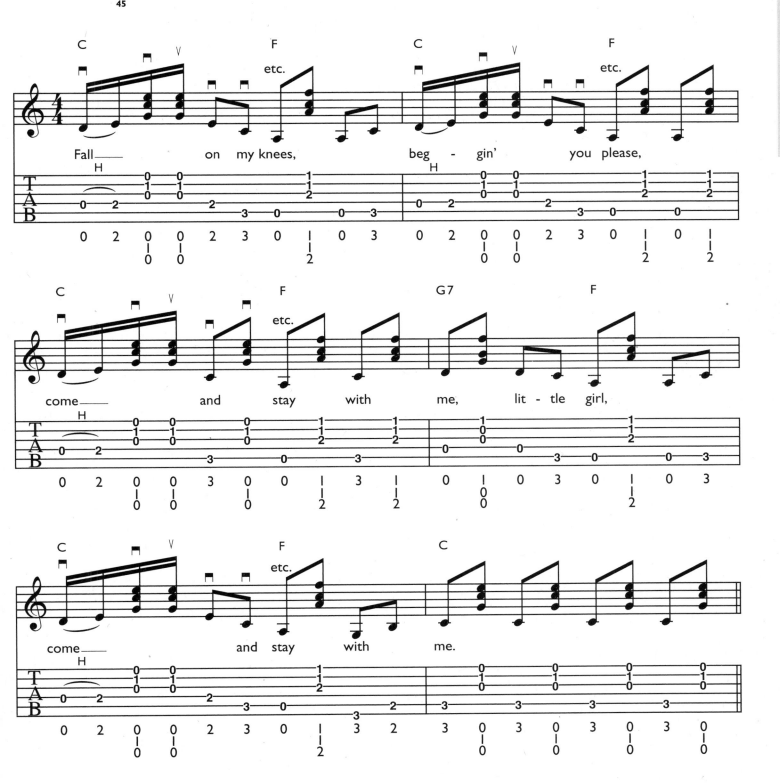

THE BLUEGRASS BACKUP SOUND

Bluegrass music draws from the same traditions as old-time music, combining them with blues and early jazz influences. Bluegrass music tends to have more improvisation, where each instrumentalist plays a solo while the others play *back-up* (accompaniment).

THE IMPORTANCE OF THE KEY OF G

The key of G is extremely popular among bluegrass guitarists because of its open, ringing sound and the ease of playing walking bass lines (page 86) and bluesy leads. Many bluegrass players will play most songs in the G position, using a capo to change the actual key of the song.

WALKING BASS LINES

Bluegrass rhythm guitar, like old-time, makes heavy use of "walking" bass lines, where the bass line follows the scale between the root of one chord and the root of the next. Try this version of the chords from *Fall on My Knees*, which has been transposed to the G position. In order to play the song in its original key of D, put a capo at the 7th fret.

FALL ON MY KNEES—BLUEGRASS BACKUP STYLE

Track 46

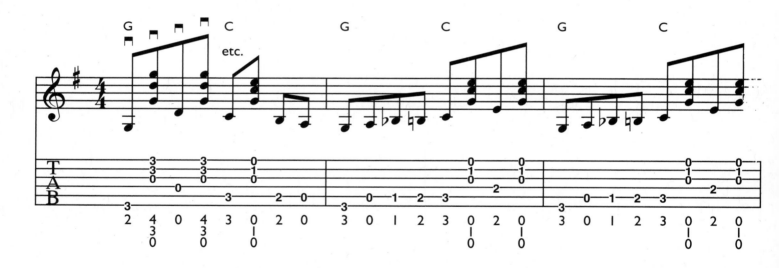

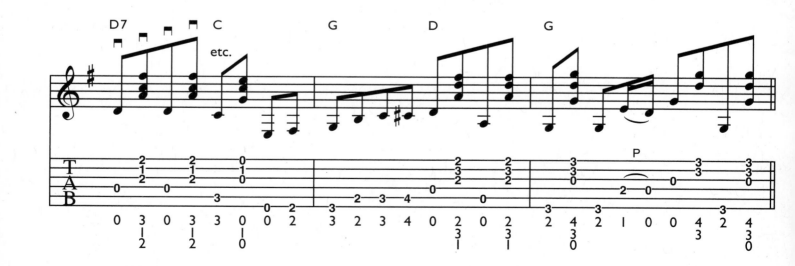

THE BLUEGRASS LEAD SOUND

Bluegrass lead playing makes use of a scale that combines the minor pentatonic scale (page 168) and the major pentatonic scale (page 174). Here is the bluegrass lead scale in the key of G:

THE BLUEGRASS LEAD SCALE IN THE KEY OF G

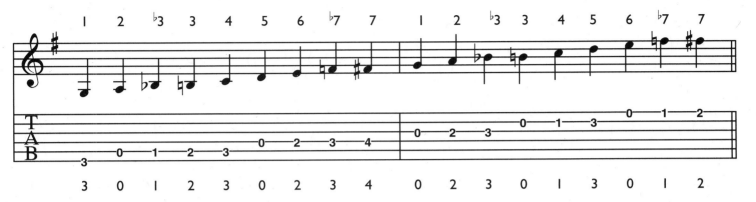

Below is a lead solo (called a *break*) based on the melody of *Fall on My Knees* in a G position. While this break is very challenging, a few tips that can make it easier to learn:

1. Work on this break one beat at a time, working on each little lick until you've got it down; then try to play two beats in a row, and so on. The licks in this break can be recombined and used in improvisations on other tunes.

2. Go slowly and remember to alternate the picking with absolute precision. This will help when you speed it up, as well as when you try other improvisations in this style.

 FALL ON MY KNEES—BLUEGRASS LEAD STYLE

Track 47

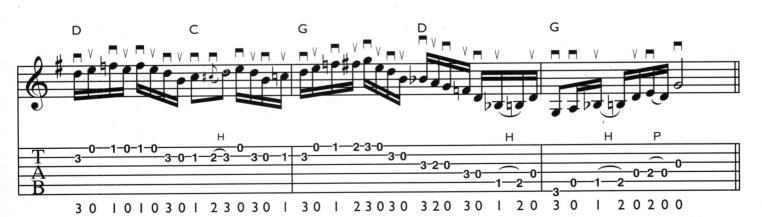

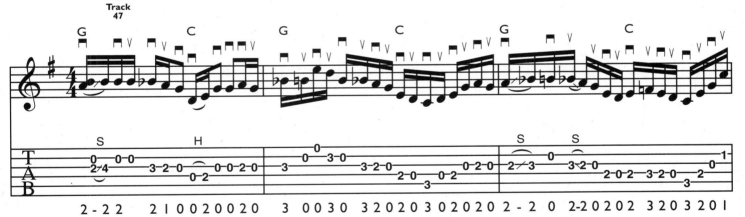

CAJUN BACKUP STYLE

Cajun music comes from the transplanted French-Canadian culture that thrives in Louisiana. Cajun folk music combines the poetry of Louisiana Cajun French dialect with fiddles, accordions and a wide variety of rhythm instruments. It is carried on today by groups such as Beausoleil, which features the guitar playing of David Doucet.

The Cajun rhythm is a driving shuffle that is mirrored in the fiddle bowing, drumming rhythms and even the pace of the lyrics. David Doucet, who plays a snare drum rhythm on guitar using split strumming, takes a fun approach to this style. Try example 38, which uses an A chord. The split strum uses a bass note, a middle zone and a treble zone (*Beginning Acoustic Guitar*, page 75). Accents are used to emphasize the rhythmic drive of the backbeat (accenting the third sixteenth-note of each four-note group, it sounds like "bo-ka-CHA-ka, bo-ka-CHA-ka").

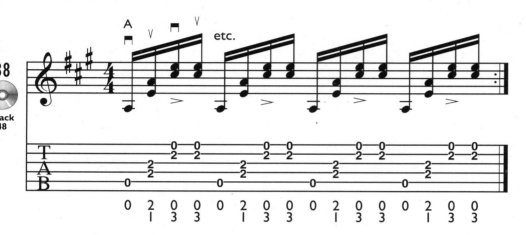

Track 48

Try the back-up strum with the chords to *Fall on My Knees*, shown in below in the key of A. In order to play the song in its original key of D, put a capo at the 5th fret.

FALL ON MY KNEES—CAJUN BACKUP STYLE

Track 49

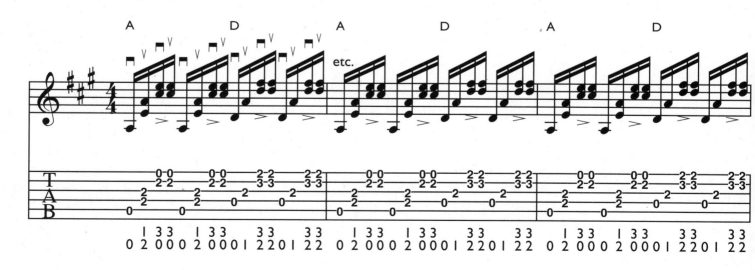

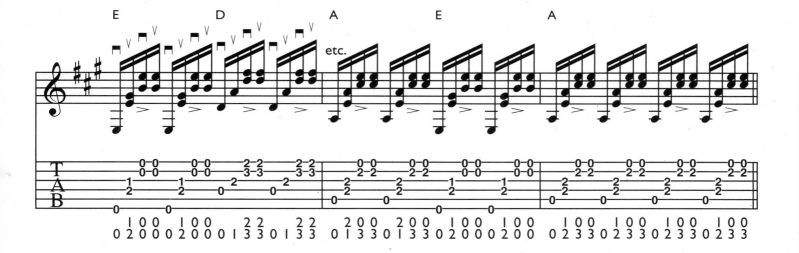

CAJUN LEAD STYLE

This version of *Fall on My Knees* uses hammer-ons and pull-offs with double stops to imitate the sound of Cajun fiddles and accordions. These licks work very well in the key of A.

Track
50

FALL ON MY KNEES—CAJUN LEAD STYLE

LESSON 9: DELTA BLUES

Delta blues guitar playing is different from any other style. African-American musicians living in the cotton-growing country of Tennessee, Mississippi and Louisiana developed Delta blues and spread it throughout the South. Masters of the style—such as Robert Johnson, Son House and Muddy Waters—developed their own techniques for drawing tones and sound effects out of the guitar. This results in an aggressive, soulful and often stark sound that reflects the lives of the people who made the music.

For this lesson, try playing without a pick. With practice, you will gradually be able to keep separate rhythms in your thumb and fingers.

REVIEWING THE TWELVE-BAR BLUES

The *twelve-bar blues* was introduced on page 62 of *Beginning Acoustic Guitar*. Let's play through this blues progression using chords in the key of E. The primary chords in E are E7 (I), A7 (IV) and B7 (V). Here are some handy chord forms to use:

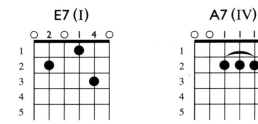 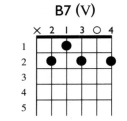

Play this progression by strumming downstrokes with *p* (the thumb of your right hand). The chord analysis is shown below the chords (in Roman numerals) to help you remember the progression. This particular blues does not go to IV (four) in the second measure. This is a common variation of the twelve-bar form.

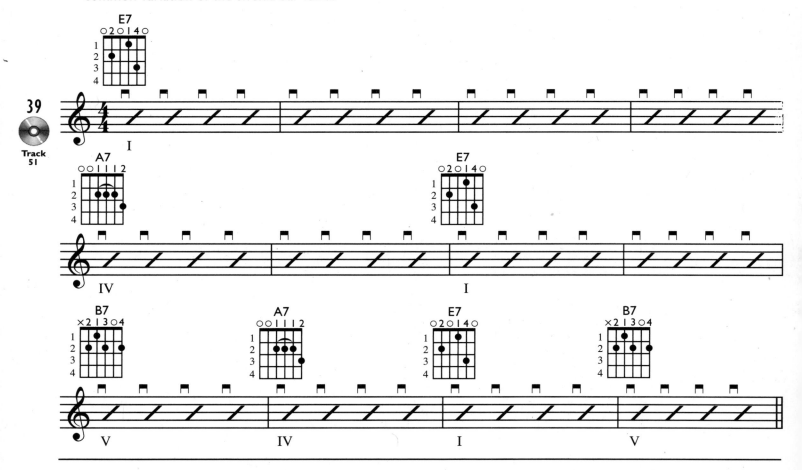

THE HEARTBEAT OF THE DELTA

A unique quality of the Delta blues is the steady, heartbeat-like pulse of the right-hand thumb on the bass notes. The thumb plays even quarter notes, regardless of the other fingers. Use the heel of your right hand to mute the strings at the bridge for a percussive, staccato effect.

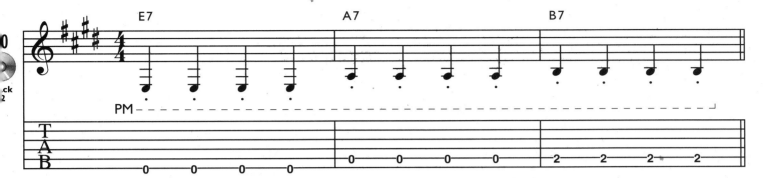

"THWACK!"

A cool trick to use with the thumb is to occasionally accent a beat by "popping" the string. To do this, reach your thumb under the bottom of the string, then "pop" the string by pulling the string away from the guitar and letting it go while keeping the heel of your hand in the mute position. The resulting sound is a resounding *thwack*! Note: You cannot possibly be too obnoxious with this. The more the better!

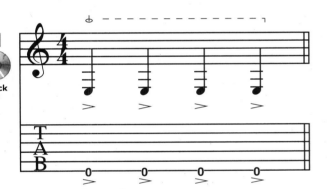

ADDING CHORDS

You can pluck sustained chords with the right-hand fingers while keeping the steady thumb-beat in the bass. You can either use one finger per string or *brush* one finger across several strings. You can play with the bass note (a *pinch*) or between bass notes. Try the pattern in example 42 below. It starts with a pinch, then sounds the chord again on the "&" of beat 2. Try it with the E chord, then try it with A7 and B7. The thumb notes are shown with stems down, while the chords (to be played with the fingers) are shown stems up.

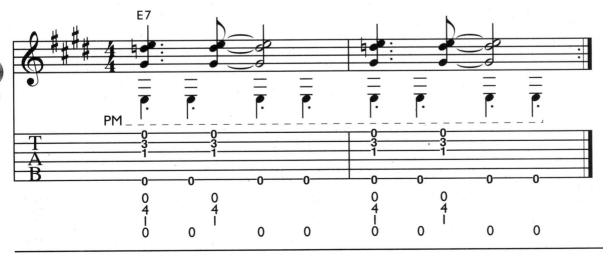

A COUPLE OF LEAD LICKS

The trick in Delta blues is to keep the thumb going even while playing lead licks up on the neck. Try these two licks in the key of E. The first measure shows a double stop where the lower note gets bent slightly sharp—not quite a half-step bend. We call this a *quarter-tone* bend (marked ¼). The second measure shows a *unison slide*, where a note on the 2nd string is slid up to the note in unison with the open 1st string.

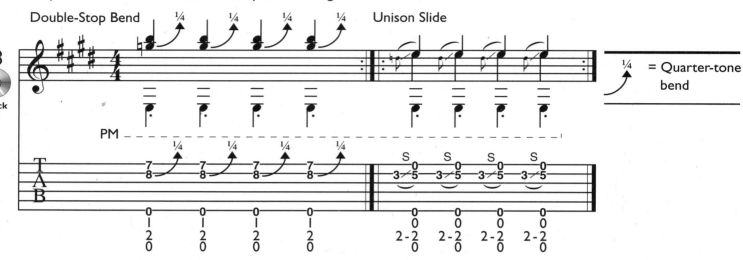

THE TURNAROUND

A *turnaround* is a melody in the last two bars of the twelve-bar blues that helps bring you back to the beginning of the form. In the two examples below, you kick it off on the first beat with a thwack on the 6th string (low E). The notes to the Low Turnaround are easy to find. Just find an open E7 chord, move it up three frets higher and start there. Then, move it down one fret with each beat. The high turnaround is very common in Robert Johnson's music. Both turnarounds end on the B7, or V (five) chord.

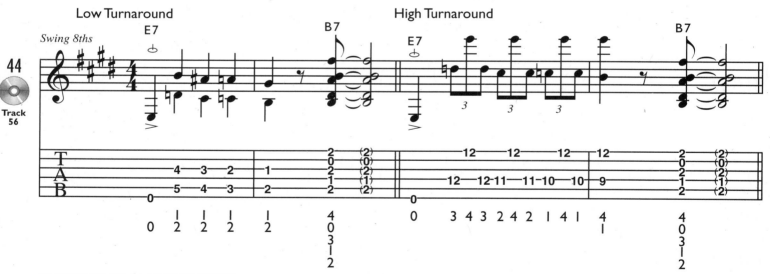

PUTTING IT ALL TOGETHER

In *Baby Blue Blues* on page 147, you will put together all of the elements shown in this lesson. This blues starts off with the two lead licks from example 43 over the E chord. Then, in the second and third lines, you will play the chord pattern from example 42 on page 145, followed by the turnaround. Note the first and second endings (introduced on page 85). The first time through, play the 1st ending (the first turnaround from example 44 above), then repeat the song. The second time through, skip the 1st ending and go straight to the 2nd ending (the second turnaround from example 44 above), which will end on an E7 chord—a good stopping place. Have fun and keep the thumb going!

BABY BLUE BLUES

CHAPTER 4

Working Your Way up the Neck

LESSON 1: MAJOR SCALE POSITIONS

REVIEWING THE MAJOR SCALE

The major scale is a useful tool for learning about improvisation and the layout of the guitar fretboard. It has seven different notes arranged by whole steps and half steps in the following order:

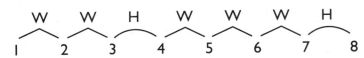

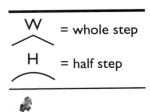

W = whole step

H = half step

You can build a major scale in any key using this formula. To show a consistent view of the relationships between scales, triads and pentatonic scales, this section of the book will concentrate on the key of A Major.

BASIC MAJOR SCALE POSITIONS

Below are three basic positions for the major scale. Each position is shown in A with its fingering, notes, scale degrees and a fretboard diagram. Note that each position has two octaves of the scale.

POSITION #1

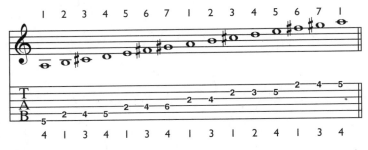

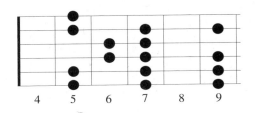

POSITION #2

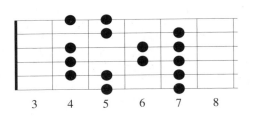

POSITION #3

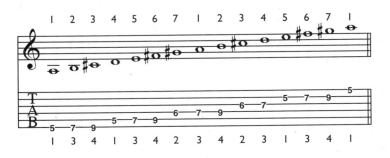

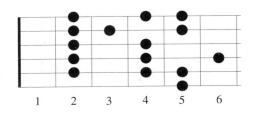

LEARN THE SCALE DEGREES

The scale degrees are simply the notes of the scale numbered 1 through 8 (eight is an octave higher than 1). It is important to learn the scale degrees and their relationships. For example, remember that there is only a half step between notes 3 and 4, and between notes 7 and 8 (1). All the other scale degrees are a whole step apart. Learning the scale degrees will help your ear training as you learn to recognize melody notes by their location within the scale. For example, when you put the scale degrees 3, 2 and 1 together, they sound the melody of *Three Blind Mice*.

IMPROVISING WITH THE MAJOR SCALE

Here is a sample solo and chord progression you can use to practice your *improvising* in the key of A Major. Improvising is the act of spontaneously creating melodies. The first line uses Position #1, the second line uses Position #2, and the third line uses Position #3. Each of these positions gives you access to a different range of the scale. Create your own improvisations using the same chord progression.

REVIEWING WHOLE-STEP AND HALF-STEP FINGERINGS

While it is important to know the basic scale positions, the imaginary "boxes" that the positions make can be restrictive. Remember that the scale is only a series of whole steps and half steps. On one string, a half step is one fret; a whole step is two frets.

Here are the shapes for whole steps and half-steps on adjacent strings:

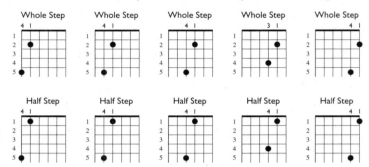

KEEP TRACK OF WHERE YOU ARE—CREATING SCALE RUNS

A *scale run* is a passage in a piece or improvisation where the notes of a scale are played in order. It is a commonly used technique for moving from one part of the neck to another. The secret to moving up and down the neck as you improvise is knowing where you are in the scale at all times. This includes knowing the scale degrees you are playing, and where the whole steps and half steps are. This will make you free to choose how far up one string you want to play the scale, and when you want to switch to the next string. Below are several examples of this technique. Try them forward and backward, and in several keys. Then make up your own scale runs to suit your music!

SCALE RUN #1

This shows one octave of a major scale starting on the 1st finger. You will use the 3rd finger to change positions on the 6th string. This scale position crosses between the 6th string and the 5th string at the whole step between scale degrees 4 and 5, then finishes the scale on the 5th string. It is shown using music, TAB and a fretboard diagram.

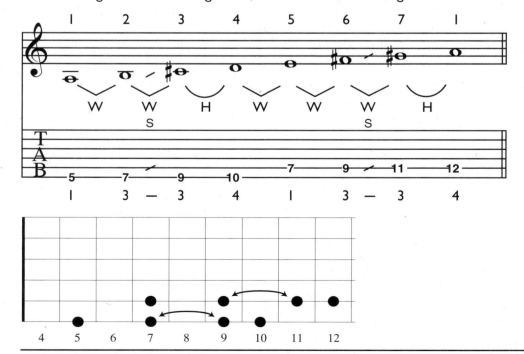

← → = slide

SCALE RUN #2

This fingering starts on the 2nd finger, and changes strings between scale degrees 2 and 3 (whole step) and between degrees 6 and 7 (whole step). Slide your 4th finger to change positions.

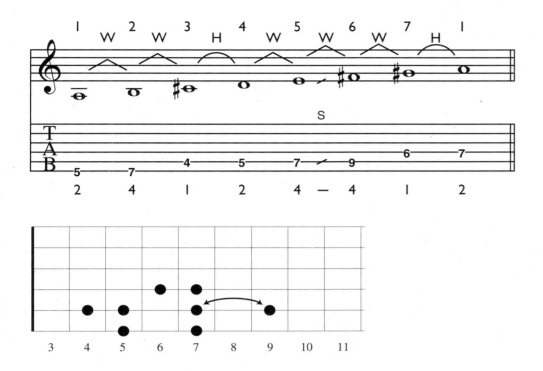

SCALE RUN #3

This fingering starts on the 3rd string with the 1st finger. The fingering changes strings at the whole step between scale degrees 2 and 3, then uses the 4th finger to change positions on the 2nd string. As in Scale Run #2, this fingering also changes strings between degrees 6 and 7 (whole step).

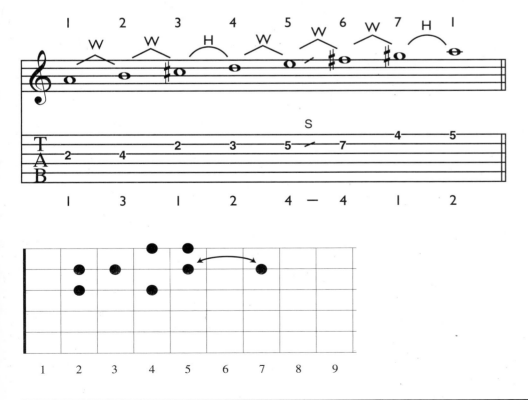

SCALE RUN #4

This fingering shows a complete, three-octave major scale starting on the 4th finger. Note the position changes and fingerings carefully. You may have to reach around the neck to make it up to high A. Don't forget to try this one going backward (read from right to left!).

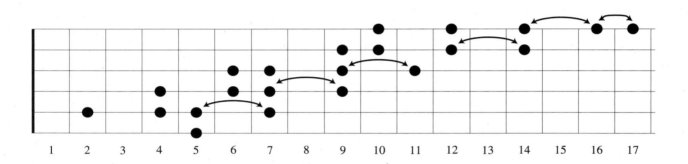

IMPROVISING WITH CONNECTED SCALE POSITIONS

Following is a sample solo and chord progression using scale runs. Scale Run #4 (shown above) makes a special appearance in the last line. The licks demonstrated in the sample solo reflect a country and bluegrass-influenced rock sound. This style of soloing can be heard in the playing of Jerry Garcia, The Allman Brothers and The Band. It's time create your own solos. Have fun!

SAMPLE SOLO

CHAPTER 5

Harmony

LESSON 1: MAJOR TRIADS UP THE NECK

REVIEWING MAJOR TRIADS

Triads are three-note chords built in 3rds. The chord tones of a triad are called the root, the 3rd and the 5th.

Major Triad Intervals

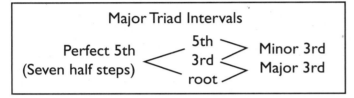

Here is a C Major triad:

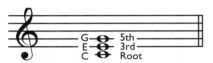

INVERTING TRIADS

To *invert* a triad is to rearrange the chord tones in such a way as to make something other than the root the lowest note. A triad may have the root, 3rd or 5th in the bass. Triad inversions allow guitarists to play the same chord on different parts of the neck. Here is an A Major triad and its inversions.

46

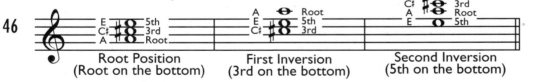

LEARNING INVERSIONS UP THE NECK

Learning the inversion *shapes* (chord forms) up the neck can greatly expand your knowledge and understanding of the neck. Inversions high or low on the neck get different sounds, and you will find that different styles of music tend toward one or the other. Each set of three strings has three possible inversion shapes. Try to learn them all.

THE A MAJOR TRIAD INVERSIONS—STRINGS 1, 2 AND 3

Practice going up and down the neck with these shapes until you know them. The roots, 3rds and 5ths are marked below each diagram.

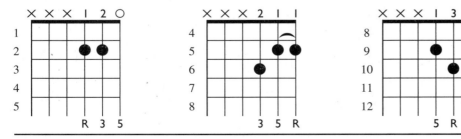

THE A MAJOR TRIAD INVERSIONS—STRINGS 2, 3 AND 4

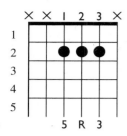
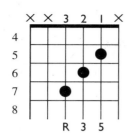
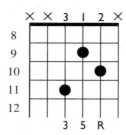

THE A MAJOR TRIAD INVERSIONS—STRINGS 3, 4 AND 5

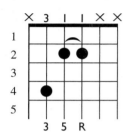
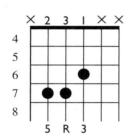
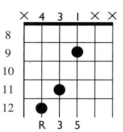

THE A MAJOR TRIAD INVERSIONS—STRINGS 4, 5 AND 6

You may notice that the shapes are the same as for strings 3, 4 and 5, but in different positions. This is because the distances between the adjacent open 3rd, 4th, 5th and 6th strings are all perfect 4ths. This means that the interval relationships between these four strings will always be the same, and they will use the same chord shapes.

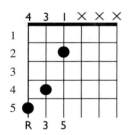
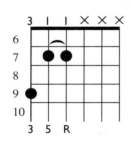
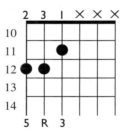

ALL OF THE ROOTS, 3RDS AND 5THS OF AN A MAJOR TRIAD IN THE FIRST TWELVE FRETS

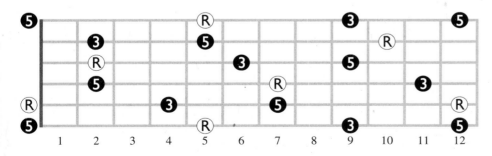

I-IV-V PROGRESSIONS IN TRIADS

Once you've learned the triad positions of an A Major chord—which is I in the key of A—learn the locations of the IV chord (D) and V chord (E).

Chord	A	D	E
Position in Key	I	IV	V

The D Chords on the First Three Strings

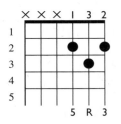 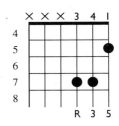 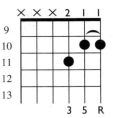

The E chords on the First Three Strings

These are easy to find. They are one whole step higher than the D chords. Remember that this relationship is true anywhere on the neck: The V chord (in this case, E) can always be found one whole step higher than the IV chord.

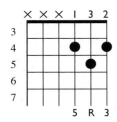 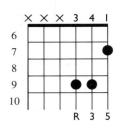 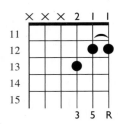

Now try these sets of I, IV and V chords. Practice them so that your fingers become used to moving up and down through these inversions. Triad progressions like these are used heavily in reggae, soul and rock music. Try picking the notes separately to play the chords as arpeggios. Try some of the alternate picking patterns you learned in Chapter 2 (page 104).

THREE WAYS TO PLAY I-IV-V WITH TRIADS IN A

#1

I — IV — V

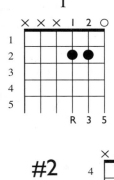 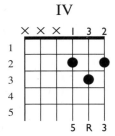 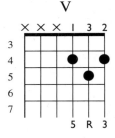

#2

I — IV — V

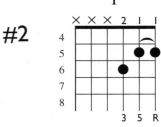 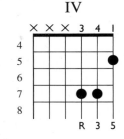 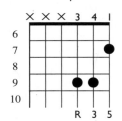

#3

I — IV — V

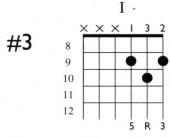 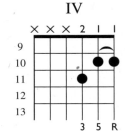 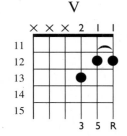

IMPROVISING WITH MAJOR TRIADS

Below is a chord progression to try using I, IV and V chords in the key of A on the first three strings. The arpeggio patterns give the triads a jangly, music-box quality. This style can be heard in the playing of Peter Buck, guitarist for R.E.M.

Watch carefully for fingering changes! The inversions occasionally switch an eighth note early. Notice how the triad inversions give the chord progression a sense of melody and motion. Try this progression with other inversions too.

Track
60

WINDCHIMES AND BOTTLECAPS·

Minor triads are constructed just like major triads with one glaring exception: The 3rd of the chord is minor. In musician jargon, this is referred to as $^\flat 3$ (flat three). This means that the 3rd of the chord is one half step lower than it was in the major triad. The 5th remains the same distance from the root, a perfect 5th (seven half steps).

Here is a comparison of A Major and A Minor triads:

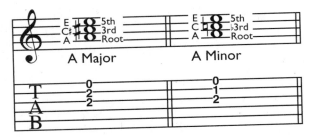

MINOR TRIAD SHAPES

Taking any major triad shape and lowering the 3rd by one half step (one fret) can form minor triads.

THE A MINOR TRIADS ON STRINGS 1, 2 AND 3

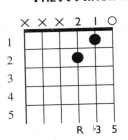
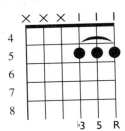
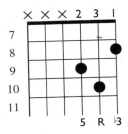

THE A MINOR TRIADS ON STRINGS 2, 3 AND 4

Compare these with the major triad shapes you learned on page 155 to see how the 3rd has been lowered.

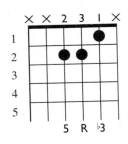
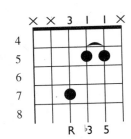
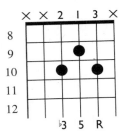

THE A MINOR TRIADS ON STRINGS 3, 4 AND 5

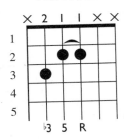
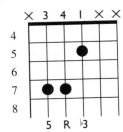
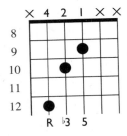

PART TWO—IMPROVISATION

47

THE A MINOR TRIADS ON STRINGS 4, 5 AND 6

Notice that the shapes are the same as the set on strings 3, 4 and 5. Only the positions have changed.

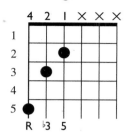
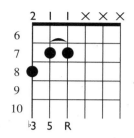
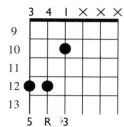

Skanking the Triads is a reggae-style tune using major and minor triads. In the first part, rest on beats 1 and 3 but strum a quick, staccato "chop" on beat 2 and 4.

Track 61

SKANKING THE TRIADS

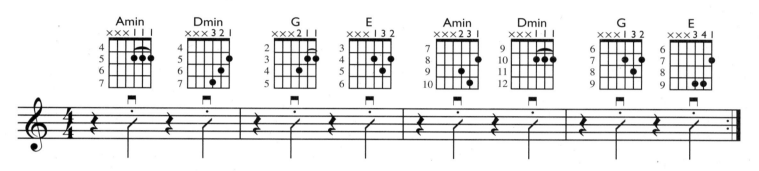

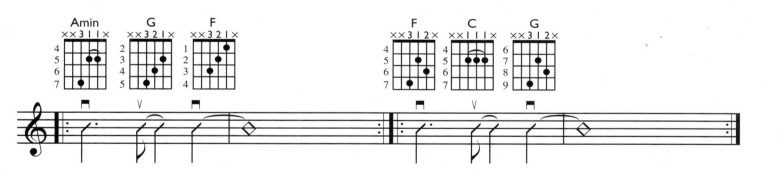

LESSON 3: MAJOR SCALE HARMONY

REVIEW—HARMONIZING THE MAJOR SCALE

This concept was first introduced on page 58. You can build triads on each note of the major scale using the scale degrees as root notes and stacking two 3rds on top of each. Use only notes in the scale for the other chord tones. This is called *harmonizing* the major scale. This is how we determine the *diatonic* harmony for the key. Diatonic means "of the key."

THE A MAJOR SCALE HARMONIZED IN TRIADS

○ = Diminished

The triads are numbered with Roman numerals based on the scale degrees of the root notes. For example, the root of the I (one) chord is the first scale degree. The root of the ii (two) chord is the second scale degree. Upper-case Roman numerals designate major triads; lower-case numerals designate minor and diminished triads.

The diatonic harmony of a major scale includes three major triads (I, IV and V), three minor triads (ii, iii and vi) and one diminished triad (vii°).

FIRST POSITION DIATONIC TRIADS ON THE FRETBOARD

Here are the diatonic triads of the key of A starting with a first inversion triad (3rd on the bottom, see page 154) on strings 1, 2 and 3. Notice that the diatonic triads maintain the same inversion structure (3rd, 5th, root), even though some are major, some are minor and one is diminished. Practice going up and down the neck with these chords. You may find that the chords in higher positions (V, vi and vii°) are hard to play on your guitar. If you have trouble fretting these chords, try the alternate positions of the V, vi and vii chords. They are the same triad inversions, just lower on the neck. Notice that the vii chord is just like a minor triad with a lowered 5th (♭5).

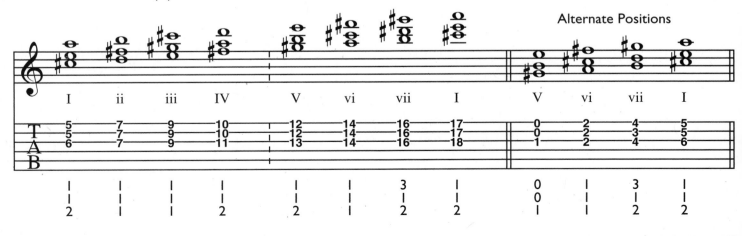

Alternate Positions

160   Intermediate Acoustic Guitar

HARMONIZING A MELODY WITH DIATONIC TRIADS

It's very effective and fun to harmonize a melody with triads. Example 49 is a short melody using notes of the major scale on one string (the 4th string). The scale degrees are shown above.

Below is an example of the melody harmonized with root-position triads. The melody notes have become the roots of the chords (even though the melody notes are still on the 4th string). This is the simplest way to harmonize a melody with triads.

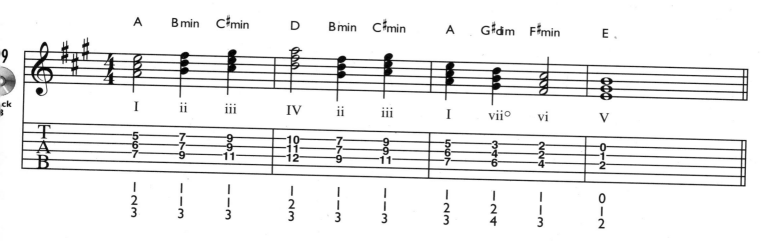

This time, the melody notes (and chord roots) are an octave higher on the 1st string, so the triads have been inverted to first inversion. In your practice, try to construct a harmonized scale starting from any inversion shape. Just locate the root and follow the scale up that string, adjusting the 3rds and 5ths of the chords to make the proper chord qualities (major, minor or diminished) based on the proper diatonic harmony for the key.

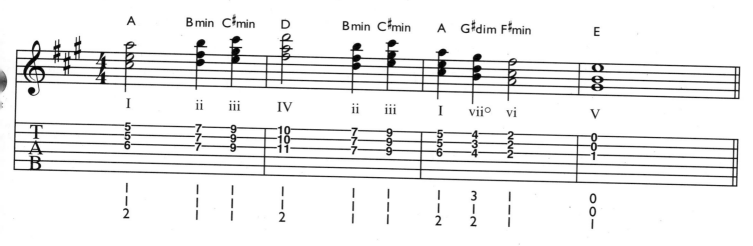

USING DIATONIC TRIADS TO SPICE UP A CHORD PROGRESSION

Once you have learned the inversions of the diatonic triads, you can mix and match them to play chord progressions. The more triad inversions you know, the more freedom you have to play a simple progression in different ways. Jimi Hendrix often used triad voicings (arrangements of chord tones) up and down the neck when playing chord progressions. This would allow him to play a chord progression many different ways without repeating the same series of voicings.

For a little variety, in this part of the lesson you will be working in the key of C. Below is a simple chord progression in C to try. The chord analysis (Roman numerals) is provided. Use the chord fingerings you are most familiar with.

BRUTHA T'S VISION

Track 65

In order to play *Brutha T's Vision* using diatonic triads and their inversions, simply choose inversions of the chords you need (IV, vi, I and V) to play the progression. Below are all of the inversions of diatonic triads in C on strings 2, 3 and 4. Practice going up and down the inversions to get used to them.

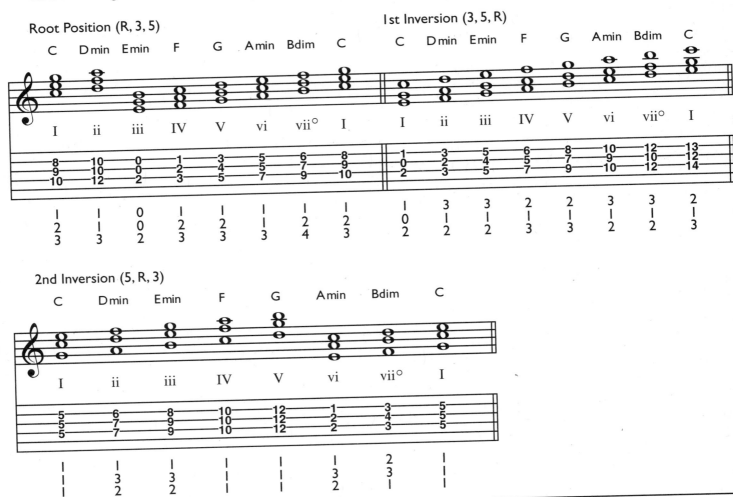

MIXING INVERSIONS FOR BETTER VOICE LEADING

When a singer sings a part in a choir, they are always singing one, individual *voice* in a harmony. Your guitar is the choir. Each note in each chord is an individual voice. *Voice leading* is the logical movement, from chord to chord, of the individual voices of each chord. The best voice leading is mostly stepwise—the individual voices do not have to make wide melodic leaps.

Here is *Brutha T's Vision* shown using triads on strings 2, 3 and 4. The triad inversions have been mixed and matched to provide the best possible voice leading. Notice, for example, how the F chord and the Amin chord have the notes A and C in common. Therefore, only one note changes between them (F moves to E). Try the progressions in example 52, then make up your own. Use this technique with any chord progression. You can even add suspensions, arpeggios, slides and slurs.

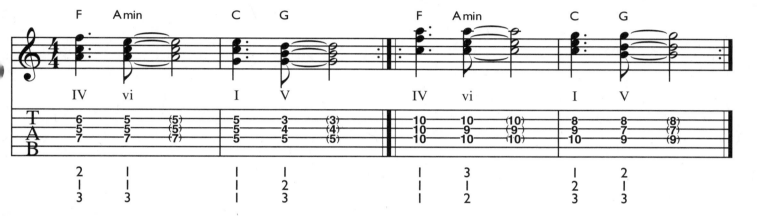

LEARNING THE CYCLE OF DIATONIC TRIADS IN ALL MAJOR KEYS

Let's call the diatonic triads for any major key played in numerical order *the cycle of diatonic triads*. The series of diatonic triads is: major, minor, minor, major, major, minor, diminished.

Here are the diatonic triads in each major key. Try them with the inversions you have learned.

Major Key	I	ii	iii	IV	V	vi	vii°
A	A	Bmin	C#min	D	E	F#min	G# dim
B♭	B♭	Cmin	Dmin	E♭	F	Gmin	A dim
B	B	C#min	D#min	E	F#	G#min	A# dim
C	C	Dmin	Emin	F	G	Amin	B dim
D♭	D♭	E♭min	Fmin	G♭	A♭	B♭min	C dim
D	D	Emin	F#min	G	A	Bmin	C# dim
E♭	E♭	Fmin	Gmin	A♭	B♭	Cmin	D dim
E	E	F#min	G#min	A	B	C#min	D# dim
F	F	Gmin	Amin	B♭	C	Dmin	E dim
G♭	G♭	A♭min	B♭min	C♭	D♭	E♭min	F dim
G	G	Amin	Bmin	C	D	Emin	F# dim
A♭	A♭	B♭min	Cmin	D♭	E♭	Fmin	G dim

A *double stop* is two notes played simultaneously on a single instrument. Double stops allow you to harmonize your melody with only one other note, giving you two out of three triad voices.

DOUBLE STOPS WITH 3RDS

You can use the interval of a 3rd to harmonize a melody anywhere on the neck. Below is a review of the major 3rd and minor 3rd shapes on the guitar neck. The frets shown will sound a major 3rd built on A (A and C♯), or a minor 3rd built on A (A and C).

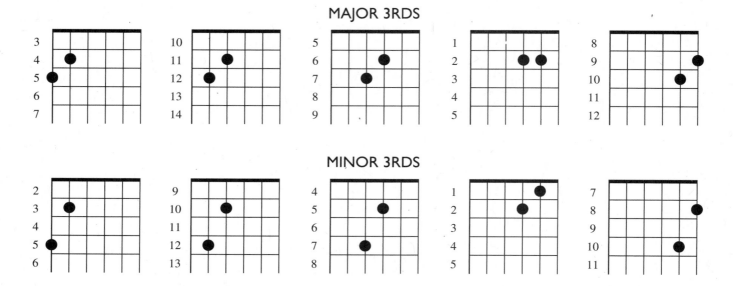

The most common way to harmonize a melody is by using the roots and 3rds of the diatonic triads. To remember when to use a major 3rd as opposed to a minor 3rd, or vice versa, just think of the cycle of diatonic triads: major, minor, minor, major, major, minor, diminished. This cycle tells you what type of 3rd interval to play (for the diminished chord, play a minor 3rd). Here is an example of an A Major scale harmonized on strings 2 and 3:

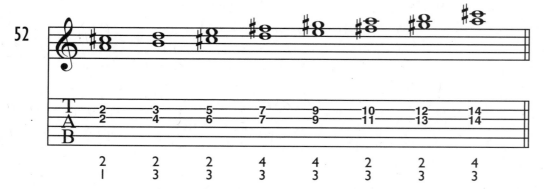

Try creating melodies that go up and down this cycle of 3rd intervals. Also try it in other places on the neck (in other keys).

This type of harmony on the guitar invokes the sound of Mexican *Mariachi* and *Conjunto* music. Try *Oaxoca Juan's Waltz* on page 165. It uses major and minor 3rds that are diatonic to the A Major scale. The fingerings cover the entire range of the guitar fingerboard. Watch out for the *D.C. al Fine* (Da Capo al Fine) at the end. This means go back to the beginning and play until the *"Fine"* (pronounced *"fee-nay"*). *"Fine"* means "end."

PART TWO—IMPROVISATION

Notice the time signature. Count three beats per measure. Also, notice the pickup notes
(page 39, *Beginning Acoustic Guitar*) at the beginning. Count two beats and come in on beat 3.

OAXACA JUAN'S WALTZ

PART TWO—IMPROVISATION

DOUBLE STOPS WITH 6THS

A 6th is the inversion of a 3rd (interval inversion was introduced on page 51 of *Beginning Acoustic Guitar*). For example, A to C♯ is a major 3rd, while C♯ to A is a minor 6th. 6ths have a more open quality than 3rds and sound great sliding around on the guitar. Below is a review of the major 6th and minor 6th shapes. The frets indicated sound a major 6th with A on top (C and A) and a minor 6th with A on top (C♯ to A).

MAJOR 6THS

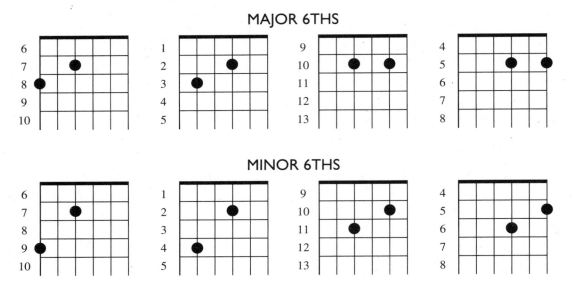

MINOR 6THS

Try this A Major scale harmonized in 6ths. Notice that these are just the outer two voices of the diatonic triads you learned in this chapter. The roots are in the top voice, the 3rds on the bottom. Again, if you have trouble above the 12th fret, try the alternate positions lower on the neck. These are particularly useful if your melody starts on the root and descends.

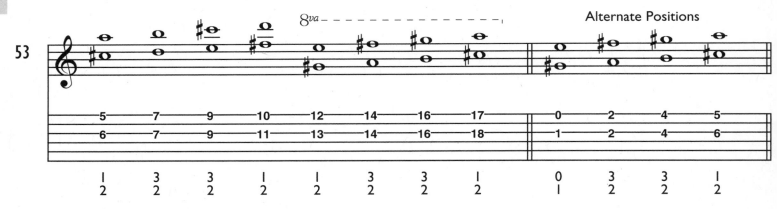

Try this set of 6ths using the 5ths of the triads on the bottom and the 3rds on top. These are the outer two voices of the second inversion (5th on the bottom) triad set on strings 2, 3 and 4.

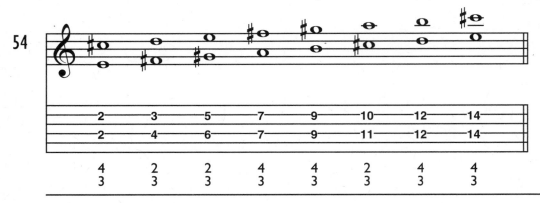

SLIDING 6THS

The sound of harmonized 6ths sliding around on a guitar is instantly recognizable in country, gospel and soul music. The following example includes a workout of 6ths all over the neck, plus a couple of cool sliding-6th licks to use in the key of A Major. Try moving these licks around to other keys.

6TH SENSE

CHAPTER 6

Pentatonic Scales

LESSON 1: MINOR PENTATONIC SCALE

Part Two—Improvisation

The minor pentatonic scale was introduced in *Beginning Acoustic Guitar* (page 66) as a good scale to use for blues improvisation. The minor pentatonic scale has five notes which are numbered 1, b3, 4, 5 and b7 for the major scale degrees they are closest to. This scale does not have scale degrees 2 or 6. Here are the notes and interval series of the A Minor Pentatonic scale:

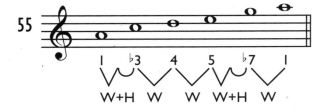

LEARNING PENTATONIC SCALE POSITIONS UP THE NECK

The pentatonic interval series (whole+half, whole, whole, whole+half, whole) is very common in folk music from many cultures. Some of the earliest melodies known are in pentatonic scales. The pentatonic scale is found on the guitar in five positions. Each position starts with a different one of the five scale degrees (1, b3, 4, 5 or b7).

POSITION #1— STARTING ON 1

Below is the A Minor Pentatonic scale starting on the A note on the 5th fret of the 6th string. This is the most well-known position for this scale. The notes, scale degrees, frets, fingering and neck diagram are shown. The tonic notes (1) are highlighted to help you keep the key in mind.

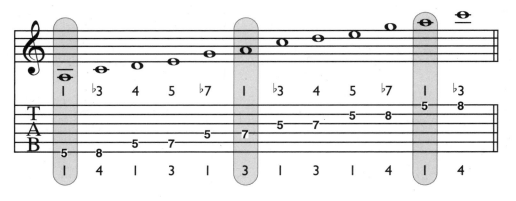
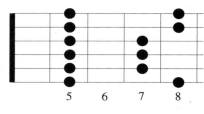

Try this example of a blues lick using Position #1. Blues solos often use minor pentatonic melodies against major or dominant chords. The ♭3 is referred to as a *blue note* because it clashes (in a good way) with the ♭3 of a major chord. The scale degrees are shown so you can identify the blue notes.

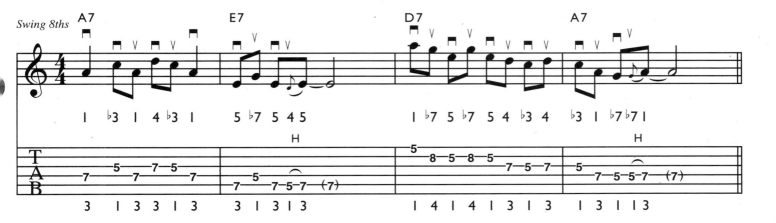

POSITION #2— STARTING ON ♭3

Here is the A Minor Pentatonic scale starting at the C note on the 8th fret of the 6th string:

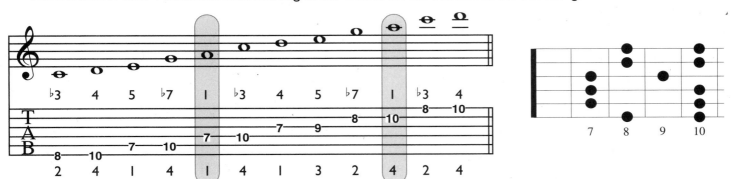

Position #2 actually makes a great *extension scale* for Position #1 (page 168). A fun trick is to play duplicate licks an octave apart using the different scale fingerings. This example shows a short bending lick as it appears in both positions (bars 1 and 2 = Position #1, bars 3 and 4 = Position #2).

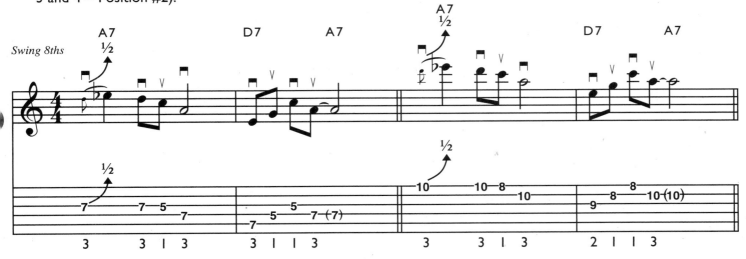

POSITION #3— STARTING ON ♭7

Below is the A Minor Pentatonic scale starting at the G note on the 3rd fret of the 6th string. This is also a very common fingering for the scale.

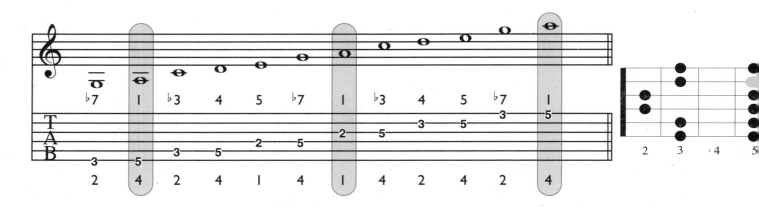

Example 59 uses Position #3 in the context of minor chords. Hear how the character of the melody changes when played over minor chords even though you are using the same scale.

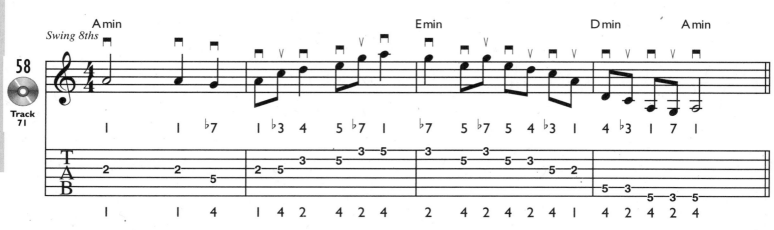

POSITION #4— STARTING ON 4

Here is the A Minor Pentatonic scale starting at the D note on the 10th fret of the 6th string.

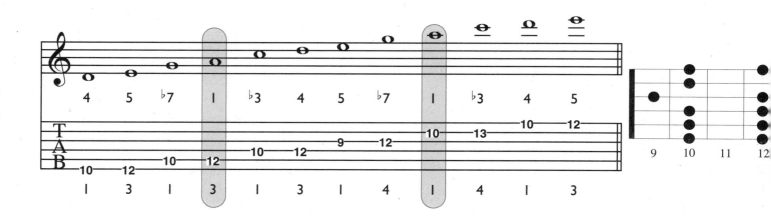

Here is the A Minor Pentatonic scale starting at the E note on the 12th fret of the 6th string.

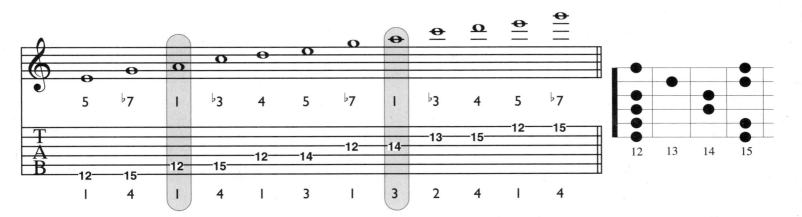

CONNECTING THE POSITIONS

You can use your knowledge of the five positions of the pentatonic scale to create melodic runs that go through more than one position of the scale. An excellent way to learn this is to practice the scale going up and down just one string. The fretboard diagram below will help you find the notes.

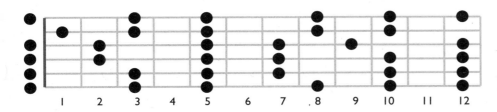

Here is a comfortable minor pentatonic scale run that uses slides with the 3rd and 4th finger to change positions. It starts on a G note (♭7) and goes through three octaves of the scale. The scale degrees, notes, frets and fretboard diagram are shown.

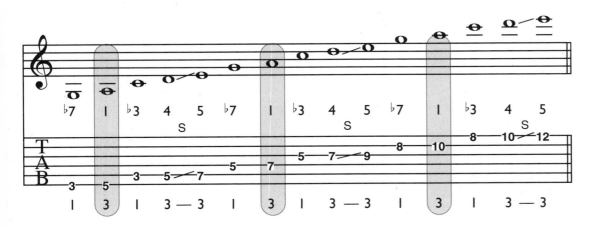

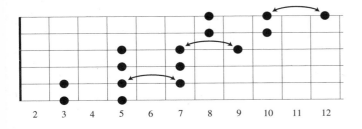

⌒ = Change positions with a slide

TIPS FOR IMPROVISING

It is tempting to learn the scale positions and then just fly up and down the scale positions in a flurry of notes. But it is far more musical to create melodies out of the scales. Here are a few tips to help you:

1. Practice going up *and* down the scale positions—learn them forwards and backwards.

2. Practice skipping around notes in the position; play them out of order without losing track of where you are. Try saying the scale degree numbers aloud as you play.

3. Try to emphasize chord tones in your improvisation. This takes some work and practice with chord spelling, but you can start by emphasizing the notes of an A Minor triad (1, ♭3 and 5) while playing in an A Minor Pentatonic scale. To emphasize a chord tone, use it as the start or end of a phrase, or make it a longer note within a phrase.

Below is a sample solo using the minor pentatonic scale positions you have learned in this lesson. It is based on the chord progression for the swing tune *Still A Minor At 32* (page 130). Try working your way through this solo, then try improvising your own solos using the minor pentatonic scale.

> ### SPECIAL BONUS
> The bridge of this solo uses triads with suspensions (page 106) to create a different effect. This helps set the B section apart from the A section.

 RETURN OF THE SON OF STILL A MINOR AT 32

Track 70

A Section

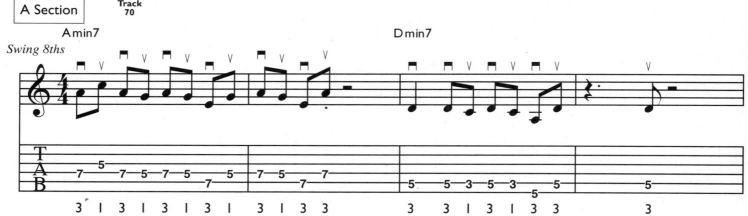

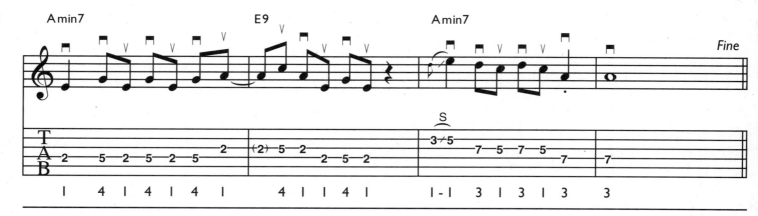

The major pentatonic scale is a good scale to use for country, bluegrass and blues improvisation when you are looking for a major sound. The notes of the major pentatonic scale are derived from the major scale. They are scale degrees 1, 2, 3, 5 and 6. Degrees 4 and 7 are omitted. Here is the A Major Pentatonic scale:

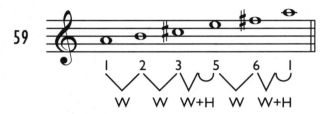

TEN POSITIONS FOR THE PRICE OF FIVE

The interval structure of the scale (whole, whole, whole+half, whole, whole+half) is the same as that of the minor pentatonic scale. It simply starts at a different point in the cycle. *Any minor pentatonic scale has exactly the same interval pattern as a major pentatonic scale a minor 3rd higher.* In other words, the fingerings for the major pentatonic scale use the same shapes on the neck as the minor pentatonic. It's just that in the major pentatonic, the scale degrees are renumbered. What was ♭3 is now 1. So, the five minor pentatonic positions, with a little shuffling around to create major pentatonic positions, are actually ten pentatonic positions.

POSITION #1—STARTING ON 6

Here is the A Major Pentatonic scale starting on the F♯ note on the 2nd fret of the 6th string. It is the same fingering shape as the A Minor Pentatonic Position #1—Starting on 1 (page 168). Now your tonic note (A) is played with your 4th finger on the 6th and 1st strings, and your 1st finger on the 3rd string.

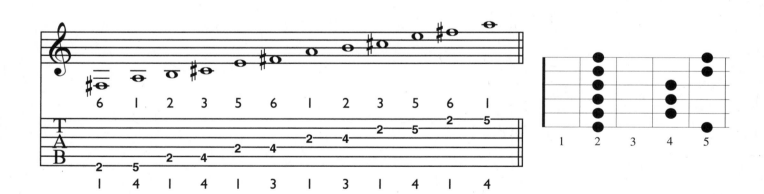

Example 61 uses the A Major Pentatonic scale in Position #1.

POSITION #2—STARTING ON 1

Below is the A Major Pentatonic scale starting at the A note on the 5th fret of the 6th string.
Compare it to the A Minor Pentatonic scale starting at the same fret (Position #1, page 168).

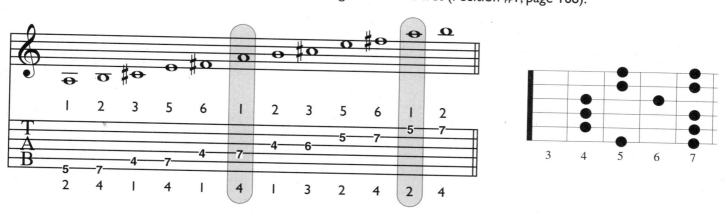

Here is a short example using Position #2 of the A Major Pentatonic scale and Position #1 of
the A Minor Pentatonic scale:

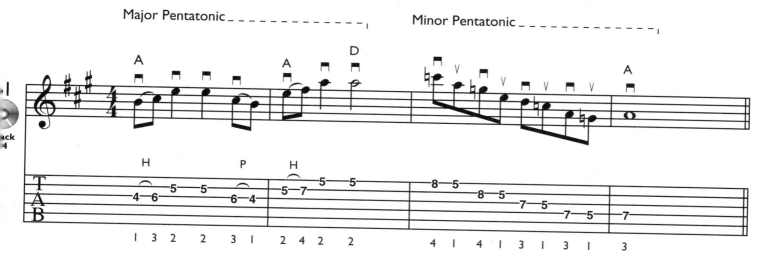

POSITION #3—STARTING ON 2

Here is the A Major Pentatonic scale starting on the B note on the 7th fret of the 6th string:

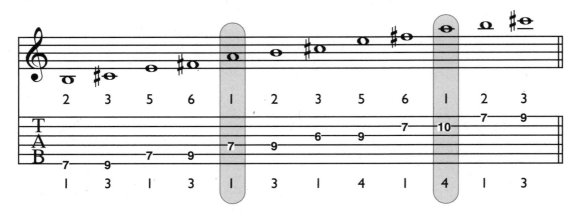
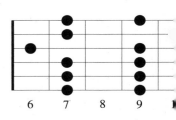

POSITION #4—STARTING ON 3

Here is the A Major Pentatonic scale starting on the C♯ note on the 9th fret of the 6th string:

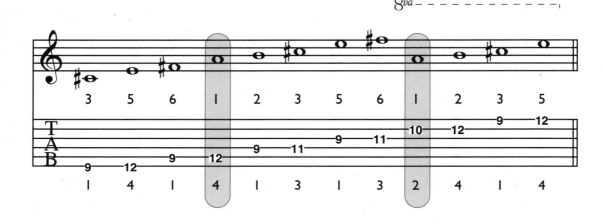
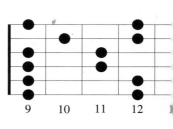

POSITION #5—STARTING ON 5

Here is the A Major Pentatonic scale starting at the E note on the 12th fret of the 6th string:

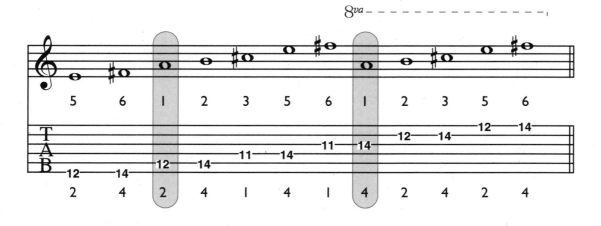
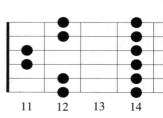

Example 63 uses the three positions you learned on page 176 (Positions #3, #4 and #5).

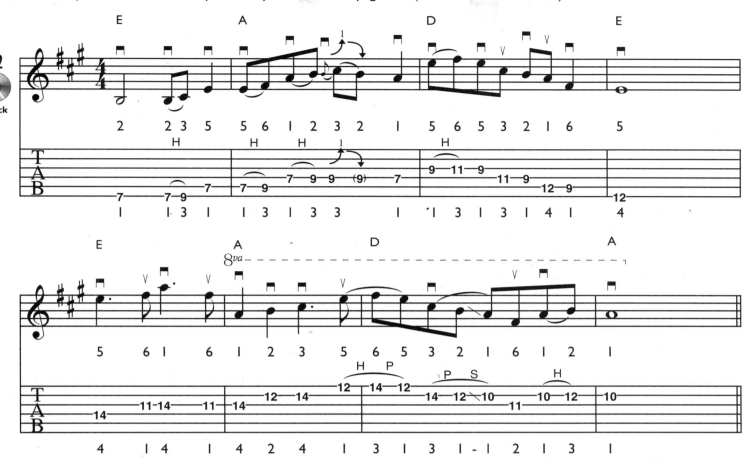

CONNECTING THE POSITIONS

Try this example of a four-octave major pentatonic scale using slides with the 3rd and 4th fingers to change positions going up the neck. Try it backwards, too!

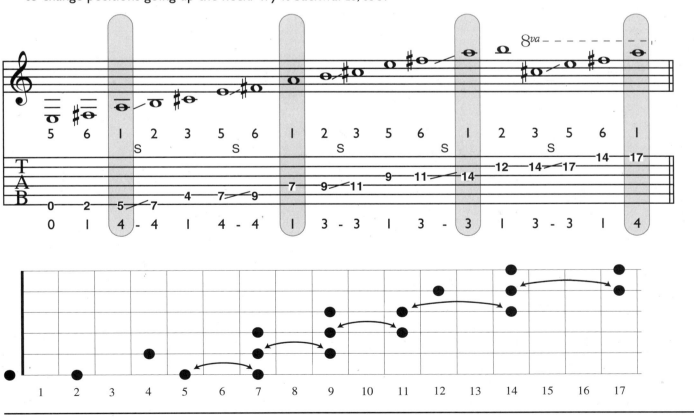

IMPROVISING USING THE MAJOR (AND MINOR) PENTATONIC SCALES

The following example solo is based on an *eight-bar blues* chord progression. There are several versions of eight-bar blues. This chord progression can be heard in the song *Key to the Highway* by Big Bill Broonzy among many other tunes. The chord analysis is shown so that you can experiment soloing over this progression and in other keys.

This solo uses the A Major Pentatonic scale in several positions.

EIGHT BALL IN THE CORNER BLUES—SOLO #1

Track 76

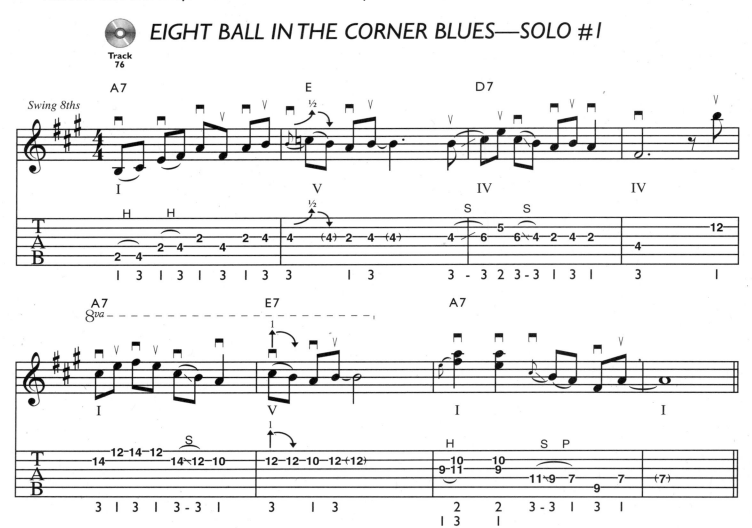

This example solo uses the minor pentatonic scale over the same chord progression. Notice how the character of the melody in the solo changes with the minor sound.

EIGHT BALL IN THE CORNER BLUES—SOLO #2

Track 77

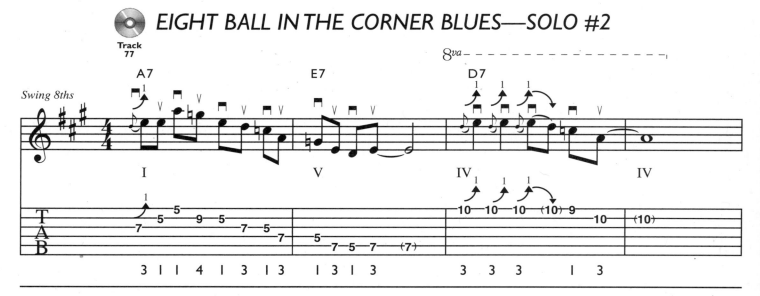

The next solo mixes the minor and major pentatonic scales in the same solo. Notice how the major pentatonic sounds great over the V chord and how the minor pentatonic helps lead the ear to the IV chord. This is because the ♭3 of the minor pentatonic scale is the same note as the ♭7 chord tone of the IV chord (D7). Also, the minor pentatonic has scale degree 4 in it which is the root of the IV chord; the major pentatonic scale does not.

EIGHT BALL IN THE CORNER BLUES—SOLO #3

Track 78

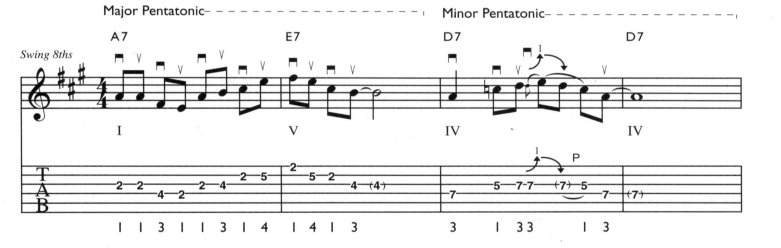

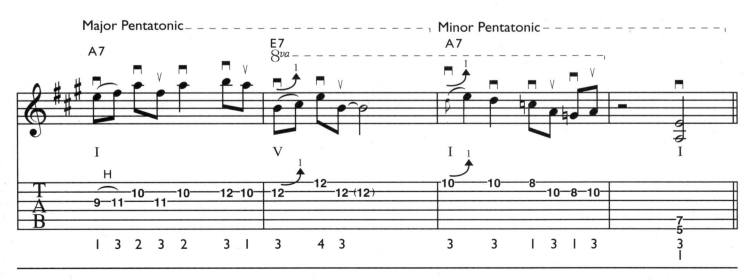

CHAPTER 7

Introducing Alternate Tunings

Any tuning other than the standard E-A-D-G-B-E tuning is an *alternate tuning*. Alternate tunings have been popular with acoustic guitarists in all styles and eras. Early blues guitarists tuned their strings to open chords (called *open tunings*) to facilitate playing with a bottleneck or slide. Acoustic rockers and songwriters such as Joni Mitchell and David Crosby pioneered the use of alternate tunings to achieve more complex and colorful chord voicings. More current players such as Michael Hedges, Ani DiFranco and David Wilcox have used alternate tunings to expand the range of tones and textures available on the guitar.

It's great fun to experiment with alternate tunings. They can help you create whole new sounds out of familiar patterns, and they can push you to develop new patterns and ideas. It can be as simple as re-tuning one string, or as complicated as developing an entirely new tuning for the instrument. This chapter will introduce a few of the most common tunings and some tips for getting new sounds without re-tuning at all. This topic is covered in more depth in *Mastering Acoustic Guitar*.

LESSON 1: GETTING CREATIVE WITH OPEN STRINGS

One of the benefits of alternate tunings is having new pitches available on open strings. This can allow new chord voicings and scale patterns. You can get an idea of how this works by experimenting with the relationships between fretted notes and open strings in standard tuning.

EXPERIMENTING WITH CHORDS

This is a very simple technique that can add a whole new flavor to your playing. Try moving some standard open chords—chords that include open strings—up and down the neck, allowing the open strings to ring. You used this technique in *The Rocky Road to the Foggy Cliffs of Erin's Green Shamrock Shore* on page 137. In that tune, you used E and A chord forms while the first two strings rang open. Here are some more examples of this idea at work:

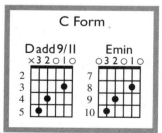

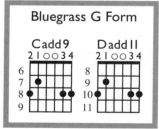

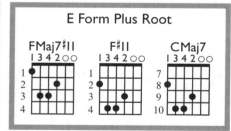

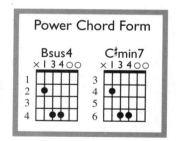

Here is an example using C and G shapes. When you use open strings in chords going up the neck, sometimes they create color tones such as 9s, 11s and 13s. The chord names can get quite complex but the fingerings are very basic.

 ## SPARE CHANGE FOR A NEW CHORD

Track 79

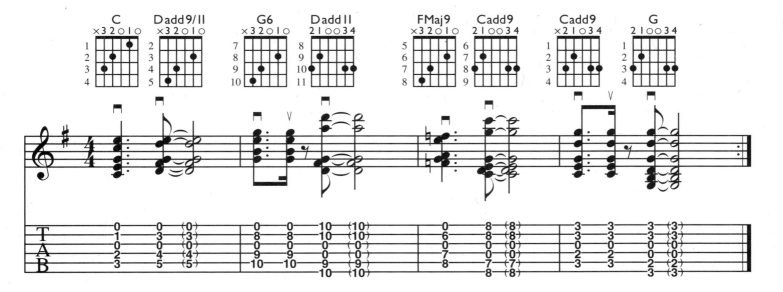

THE MOUNTAIN DULCIMER EFFECT

The mountain dulcimer, or *lap dulcimer*, is a common instrument in Appalachian folk music. Players such as Joni Mitchell and Peter Buck have also used it in rock music. On a simple four-string dulcimer, a pair of strings is fretted for the melody while the other two are open, *drone* (a long, sustained note) strings. You can get this effect on the guitar in standard or open tunings by fretting a melody up and down one string while an adjacent string (or pair of strings) acts as a drone. The mountain-dulcimer style often uses a regular strum pattern to simulate the rhythm of a fiddle bow "shuffle." In this example, the melody notes are black so that you can distinguish them from the drone notes which are gray.

SHUFFLIN' SUCCOTASH

Track 80

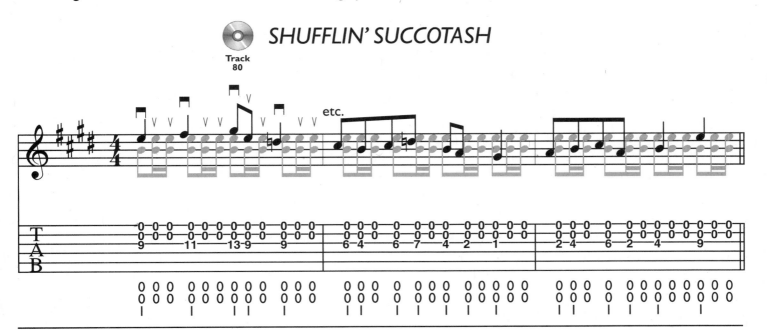

Chapter 7—Introducing Alternate Tunings   **181**

Drop D tuning is the simplest and most common alternate tuning. Simply "drop" your 6th string down one whole step to D. Example 63 shows the tuning of your open strings in drop D. Also shown, in gray, are the matching notes on adjacent strings to use for tuning your guitar to drop D. Note that your open 5th string matches the 7th fret of the 6th instead of the 5th fret.

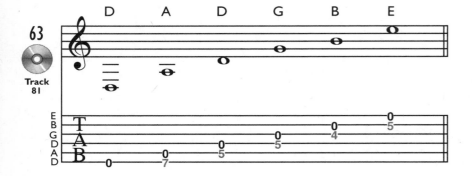

TUNING TIPS

When using alternate tunings, you will have to find new ways to match your strings to each other for tuning. Most alternate tunings will leave one or more of the standard strings intact, allowing you to use them as a point of reference. In addition, you will often retune a string to a note that is an octave above or below one of the standard strings. For example, the "drop" D in this tuning is an octave below the 4th string (D). Try to match these strings by octave using your ears. You can also match the 12th fret harmonic of the 6th string to the open 4th string. With practice, you will get used to hearing the octaves and be able to fine-tune them to each other.

NEW CHORD FORMS IN DROP D

One of the best first steps in dealing with a new tuning is to learn some basic chords. Here are the basic chords in drop D:

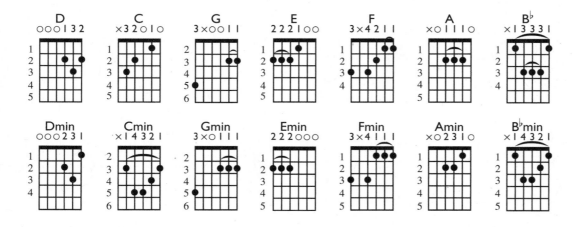

SPECIAL FEATURE—BARRED POWER CHORDS

Every alternate tuning has some "special features" that offer you new sounds, or an easier way to play old sounds. There are several tunings with the lowest three strings tuned D, A, D. In any of these tunings, power chords are found when all three strings are played at the same fret. This means you can play a full power chord (root, 5, root) with one finger. Try the examples on the right:

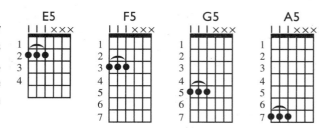

This tune uses the F, E and G power chords shown above, plus major triad fingerings on strings 2, 3 and 4. The rhythm is very syncopated but if you count it out, you'll get the funk!

DROP D NOISE, DROP D FUNK

Track 82

This example uses major triads on the first three strings. It is in the style of Stephen Stills' *Love the One You're With*.

BEGGARS CAN'T BE CHOOSERS

Track 83

Chapter 7—Introducing Alternate Tunings   **183**

IMPROVISING OVER A PEDAL TONE

You may have noticed that it can be difficult to practice your scales and improvising without someone playing chords. Drop D tuning can be a great remedy for this. You can use the lower three strings (D, A, D) as a sustaining drone, or *pedal tone*, while you improvise with scales and chords on the first three strings. You can either play to a regular beat, or use a free rhythm to evoke the sound of bagpipes or Indian *sitar* music.

Below are two scale fingerings for improvising in drop D tuning, the D Major scale and the D Minor pentatonic. They are shown over a low D pedal tone.

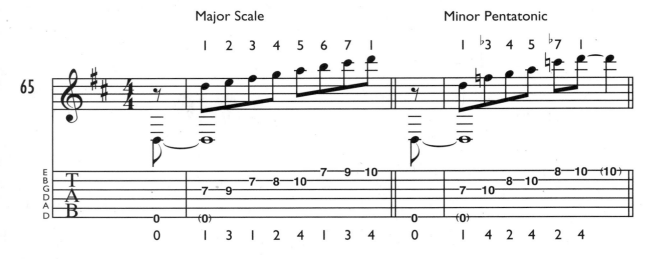

Example 66 uses the D Major scale. The pedal tones are struck on the "&" before the downbeat and allowed to ring for nearly two measures. Try this technique with your own improvisations and scale fingerings.

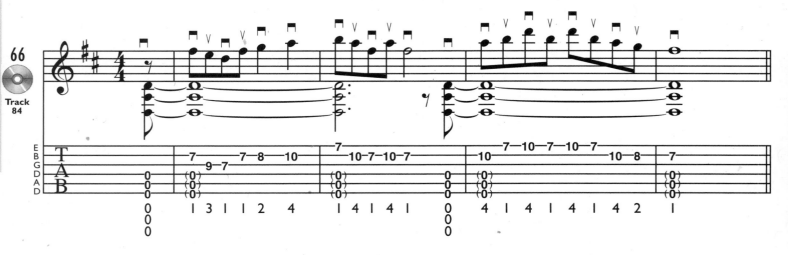

This example uses the D Minor pentatonic scale in a free rhythm (no time signature). The note values are merely suggestions for the relative lengths of the notes. There is no actual "beat." The dotted bar lines are there to suggest phrases. Strum the three-note pedal chord, then prepare your pick to play the melody on the treble strings.

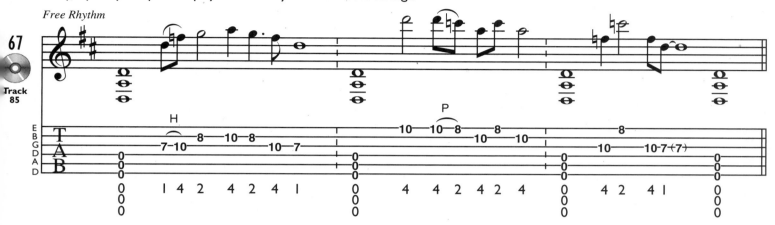

KEEPING A STEADY BEAT

You can use fingerstyle technique to keep a steady beat in your pedal tone. You have worked with this in the Delta blues section of this book (pages 144 – 147). Use *p* (the right-hand thumb) to play pedal tones on the quarter notes, while your other fingers play the scale tones.

Here's a D Major scale played with this technique to get you started:

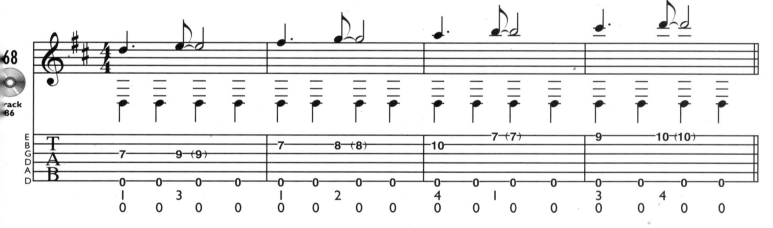

ALTERNATING BASS AND CHANGING PEDAL TONES

Once you have experimented with keeping a steady beat with *p*, try alternating between the 6th and 4th strings. Example 69 uses the minor pentatonic scale to demonstrate this technique. Notice that in measure 3, the pedal tone changes to A. This gives the impression of chord movement without creating any fingering problems.

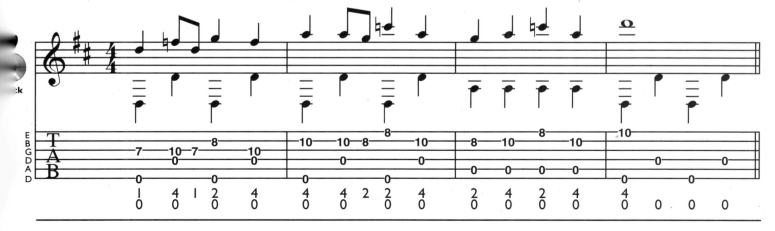

Chapter 7—Introducing Alternate Tunings   **185**

IS IT A TUNING OR A FOOTBALL PLAY?

Double drop D tuning is a variation on drop D tuning. In double drop D tuning, we tune both the 6th string (E) and the 1st string (E) down one whole step to D. Here are the open-string pitches in double drop D tuning, along with the frets for matching the notes to adjacent strings (in gray) for tuning.

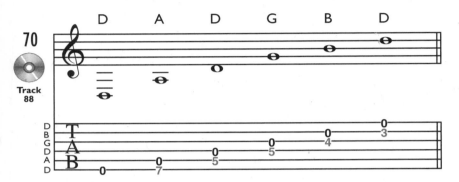

This tuning has been used extensively by Joni Mitchell and Neil Young. It is a popular alternate tuning for players who don't want to entirely relearn the guitar for a new tuning. With four strings remaining the same, it is easy to maintain your orientation on the fingerboard while still taking advantage of the new tonal colors the tuning offers.

BASIC CHORDS

Here are some basic chord fingerings for this tuning:

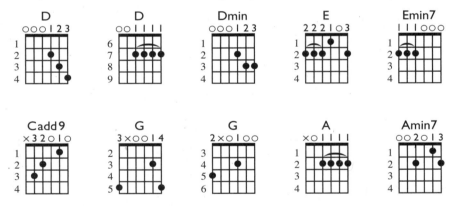

SPECIAL FEATURE – HIGH OPEN D STRING

With the 1st string now tuned to D, you have three open D strings. The 1st string can be used as a drone or as a unison with any chords using another D note. Below are some suggested voicings to try. Notice the ringing, slightly "out-of-phase" sound of playing two strings playing exactly the same pitch—this is due to the near impossibility of perfect unison tuning. (This effect is one of the main reasons a violin section in an orchestra sounds different than a solo violin.)

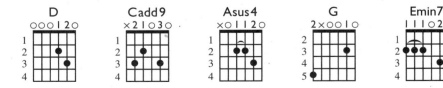

Free Cinnamon Buns in Paris, which is in the style of Joni Mitchell and Neil Young, takes advantage of the open 1st string to create a drone through the first few chord changes. It also uses one-finger power chords and a Dsus4 triad in an upper position voicing.

FREE CINNAMON BUNS IN PARIS

Track 89

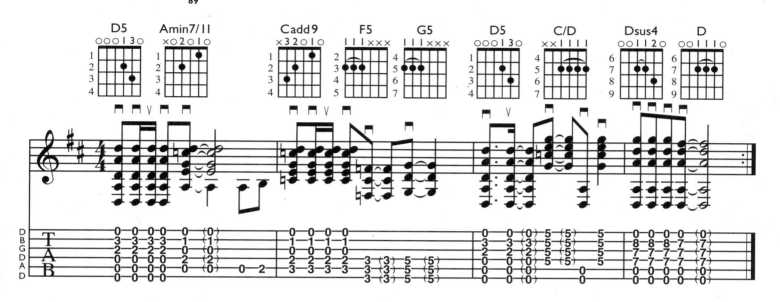

Sprinkles and Jimmies is in the style of *32 Flavors* by Ani DiFranco. It shows how simple chord fingerings, arpeggios and open strings can be combined to create spacious voicings. Double drop D tuning is great for keys other than D! This progression is in the key of G.

SPRINKLES AND JIMMIES

Track 90

Chapter 7—Introducing Alternate Tunings **187**

Open G tuning is one of the most popular alternate tunings. It is called "open G" because the strings are tuned to the notes of a G triad (G, B and D). An easy way to remember how to get to this tuning is this: *tune each string to the closest note in a G triad and only tune down.*

Here are the open string notes and matching adjacent notes (in gray) for open G and a few harmonic tone matches to help you fine tune:

Track 91

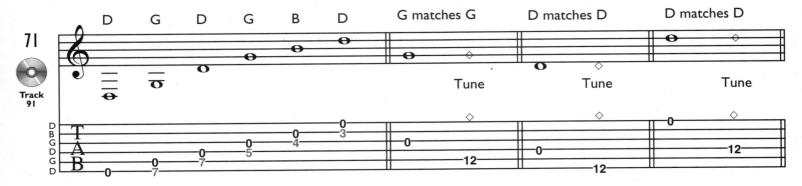

Open G tuning can be heard in the playing of Robert Johnson, Son House, The Rolling Stones, The Black Crowes and countless others. It is popular with slide players because it allows you to sound a full major chord by barring all the way across one fret.

Here are some of the basic chords in open G:

Here are the power chord fingerings (root, 5, root) in open G (these are movable):

Here are some other movable chord fingerings for this tuning:

SPECIAL FEATURE: TRIADS ON STRINGS 2, 3, AND 4

In open G tuning, strings 2, 3 and 4 remain the same as they are in standard tuning. You can play all of the same triad shapes and harmonized scales on these strings as you would in standard tuning. This can help you find chords up and down the neck, and help keep you oriented when learning this tuning.

Here is a harmonized G Major scale using triads in open G:

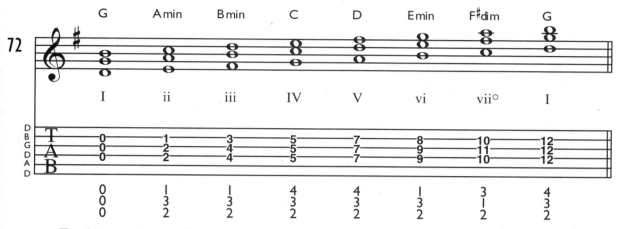

Try this tune in open G tuning. It is in the playing styles of The Rolling Stones, The Black Crowes and The Faces. It uses many of the popular chord voicings and triads available in open G. The second line features parallel octaves (page 52) played on strings 3 and 5, and on strings 4 and 6. Notice that it is easy to play parallel octaves in this tuning by playing the same fret on any two strings that are tuned to the same pitch class, such as the 6th string (low D) and the 4th string (middle D).

BATS IN THE BARRELHOUSE

Track 92

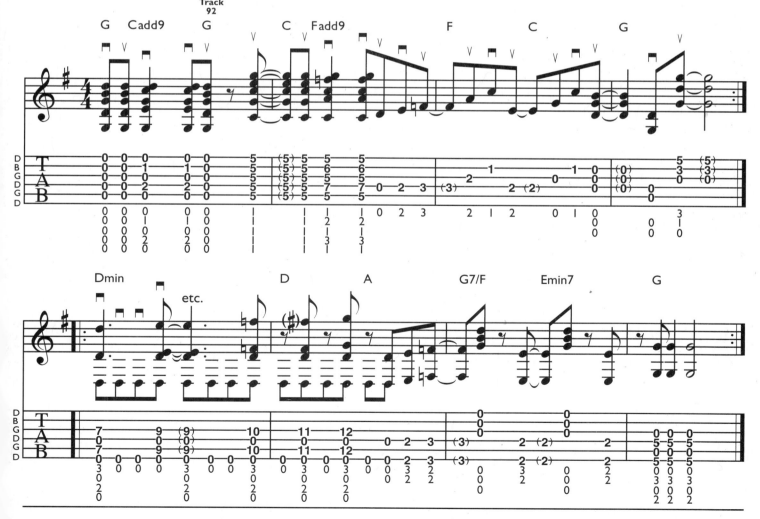

Open D tuning is another very popular tuning. It is called "open D" because the strings are tuned to the notes of a D Major triad (D, F#, A). Tune each string to the closest note in a D triad and only tune *down*.

Here are the open-string notes and matching notes (in gray) on adjacent strings for tuning, plus a few harmonic tone matches to help you fine tune:

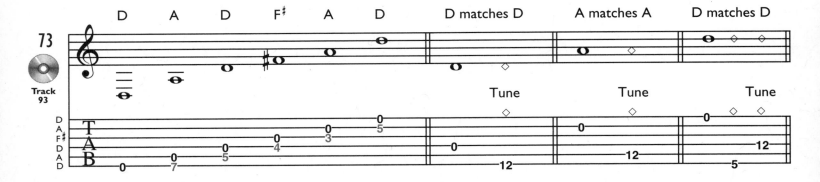

Track 93

SECRETS OF THE MASTERS—FOUR TUNINGS FOR THE PRICE OF TWO!

Open A tuning is identical to open G but everything is one whole step higher. The tuning is: E, A, E, A, C#, E. The chord forms are the same as for open G tuning.

Open E is identical to open D, but one whole step higher. The tuning is: E, B, E, G#, B, E. The chord forms are the same as for open D tuning.

Open D tuning can be heard in the playing of The Rolling Stones, Joni Mitchell, Ry Cooder and many others. Like open G, it is a great tuning for slide playing and the blues.

Here are some basic chords in open D:

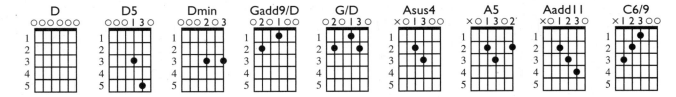

Here are the power chord fingerings (root, 5, root) in open D (these are movable):

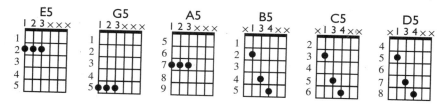

Here are some other movable chord fingerings for this tuning:

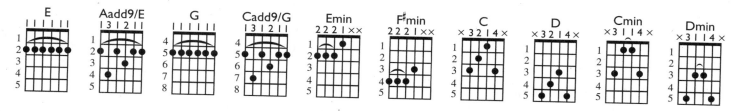

SPECIAL FEATURE: TRIADS ON STRINGS 3, 4 AND 5

In the open G tuning section (pages 188 and 189), you learned that you can still play triads on strings 2, 3 and 4 just as you did in standard tuning. In open D tuning, these triad forms move to strings 3, 4 and 5 and transpose to the key of D.

Here is a harmonized D Major scale using triads:

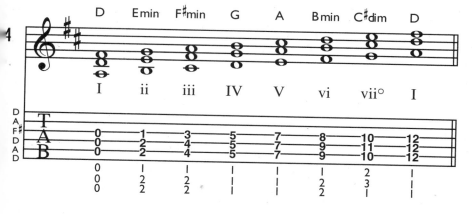

Don't Talk to Strangers is in the style of The Black Crowes' *She Talks To Angels*. Notice that it uses chords that feel similar to those used in open G, except that they are moved to the next lower string. Also, note the use of full harmonic chords at the end of the first line. Play these by touching the harmonic nodes across all six strings with one finger and then strum.

The harmonics in this tune are simple, although there are some added decorative notes. The basic harmonies are shown, and some fingering tips for the decorative notes are shown below. Have fun!

DON'T TALK TO STRANGERS

Track 94

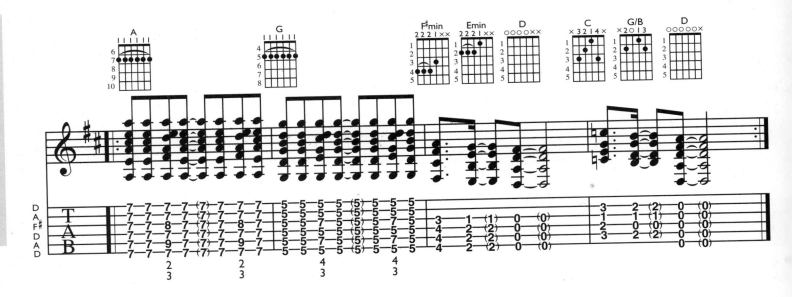

Congratulations! You've accomplished a lot to get to this point. Don't stop now—

PART THREE—ALTERNATE TUNIGS

192   Intermediate Acoustic Guitar

MASTERING ACOUSTIC GUITAR

This book was acquired, edited, and produced
by Workshop Arts, Inc., the publishing arm of
the National Guitar Workshop.
Nathaniel Gunod, acquisitions, managing editor
Timothy Phelps, interior design
Gary Tomassetti, music typesetter
CD recorded and mastered by Collin Tilton at Bar None Studio, Cheshire, CT

TABLE OF CONTENTS

00

Track 01

An MP3 CD is included with this book to make learning easier and more enjoyable. The symbol shown at bottom left appears next to every example in the book that features an MP3 track. Use the MP3s to ensure you're capturing the feel of the examples and interpreting the rhythms correctly. The track number below the symbol corresponds directly to the example you want to hear (example numbers are above the icon). All the track numbers are unique to each "book" within this volume, meaning every book has its own Track 1, Track 2, and so on. (For example, *Beginning Acoustic Guitar* starts with Track 1, as does *Intermediate Acoustic Guitar* and *Mastering Acoustic Guitar*.) Track 1 for each book will help you tune your guitar.

To access the MP3s on the CD, place the CD in your computer's CD-ROM drive. In Windows, double-click on My Computer, then right-click on the CD icon labeled "MP3 Files" and select Explore to view the files and copy them to your hard drive. For Mac, double-click on the CD icon on your desktop labeled "MP3 Files" to view the files and copy them to your hard drive.

INTRODUCTION

Welcome to *Mastering Acoustic Guitar*! This book takes us deeper into the concepts and techniques introduced in *Beginning Acoustic Guitar* and *Intermediate Acoustic Guitar*.

WHO SHOULD USE THIS BOOK

This book is designed for advanced students. You need to be familiar with the construction of the major scale, diatonic harmony, intervals, triad inversion, 7 chords, major and minor pentatonic scale positions, sixteenth-note rhythms, drop D, double drop D, open G and open D tunings. These topics are all covered in either *Beginning Acoustic Guitar* or *Intermediate Acoustic Guitar*. You do not need to be able to read music to use this book. However, a basic knowledge of music reading will greatly help your understanding of the scales, chords, rhythms and modal keys discussed.

HOW TO USE THIS BOOK

This book is organized in four major sections:

PART ONE—BAG OF TRICKS

This section covers new playing techniques in funk, rock and swing styles, new chord voicings and an introduction to odd time signatures and polyrhythms. You will also be introduced to right-hand tapping and slap harmonics.

PART TWO—MODAL SOUNDS

This section gives an in-depth view of the Mixolydian, Dorian and Aeolian modes. These are the three most commonly heard modes in modern folk and rock music. Each has its own signature melodic sounds and harmonic character.

PART THREE—ALTERNATE TUNINGS

This section adds to the alternate tunings covered in *Intermediate Acoustic Guitar*, including D Minor tuning, DADGAD, C tuning and radical tunings used by pioneers such as Michael Hedges and Ani DiFranco.

PART FOUR—COMPOSITION AND ARRANGING

This section takes you through the process of creating a composition or arrangement, from melodic and harmonic fragments to a full-blown arrangement in an alternate tuning.

This book is designed so that you can study Parts One, Two and Three simultaneously or sequentially. Part Four brings together skills learned in the previous parts and should be used after completing the other three sections.

WHERE TO GO FROM HERE

This three-book method was designed to give you a foundation of techniques and improvisational theory to help you play the sounds heard in modern acoustic music. You can build your understanding by applying the lessons in this method to other keys and positions, and by creating your own compositions, arrangements and new techniques.

This volume is dedicated to the memory of Michael Hedges, and
to all the other masters for their gifts of music and inspiration.

CHAPTER 1

New Techniques

LESSON 1: BUILDING SPEED AND AGILITY

ACCURACY AND ECONOMY

Accuracy and economy of motion are the keys to building speed and agility in your playing. Try to identify the specific muscle movements required to play specific passages on the guitar, and then eliminate any extra motion in your playing that detracts from your efficiency. Here are three crucial points to improving your technique:

1. Be observant of your playing technique. Pay attention to how you hold the guitar, your hand positions, your finger movements and your breathing.

2. Strive for economy of motion in your playing. Play with as little movement as possible, and try to avoid tension. Stay loose and relaxed.

3. Practice exercises that address specific movements or techniques, and concentrate on the effects that the exercises were designed to achieve. Exercises have little effect if you simply try to play them as fast as possible.

Below are some exercises you can use to warm up your fingers and to build speed and accuracy. To get the maximum effect of these exercises, follow these pointers:

1. Concentrate on the motion of your fingers. Keep them "floating" close to the frets. Move them up and down like pistons in a car engine. Don't play too fast! It is better to play slowly and to focus on technical improvement than it is to conern yourself with simply being able to play fast.

2. Concentrate on synchronizing your picking hand with your fretting fingers. Feel the simultaneous "twitch" in both forearms that makes each note.

3. Practice these exercises for a few minutes at the beginning of each practice session. This will allow you to start off with the best technique possible. Soon the technique you develop in the exercises will start to show up in your regular playing.

PISTON EXERCISE #1

This exercise is shown on the 3rd string, but practice it on each string.

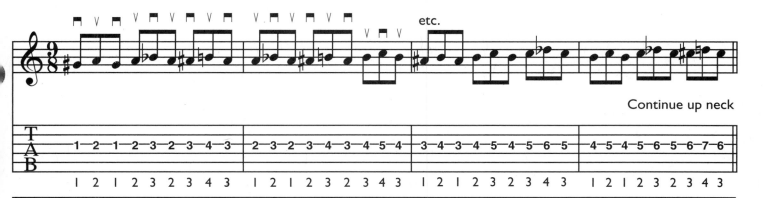

PISTON EXERCISE #2

Like Piston Exercise #1, this exercise is shown on the 3rd string, but practice it on each string.

The following exercises will help you stretch your fingers and develop an efficient left-hand position. Make sure that your hand is not turned away from the neck, causing your pinky to stretch. If you feel pain as you practice these exercises, stop immediately! Evaluate your hand position. You may be bending your wrist too sharply, or bending backwards at your *knuckle joint* (the one that connects your finger to your hand). Relax and go very slowly!

Try moving all these exercises to different positions on the neck.

STRETCHING EXERCISE #1

Try to keep all your fingers down until it's time to move your 1st finger again. Keep the notes sustained and connected.

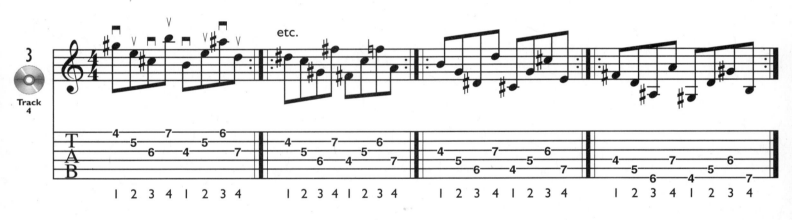

STRETCHING EXERCISE #2

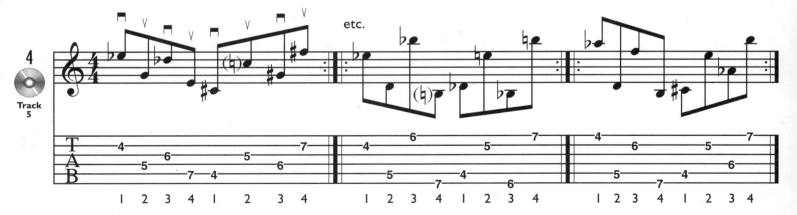

The term *pedal tone* refers to a pipe organ technique in which a note is sustained with a foot pedal while the organist plays changing melodies or harmonies above it. As a musical device, pedal tones can sound in the bass, middle or treble regions of a chord or melody. Another term for a pedal tone is a *drone*.

Contemporary acoustic guitar music relies heavily on pedal tones, as both rhythmic and harmonic devices. Players such as Dave Matthews, Shawn Colvin, Patty Larkin and Joni Mitchell use this technique to create the impression of multiple guitars playing together.

PEDAL TONES IN THE LOWER VOICE

You can use pedal tones in a variety of contexts. For example, try droning on a bass string while playing a melody on an adjacent string. This technique is sometimes heard in heavy metal music, and is also popular in contemporary Celtic playing. Another common technique is to play a chord progression over a static pedal tone.

Pedal to the Metal uses both techniques described above. Notice the *D.C. al Fine*. After playing the second line, return to the beginning and play until the *Fine* (in this case, observing the repeat sign). Notice that the rhythms are stemmed in opposite directions. This is how music in two parts is usually written.

PEDAL TO THE METAL

Track 6

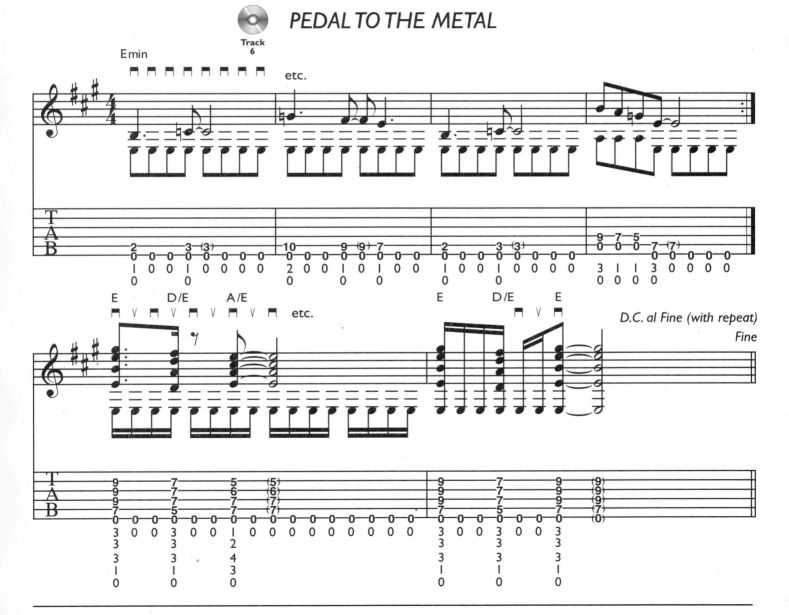

Part One—Bag of Tricks

PEDAL TONES IN THE UPPER VOICE

Pedal tones can also sound great in the higher notes of a chord (the upper voices). This is a very common technique in acoustic guitar playing. Keeping a drone in the high notes while the bass line or chords change creates a jangling, folk-rock kind of sound. Listen to the playing of Joni Mitchell, Peter Buck (of R.E.M.) and David Crosby to hear this technique.

Splash Into the Pool is in the style of Dave Matthews Band's *Crash into Me*. It uses a moving bass line against pedal tones on the first two strings. The moving bass line creates the impression of a chord progression without the use of full chords.

 # SPLASH INTO THE POOL

Track
7

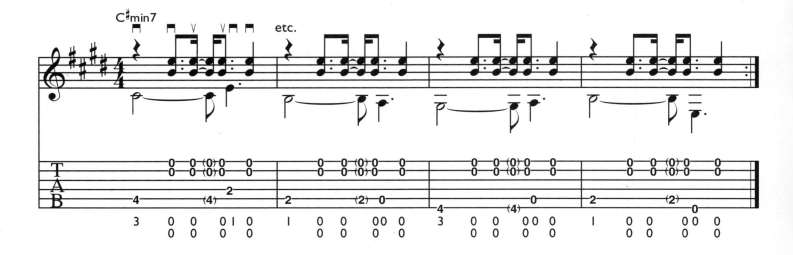

The **Dave Matthews** Band emerged in the 1990s with a jazz-inflected rock sound driven by funky acoustic guitar riffs. Matthews released a live album of duo performances with Tim Reynolds, "Live at Luther College, 1996." Reynolds' eclectic and fluid lead work combined with Matthews' driving rhythms and songwriting to create a benchmark of modern acoustic rock.

It is a little trickier to hold a pedal tone on a fretted note, but it sounds great! This tune is in the style of the Beatles' *Norwegian Wood*, and uses a droning D in the upper voice to tie the riff together.

ISN'T IT FINE, SCANDANAVIAN PINE

Track 8

PEDAL TONES IN THE MIDDLE VOICE

Drone notes in the middle voice allow you to hear a bass line and melody while a common tone acts as sonic "glue" in the chord progression. The next tune is in the style of Dave Matthews Band's *Tripping Billies*. It uses the interval of a 10th, which is an octave plus a 3rd. By moving major and minor 10ths up and down the neck, you get the sound of a very open harmonized scale.

The first four bars have 10ths in the key of D while a pedal tone drones on the open D string. Use your 2nd and 3rd finger to play the major and minor 10ths on the 6th and 4th strings, leaning your 2nd finger over just slightly to mute the 5th string. The next four bars has a chord progression of syncopated power chords, providing lots of contrast with the first four bars. This kind of contrast is good for separating sections of a song, such as verses and choruses.

THE RISE AND FALL OF THE UNCOORDINATED WILLIAM

Track 9

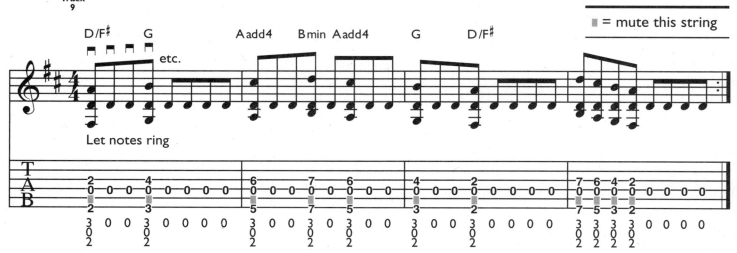

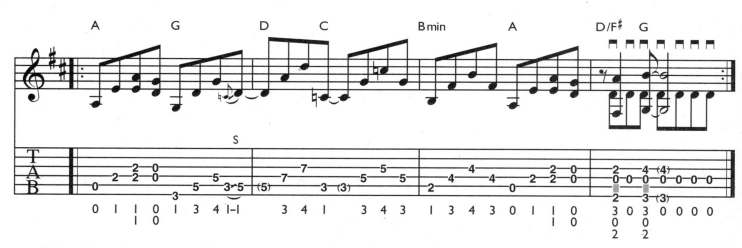

I'll Pedal, You Steer on page 203 combines all of the pedal-tone techniques and places them in the key of G Major. A new technique is added in bar 8. Fretted notes on one string are pulled-off to the open note, then the open note is picked. This technique is useful in improvisation, allowing you to use a few simple moves to create the impression of a very rapid passage.

Notice the use of *scratch* symbols ×. When you see this symbol, release your left-hand fingers from the chord just enough to lift the strings from the frets, causing a percussive un-pitched sound. Palm muting (PM) is used as well. Use the right side of your right hand to dampen the sound a slight amount.

× = Scratch

I'LL PEDAL, YOU STEER

* PM = Palm Muting

In the mid 1980s, Michael Hedges turned the acoustic guitar world on its ear by developing an entirely new approach to composing for the instrument. Hedges used alternate tunings, traditional technique and new techniques such as *slap harmonics* and *tapping* to realize his musical vision. Other artists, such as Phil Keaggy and Preston Reed, have added to these techniques.

DOUBLE DROP D TUNING

This lesson will use double drop D tuning, in which the 1st and 6th strings are both tuned down to D (page 182). Here are the open notes of the tuning, as well as the matching notes (shown in grey) on adjacent strings to use for tuning.

5

Track 11

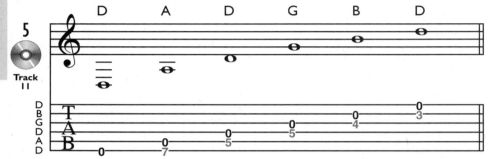

SLAP HARMONICS

One of the most dazzling effects in this style is the *slap harmonic*. A slap harmonic is achieved by striking the strings with the right hand at a harmonic *node* (page 112) in such a way as to generate an exciting, percussive harmonic chord. For example, use the *i* or *m* (the index or middle finger of your right hand) to "slap" the 12th fret, causing the strings to sound a harmonic chord. Here are some tips to help you learn the technique:

1. Keep your finger (try *m* first) exactly parallel to the fret, and strike directly on the fret.

2. Keep your wrist and finger very loose. Use a tiny snap of the wrist to lightly "bounce" your finger on the fret.

3. Don't slap too hard! You can bruise your finger by repeating this motion incorrectly for too long. Remember to *lightly* bounce off the fret. If you have trouble with your *m*, try it with the side of your *i* finger, using your *m* as support.

Slap with m.

Slap with i.

Try the harmonic slaps in example 6, A through D. You will be slapping full chords as well as power chords on the lowest strings. Be patient and stay relaxed!

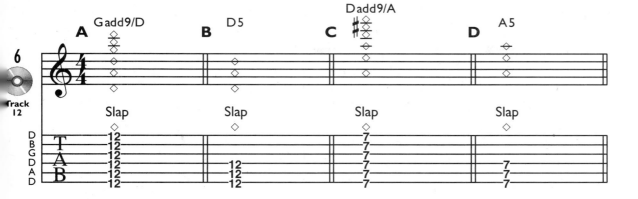

LEFT-HAND TAPPING

By using strong hammer-ons and pull-offs, you can sound notes on the fingerboard without plucking the strings. This is called *tapping* and is designated in tablature with a "T."

Try the repetitive tapping patterns in example 7, below. Hammer straight down on the note, then pull-off with a slight snap of the finger. *Don't use your right hand at all!* Hammer-ons are designated with "H," pull-offs with "P."

T = Tap

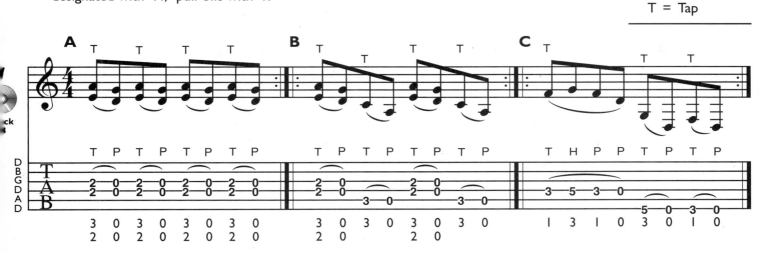

Michael Hedges' 1981 debut "Breakfast in the Field," and follow-up masterpiece "Aerial Boundaries," introduced a new vision of the possibilities for acoustic guitar. Hedges used slapping, tapping, harmonics, alternate tunings and a meticulously engineered amplification system to wrench new sounds and textures from his Martin D-28. Hedges went on to record albums featuring vocals and other instruments, creating new techniques to accommodate the demands of his compositions.

RIGHT-HAND TAPPING

You can also tap notes on the fingerboard with your right-hand fingers. Hammer down quickly and firmly directly behind the fret with the pad of any right-hand finger, just as you would if you were hammering-on with your left-hand fingers. You may want to touch your thumb to the edge of the fingerboard to stabilize your hand position.

Tapping with i.

RH = Right hand
LH = Left hand

Try these examples:

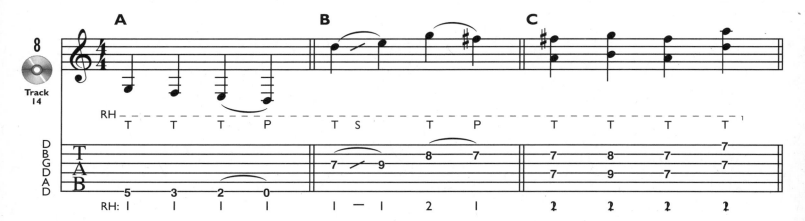

COMBINING RIGHT- AND LEFT-HAND TAPPING

You can create the effect of two guitars playing at once by playing an *ostinato* (a repeated accompaniment pattern) with your left hand while tapping a melody with your right. When first attempting this technique, it is easiest to "get going" with your left hand before you add your right. Try example 9 slowly and patiently!

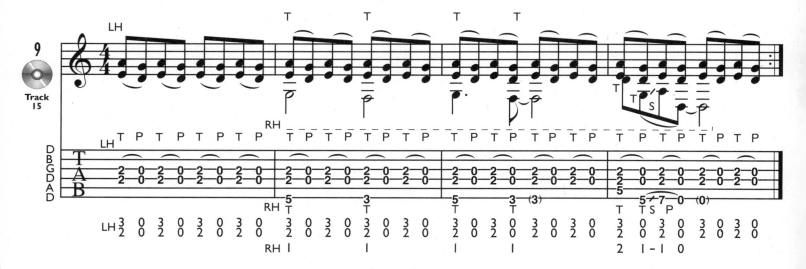

---

206   *Mastering Acoustic Guitar*

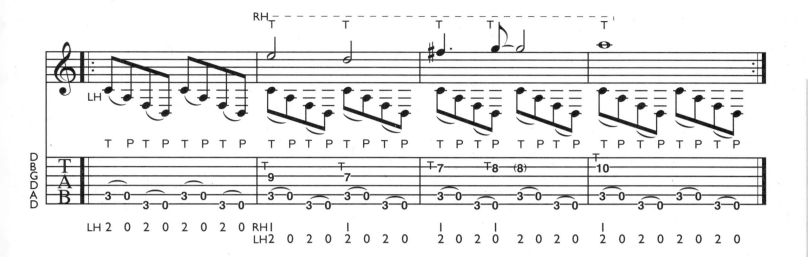

LEAP-FROG PULL-OFFS

This technique not only sounds amazing, but it looks and feels incredibly cool! Play a barre chord on the lower three strings with your left hand. Then fret a barre chord *with your right hand* (!) a whole step lower. Pull-off from the left-hand chord to the right-hand chord. Then "leap frog" your left hand one fret below your right hand, and pull-off your right-hand chord to the new left-hand chord.

Pulling off from a chord on the 7th fret to a chord on the 5th fret.

Pulling off from a right-hand chord on the 5th fret to a chord on the 3rd fret.

Try these examples:

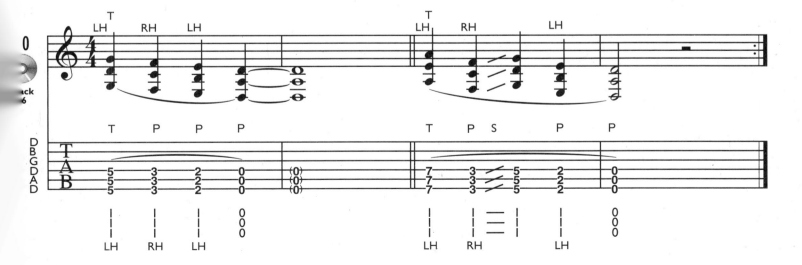

PULL-OFF HARMONICS

You can sound a harmonic with a pull-off of your left hand by using the *i* finger of your right hand to lightly touch the harmonic node at the 12th fret. This is a tricky technique. You need a great deal of "snap" in your left-hand pull-off or you won't hear anything. Think of this as using your left-hand 1st finger to literally pluck the strings while your right hand touches the harmonic node.

Preparing right-hand harmonic and left-hand chord.

Pulling off from chord with left-hand to sound right-hand harmonic.

Try these examples:

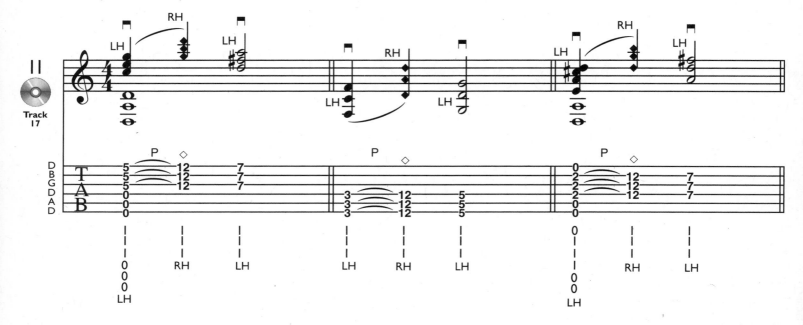

Track 17

PUTTING IT ALL TOGETHER

The tune on page 209 uses all of the new slapping and tapping techniques introduced in this chapter. The first four bars has slap harmonics, leap-frog pull-offs and pull-off harmonics, plus a couple of harmonic chords strummed with downstrokes. The next four bars begin with an ostinato pattern with left-hand tapping, and adds a few *artificial harmonics* (page 114) played with the right hand. The following four bars combine a left-hand ostinato with a harmonized melody tapped by the right hand. The last four bars have a new ostinato pattern, with the right-hand melody moving to the bass string. The final two measures reprise the original left-hand ostinato from the second four bars.

Work on each small segment of the piece separately, patiently and *slowly*! You may want to work on the right- and left-hand parts separately before putting them together. Make sure to count the rhythm carefully.

Fine

D.C. al Fine

CHAPTER 2

New Chords

LESSON 1: 7 CHORDS

You have already worked with dominant 7 chords in *Intermediate Acoustic Guitar* (page 110), so some of this will be a review. There are, however, four other qualities of 7 chord: *major 7, minor 7, diminished 7* and *half-diminished 7* (*minor 7 ♭5*).

A *7 chord* is a four-note chord built in 3rds. Another way to think of it is as a triad with an added note that is a 7th above the root.

Here are all the types of 7 chords shown with C as the root:

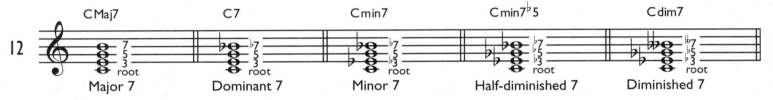

| CMaj7 | C7 | Cmin7 | Cmin7♭5 | Cdim7 |
| Major 7 | Dominant 7 | Minor 7 | Half-diminished 7 | Diminished 7 |

Note: All of the following chords are in standard tuning.

MOVABLE MAJOR 7 CHORDS (Maj7)

The major 7 chord is a major triad with an added major 7th interval. The major 7th interval can be thought of as eleven half steps above the root, or one half step below the octave. The construction of the chord is root-3-5-7. Below are some movable fingerings for major 7 chords. Make sure to note where the roots are (indicated under the diagrams). This will allow you to move these forms anywhere on the neck to find major 7 chords on any root.

♭♭ = Double Flat.
Lower the note one whole step.

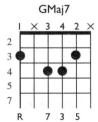
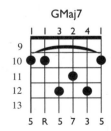
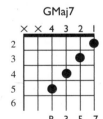
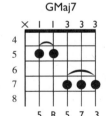
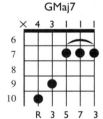

MOVABLE MINOR 7 CHORDS (Min7)

The minor 7 chord is a minor triad with an added minor 7th interval. The minor 7th interval can be thought of as ten half steps above the root, or one whole step below the octave. The construction of the chord is root-♭3-5-♭7. Here are some movable minor 7 fingerings:

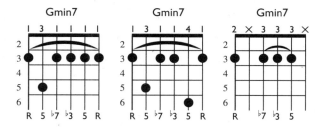

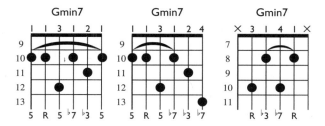

MOVABLE DOMINANT 7 CHORDS (7)

A dominant 7 chord is a major triad with an added minor 7th interval. The minor 7th interval is ten half steps above the root, or one whole step below the octave. The construction of the chord is root-3-5-♭7. Here are some movable fingerings:

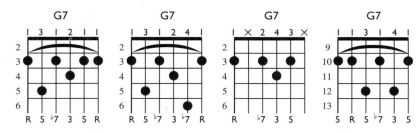

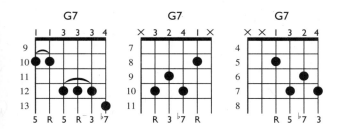

The next tune uses major 7, minor 7 and dominant 7 chords, including some open-position fingerings. There is also an A/B chord. This type of chord is referred to as a *slash chord*. Slash chords are used to indicate a chord with something other than the root in the bass. The symbol to the left of the slash designates the chord, while the letter to the right of the slash indicates the bass note. Slash chords and 7 chords are prevalent in the jazz-inflected music of groups such as Steely Dan and America.

MELLOW GROOVIN' PHAT DADDY-O DUDE

Track 19

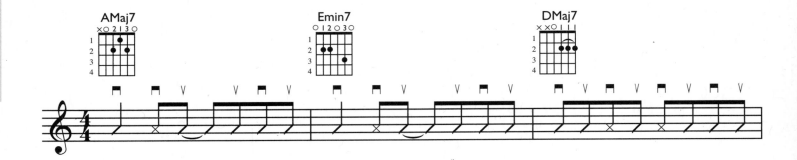

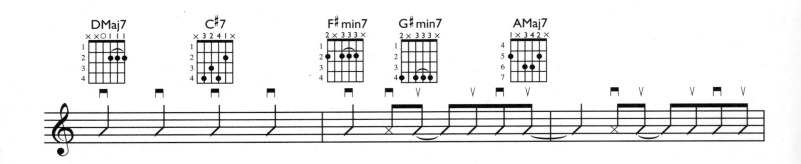

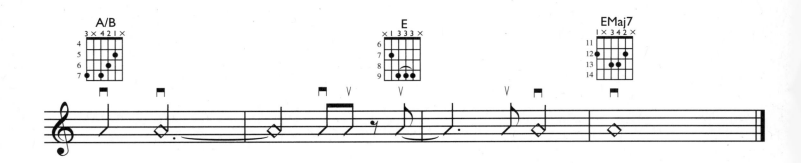

LESSON 2: AUGMENTED AND DIMINISHED CHORDS

To understand the diminished 7 and minor 7♭5 chords, it is important to fully understand augmented and diminished triads. By now, the major and minor triads are very familiar to you, so they are a great place to start.

USING MAJOR AND MINOR TRIADS TO CONSTRUCT OTHER FORMS

If you know the major and minor triad shapes very well, it is easy to transform them into the other two triad types, *augmented* (Aug) and *diminished* (dim or °).

An augmented triad is a major triad with a raised 5 (♯5).

A diminished triad is a minor triad with a lowered 5 (♭5).

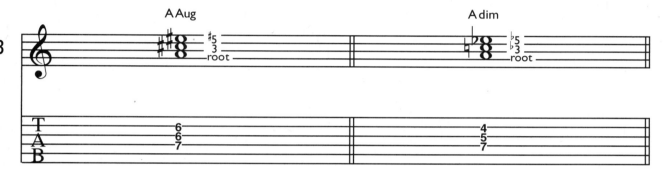

Here is an A Major triad transformed into the augmented, minor and diminished triad types.

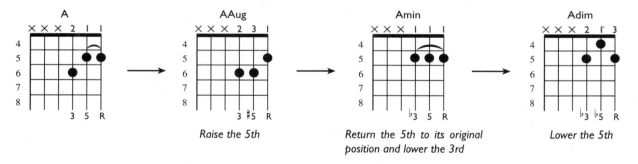

Raise the 5th   *Return the 5th to its original position and lower the 3rd*   *Lower the 5th*

AUGMENTED TRIAD CHORD FORMS

Below are the A Augmented triads on four string sets. Compare them with the major triads you learned in *Intermediate Acoustic Guitar* (pages 154-155) to see how the 5th has been raised. Notice that, on every string set, the augmented triad shape is the same in each inversion. This is because the interval distances between the root, 3, #5 and the next root are all major 3rds (four half steps).

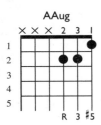

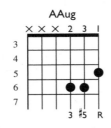

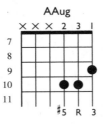

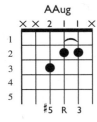

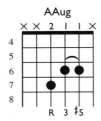

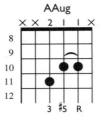

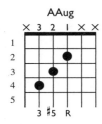

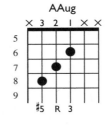

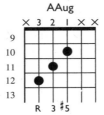

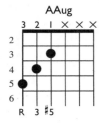

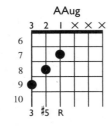

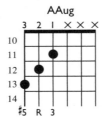

DIMINISHED TRIADS

Below are the A Diminished triads on four string sets. Compare them with the minor triads you learned in *Intermediate Acoustic Guitar* (pages 158-159) to see how the 5th has been lowered.

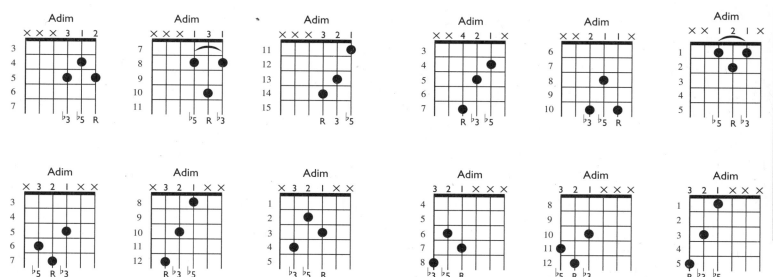

USES FOR AUGMENTED AND DIMINISHED CHORDS

Augmented and diminished triads have many uses. One is to create an unresolved, unstable sound. Another good use of augmented and diminished triads is as *chromatic passing chords*. A *passing chord* is a chord that is slipped between two main chords in a progression, connecting the chord tones melodically. *Chromatic* means "by half steps." A chromatic passing chord connects two chords (such as the I and IV chords) with notes that are one half step from the chord tones.

Here are two progressions that illustrate the use of augmented and diminished chords (try them with different inversions):

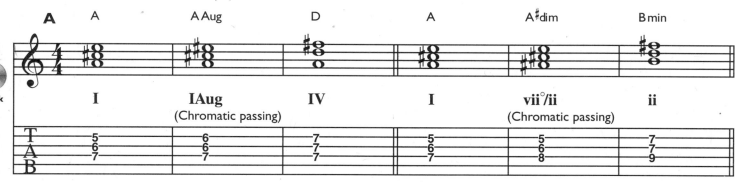

Notice that in example 14B, the A♯ Diminished chord is marked vii°/ii. This means that the chord is acting as a secondary dominant (see page 111, *Intermediate Acoustic Guitar*). A diminished chord can be thought of as a dominant-type chord because it contains the top three notes of a dominant 7 chord. In this case, the A♯dim (A♯, C♯ and E) has the top three notes of F♯7 (F♯, A♯, C♯ and E). F♯7 is the secondary dominant chord of Bmin in this example.

MINOR 7♭5 (HALF-DIMINISHED 7) CHORDS (Min7♭5 OR ∅)

The minor 7 ♭5 (half-diminished) chord is a diminished triad with an added minor 7th interval. The construction is root-♭3-♭5-♭7. Here are several movable min7♭5 fingerings.

Gmin7♭5

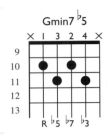
Gmin7♭5

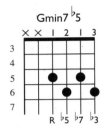
Gmin7♭5

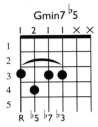
Gmin7♭5

DIMINISHED 7 CHORDS (Dim7 or °7)

Diminished 7 chords are also known as *fully-diminished* 7 chords. They consist of a diminished triad with an added diminished 7th interval above the root. The diminished 7th interval is nine half steps above the root, or three half steps below the octave. It is also a minor 3rd (three half steps) above the 5th. In fact, every chord tone in a diminished 7 chord is a minor 3rd apart. The construction of the chord is root-♭3-♭5-♭♭7*. As with the augmented triad, this symmetry has interesting effects: Since all the chord tones are the same distance apart, each one can be thought of as the root of a different diminished 7 chord. You only need to remember about *enharmonic relationships*—two notes that have the same sound but different names. A little *enharmonic respelling* goes a long way. All four chords use the same pitches. Here is an example:

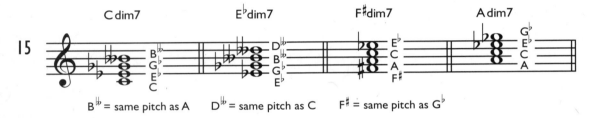

B♭♭ = same pitch as A   D♭♭ = same pitch as C   F♯ = same pitch as G♭

Another cool trick that comes with this symmetry is inverting diminished 7 chords up the neck. The chord just repeats itself every three frets (a minor 3rd). You can play the same fingering, just moving it up three frets. This is how you get that "damsel-in-distress-tied-to-the-train-tracks-while-the-evil-bad-guy-with-the-long-curled-mustache-laughs-demonically" sound from the old movies.

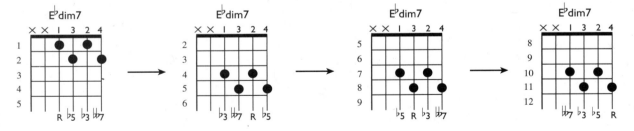

Below are a two more diminished 7 fingerings. Repeat them every three frets to hear them cycle through the inversions.

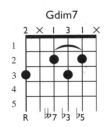
Gdim7

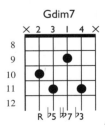
Gdim7

*♭♭ = *Double flat.* Lower the note by two half steps.

The next tune uses augmented and diminished chords to give a more complex jazz flavor to the progression. The music of Paul Simon, Willie Nelson and Tom Waits all reflects the influence of jazz and chromatic harmony. In this example, the augmented and diminished chords are used as passing chords and as *tension* chords that *resolve* to nearby triads and 7 chords.

Track 21

TOO EARLY FOR BREAKFAST

LESSON 3: ADD 9 CHORDS AND MORE

Sometimes, 7 chords and chromatic chords add too much tension to a progression. For a more open, less-tense sound, you can color triads with other intervals, such as 9ths. An *add9* chord has a sound that is similar to that of a suspended chord. The difference is that add9 chords include the 3rd (sus chords don't), so they can be built on major or minor triads.

The 9th is an octave above the 2nd degree of the scale, which is one whole step above the root. For example, the 9th of a G chord would be an A note. Notice that the 9th is a perfect 5th above the 5th of a chord, creating the sound of "stacked" 5ths in the chord. For example, in a G chord, G is the root, D is the 5th and A is the 9th (a 5th above D).

16

Try some of these *major add9* voicings. In a major add9, the 9th is a whole step above the root and, in certain voicings, a whole step below the 3rd. This creates an interesting tension, implying two stacked whole steps. The open voicings include open strings; the movable voicings don't.

OPEN VOICINGS

Aadd9   Eadd9   Cadd9   Dadd9

MOVABLE VOICINGS

Fadd9   B♭add9   D♭add9

Now try adding 9ths to minor chords. *Minor add9* chords have an interesting sound because the 9th and the minor 3rd are only one half step apart. For example, in an A Minor add9 chord, the notes are A, B, C and E (root-9-♭3-5).

OPEN VOICINGS

Amin add9   Emin add9   Cmin add9   Dmin add9

MOVABLE VOICINGS

Fmin add9   B♭min add9   D♭min add9

STACKED 4THS AND 5THS

Another unique chord color is found in *quartal harmony*. Quartal harmony is harmony built in 4th or 5ths (which are inversions of 4ths) instead of 3rds. Quartal chords have an ambiguous sound because they are not major or minor, and it is hard to tell which note is the root. Try some of these movable voicings:

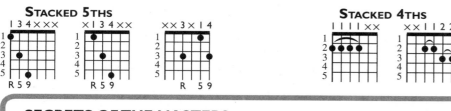

SECRETS OF THE MASTERS

All of the sus4 and sus2 chords you learned in Intermediate Acoustic Guitar (pages 106-107) can be used as quartal chords. For example, Csus2 contains the notes C, D and G. These can be rearranged to form a chord built in 5ths (C-G-D). The resulting chord, C5add9, has no 3rd, which is why it is called C5. The D above the G is the 9th above C, hence the "add9" in the name.

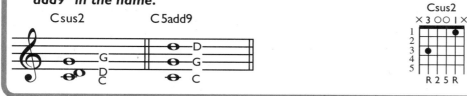

Try this tune using add9 and quartal chords.

WANDERING GHOSTS

Track 22

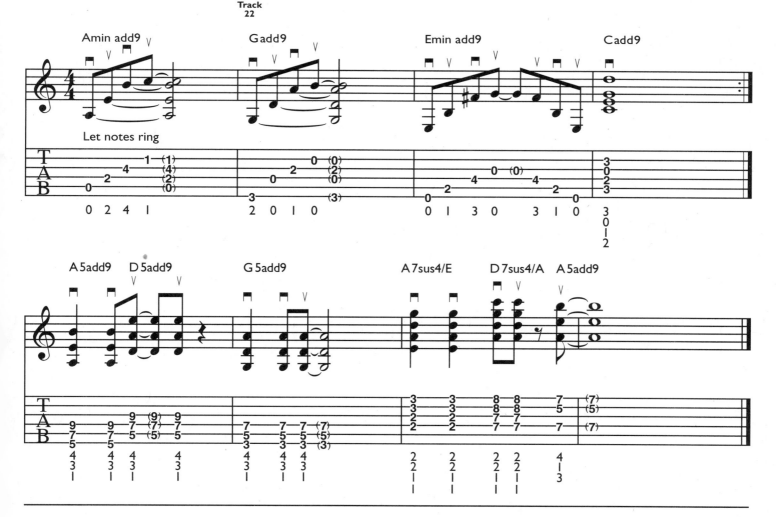

LESSON 4: DOMINANT 9 CHORDS

Including the 9th in a dominant chord adds a harmonic density that sounds particularly good in funk, jazz and blues. As you will see later in this lesson, dominant chords are particularly well suited to adding extra "tension" tones such as 9ths, 11ths and 13ths. You can add the 9th tone to major and minor 7 chords as well.

If you add another major 3rd above a 7 chord, you get a major 9th above the root. As you learned in the previous lesson, the 9th is the same as the major 2nd degree of the scale, but an octave higher. In a *dominant 9 chord*, the 9th is still one whole step above the root and one whole step below the 3rd. The difference between an add9 chord and a dominant 9 chord is that in the dominant 9 chord the ♭7 is present; in an add9 chord, it's not.

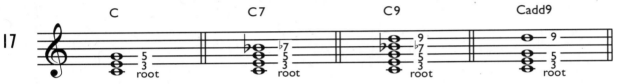

The worksheet below will give you a chance to try spelling a few dominant 9 chords. Remember that when you play them in real life, the chord tones may be placed in a different order!

DOMINANT 9 WORKSHEET					
	D9	E9	G9	F9	B♭9
9	_F_	____	____	____	____
♭7	_C_	____	____	____	____
5	_A_	____	____	____	____
3	_F♯_	____	____	____	____
Root	_D_	____	____	____	____

The correct answers are at the bottom of this page.

You can build a dominant 9 chord voicing by simply thinking of a dominant 7 voicing and raising a root tone by one whole step. Below are a few dominant 9 chord voicings. Also shown are the 7 chord voicings from which they are derived.

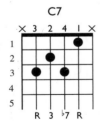 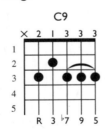 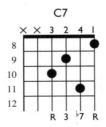 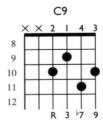 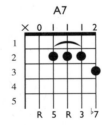 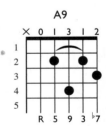

WORKSHEET ANSWERS				
	E9	G9	F9	B♭9
Root	F♯	G	F	B♭
3	B	G♯	B	D
5	B	D	C	F
♭7	D	F	E	A♭
9	F♯	A	G	C

This tune will get you used to the most common dominant 9 chord fingerings. It also includes some add9 and dominant 7 chords so that you can hear the contrast between these and the dominant 9 sound.

 MELLIFLUOUS TONES

Track
23

PART ONE—BAG OF TRICKS

11THS AND 13THS

The next two intervals of a 3rd above the 9th are the 11th and the 13th. These three tones, the 9ths, 11ths and 13th, are used to add tension to a chord. Dominant chords sound particularly good with these added tension tones.

Here's a trick for remembering 9ths, 11ths and 13ths: Subtract 7 from any one of them and this will reveal the identical tone in the scale. For example, the 9th is the same pitch as the 2nd (9-7=2). The 11th is the same as the 4th (11-7=4) and the 13th is the same as the 6th (13-7=6).

Dominant chords with a lot of tension notes sound even more interesting if some of the tensions are altered (made sharp or flat). Here is a starter set of cool alterations for dominant chords:

SHARP 11 (♯11)   **SHARP 9 (♯9)**   **FLAT THIRTEEN (♭13)**

Here they are shown in standard music notation:

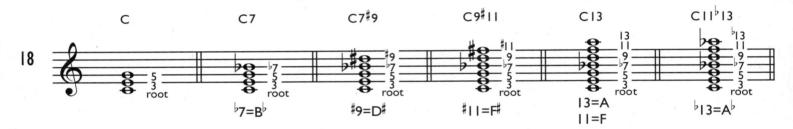

Below are some voicings that include some of these tensions and alterations. Make note of where the root in each form is, and you can move them to any root you desire.

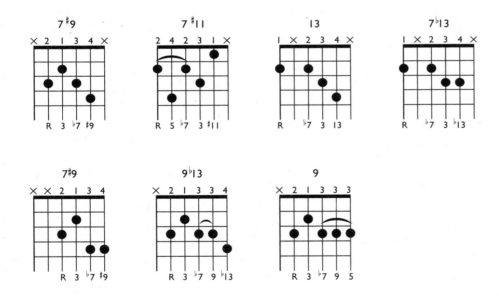

Hypertension Funk Blues on page 223 uses tension and altered chords in a funk blues progression. The chords are combined with riffs, slides and funk strumming. You can refer to the chord diagrams above to find fingerings for the altered dominant chords.

HYPERTENSION FUNK BLUES

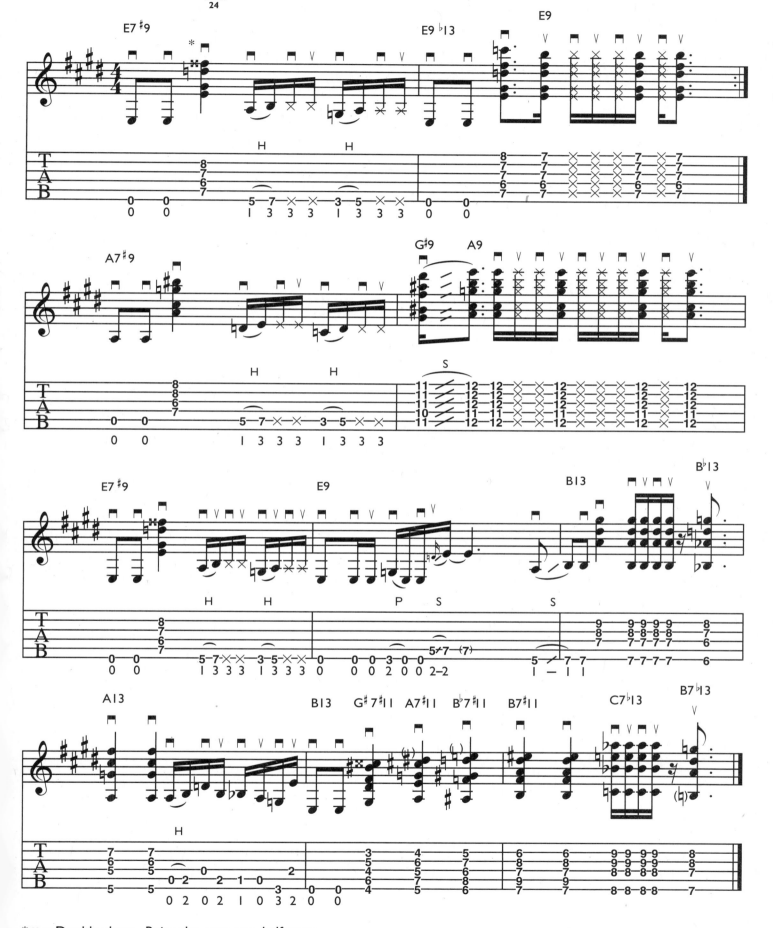

*✗ = Double sharp. Raise the note two half steps.

LESSON 6: USING TENSIONS AND ALTERATIONS TO IMPROVISE BLUES

You can incorporate 9ths, 11ths, 13ths and their alterations in your soloing. This will give you a vastly expanded pentatonic scale that you can use to spice up your improvisation.

The secret to keeping things simple when using tensions as you solo is using enharmonic relationships (page 216) and octave equivalents. The table below will help. Try to memorize these so you don't have to calculate them while you're playing.

Tension tone	Example Note (in E)	Octave Equivalent	Enharmonic Equivalent (in E)
9	F♯	2	F♯
♯9	F×	♭3	G♮
11	A	4	A
♯11	A♯	♭5	B♭
13	C♯	6	C♯
♭13	C♮	♭6	C♮

Note that ♯9 is the same as ♭3, and ♯11 is the same as ♭5. These are both common *blue notes* used in blues soloing.

Below are the tensions and alterations incorporated into an open-position E Minor Pentatonic scale. Note that the major 3rd (3) has also been included. The octave and enharmonic equivalent chord-tone names for the scale degrees are shown below the staff.

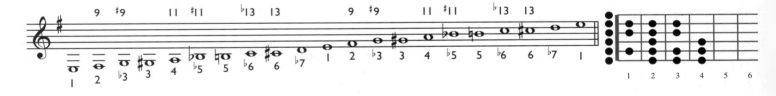

Here is another fingering for this scale in 9th position. The *Hypertension Funk Blues Solo* on page 225 is a solo for the *Hypertension Funk Blues* you learned on page 223. It uses both scale fingerings shown on this page. The use of special tension notes is shown throughout the solo.

HYPERTENSION FUNK BLUES SOLO

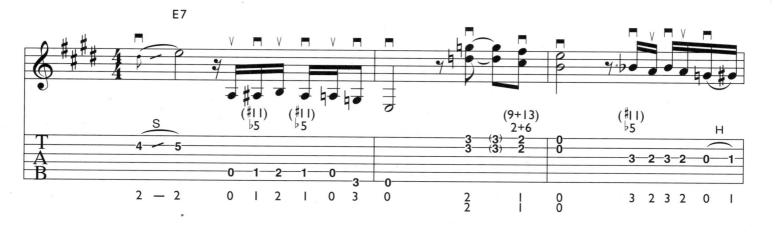

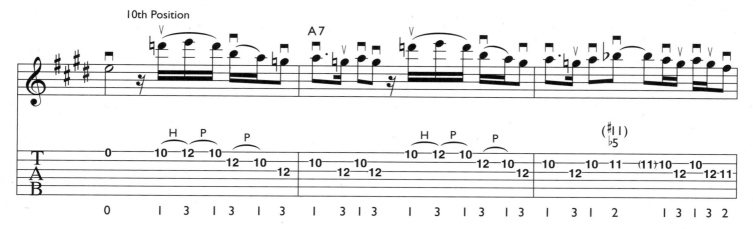

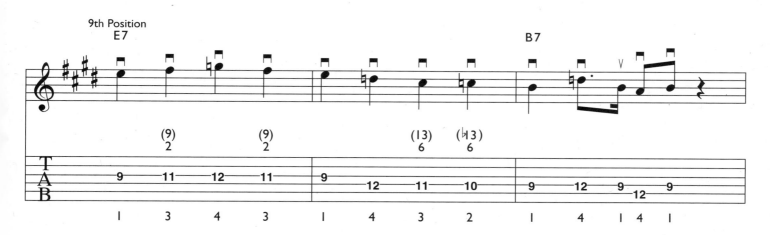

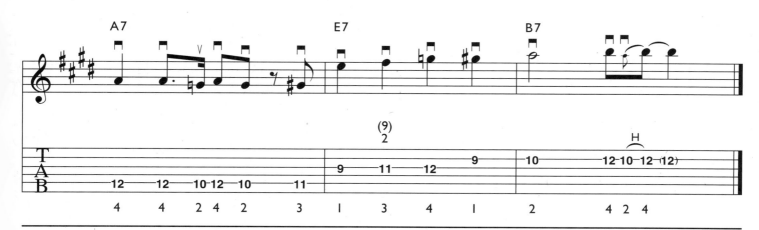

CHAPTER 3

Advanced Rhythm

LESSON 1: ODD TIME SIGNATURES

While the majority of rock, blues and folk music (and much jazz) is in $\frac{4}{4}$ time, there are other worlds of time to be explored. You have had some experience with $\frac{3}{4}$ or *waltz time* (page 38), and with $\frac{6}{8}$ time (page 136). Many other time signatures are variations of these, with beats divided in groups of two or three. The next step is to explore the *odd time signatures*. Odd time signatures are heard in the music of The Grateful Dead, Phish, the Dave Matthews Band and many others. They are also used heavily in the folk music of Brittany and Eastern Europe.

WORKING IN $\frac{5}{4}$

The secret of counting odd time signatures is to use combinations of smaller groups of beats. It can be difficult to keep track of five, seven or eleven beats, but it is easy to keep track of groups of two and three beats.

$\frac{5}{4}$ time means five quarter notes per measure. This can easily be divided into 3 + 2 or 2 + 3. Try the following exercises for counting and clapping in $\frac{5}{4}$. Clap at the × signs. Repeat each one several times.

19

1 2 3 4 5   1 2 3 1 2   1 2 1 2 3

× = Clap

Pentagroove in D is a chord progression in $\frac{5}{4}$. You can count 1-2-3-4-5, but you will hear and feel the groups of three and two beats accented by the chord changes. Also try counting 1-2-3, 1-2. Play this pattern several times through, and count to make sure you do not add extra beats! The accent pattern of 3 + 2 is shown, using dotted bar lines.

PENTAGROOVE IN D

Track 26

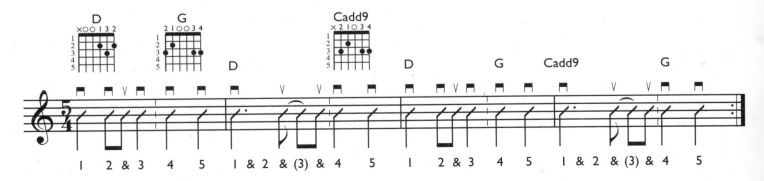

1   2 & 3   4   5   1 & 2 & (3) & 4   5   1   2 & 3   4   5   1 & 2 & (3) & 4   5

IMPROVISING IN $\frac{5}{4}$

To play melodically in $\frac{5}{4}$, you need to count! *Pentagroove in D Solo* is a solo based on the chord progression you just learned, and is also grouped 3 + 2. The scale used is the D Major Pentatonic (page 174) at the 7th position.

Track 27

PENTAGROOVE IN D SOLO

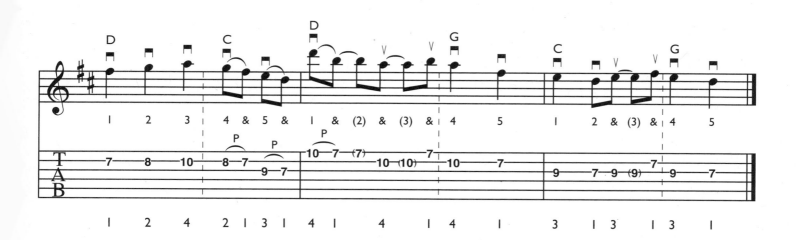

WORKING IN $\frac{7}{4}$

$\frac{7}{4}$ is much like $\frac{5}{4}$ in that you can divide it into groups of two and three beats. You get two groups of two, and one group of three that can be combined in many ways. Two combinations that occur frequently are: 4 + 3 (2+2+3); and 3 + 4 (3+2+2). Try counting these patterns:

20

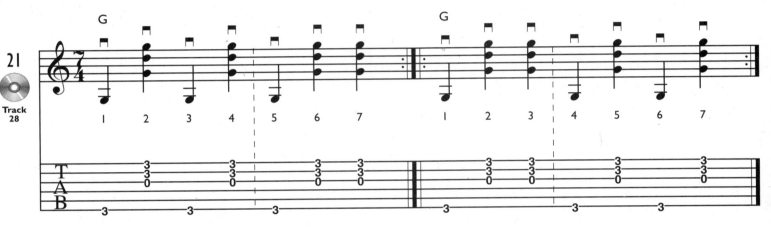

In example 21, try strumming a G chord using the accent patterns of 4 + 3 and 3 + 4. The pattern combines a bluegrass style strum (boom-chick, boom-chick) with a waltz strum (boom-chick-chick). Repeat each exercise several times. The accent groups are shown with dotted bar lines.

21

Track 28

Try *My Right Hand Has Seven Fingers*. This chord progression uses the 4 + 3 accent pattern. It is in the style of the groove to Joan Osborne's *My Right Hand Man*, which is a rock song in $\frac{7}{4}$ time. This example uses open position A, G and E chords, with some heavy syncopation, so watch your counting. Note that there are some quick, decorative sus chords made by simply adding a finger for one strum. Check the tablature.

MY RIGHT HAND HAS SEVEN FINGERS

Track 29

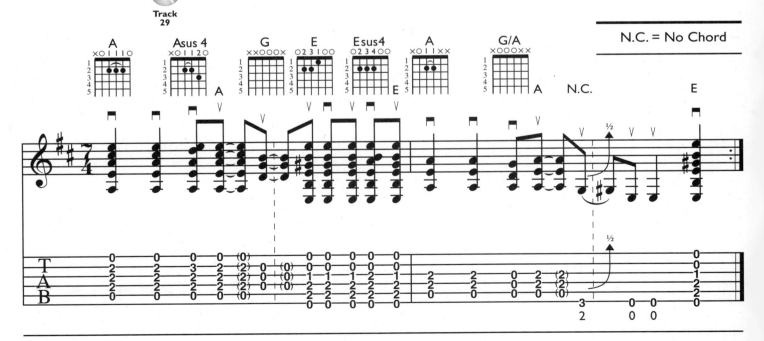

IMPROVISING IN $\frac{7}{4}$

My Right Hand Has Seven Fingers Solo is based on the chord progression you just learned on page 228. It uses the A Minor Pentatonic scale (with a few wayward additions) at the 5th position. The beat groups are shown with dotted lines (sometimes 3 + 4, sometimes 4 + 3). Also, try your own solos over the chord progression.

MY RIGHT HAND HAS SEVEN FINGERS SOLO

Track 30

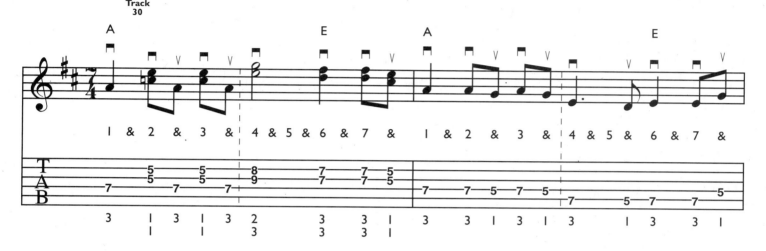

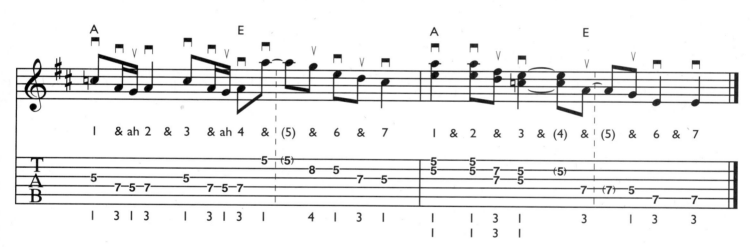

Ali Farka Toure's grammy-winning 1994 album, "Talking Timbuktu" (a collaboration with American slide master, Ry Cooder), brought world-wide attention to his unique African style. Born in Mali, Toure combines Arabic phrasing and African polyrhythms with the sounds of American blues masters such as Robert Johnson and Lightnin' Hopkins.

Chapter 3—Advanced Rhythm   **229**

WORKING IN $\frac{11}{8}$

Groups of eleven beats are easier to grasp in $\frac{11}{8}$ than in $\frac{11}{4}$. This means there will be eleven eighth notes in every measure. Remember that in most time signatures which use eighth notes as the beat, the beats are usually felt in two groups of 3, as in $\frac{6}{8}$, or three groups of 3, as in $\frac{9}{8}$. While there are many ways to count $\frac{11}{8}$, one easy way is to count it as three 3-note groups plus one 2-note group. Try this tapping exercise:

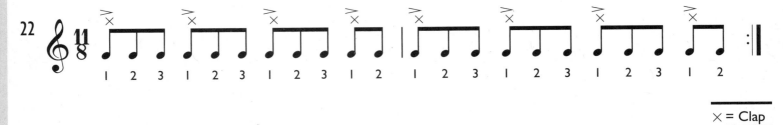

Here are a couple of licks in $\frac{11}{8}$ using a 3 + 3 + 3 + 2 accent pattern. Practice each one several times, then make up your own.

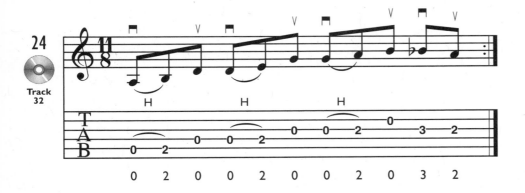

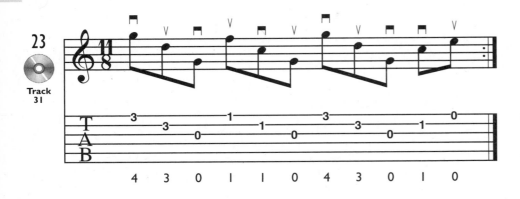

LESSON 2: WORKING IN MULTIPLE TIME SIGNATURES

Now the real fun begins. *June Bug Wings* on page 231 uses multiple time signatures to achieve a funky, shifting groove. Watch carefully for changing accent patterns. Again, try to count in groups of 2 and 3. Bar 6 is in $\frac{5}{8}$, and is followed by two bars of $\frac{4}{4}$. Don't be alarmed when the lower number of the time signature changes; the eighth notes will stay at the same tempo. Try counting example 25 to get the idea. Keep all of the eighth notes exactly equal in duration:

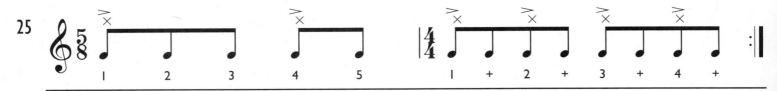

Now try *June Bug Wings*. Take it slowly, line by line. Think of each line as a separate, independent groove idea. You may even want to learn each measure separately before putting a whole line together. Have fun!

JUNE BUG WINGS

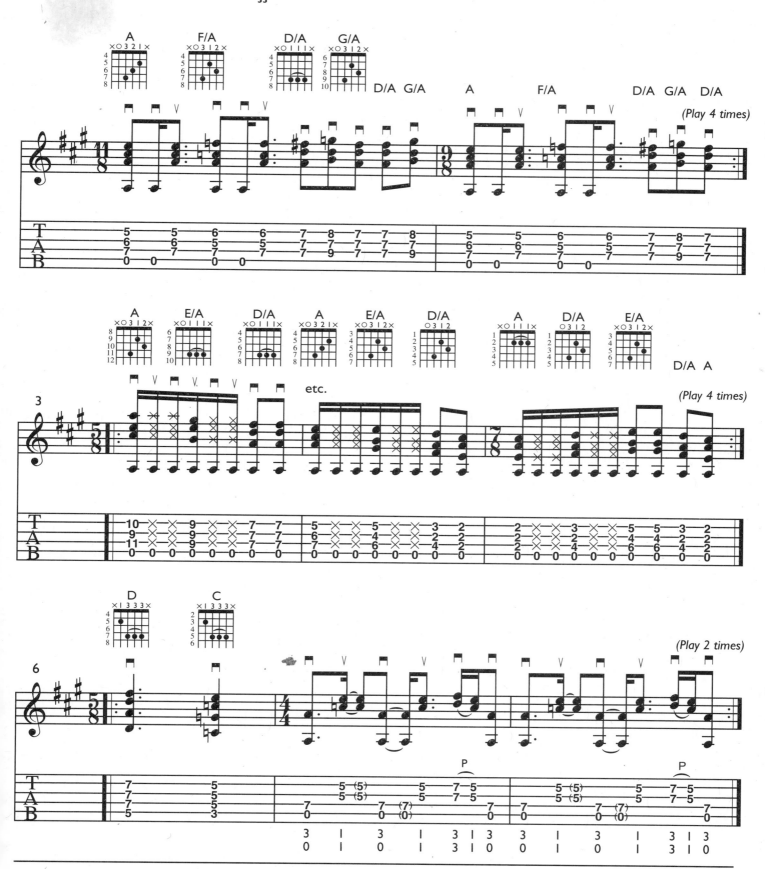

Polyrhythms are two or more distinct time signatures played at the same time. Imagine two drummers—one is playing two beats to every measure, the other is playing three beats to every measure, but the measures are the same length! This creates a *two against three* polyrhythm.

Polyrhythms can be simple or incredibly sophisticated. They are the primary structural feature of African folk music and are a key part of Cuban, Brazilian and other Latin musics. Polyrhythms sound very cool when played on solo guitar. A master of this style is the African guitarist, Ali Farka Toure.

Any polyrhythm can be worked out on paper by following these steps:

1. Multiply the two numbers you want to set against one another. This gives you the number of counts it takes before they join together again on beat one. For two against three, you get a multiple of six counts.

2. Write out the total counts (for two against three, that's 1 2 3 4 5 6).

3. Divide the total number of counts by the first rhythm (for two against three, 6 ÷ 2 = 3). This means that the first rhythm (two) will appear every three counts. Mark below these counts with ✕'s.

4. Divide the total number of counts by the second rhythm (for two against three, 6 ÷ 3 = 2). This means the second rhythm appears every two counts. Mark these on a second line.

Here's what you end up with:

TWO AGAINST THREE						
Count:	1	2	3	4	5	6
Left Hand:	✕			✕		
Right Hand:	✕		✕		✕	

Try playing this rhythm by counting aloud, and tapping your hands on your thighs or a table whereever there is an ✕. Then, switch hands!

Example 26 uses a D octave in open position and is written in $\frac{6}{8}$. It alternates between three notes per measure and two notes per measure.

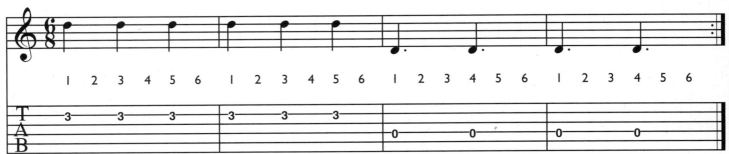

The following examples will get you playing the two against three polyrhythm. You can fingerpick the examples using your thumb for the low note, or use a pick for the low note and play the high notes with your fingers.

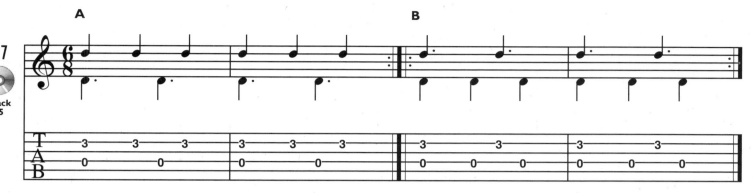

These examples incorporate some harmonic movement, creating a I-IV-V progression in the key of D. We will gradually add more melodic activity to make the licks more interesting. Play each example as a separate exercise. When you master them all, try mixing and matching them.

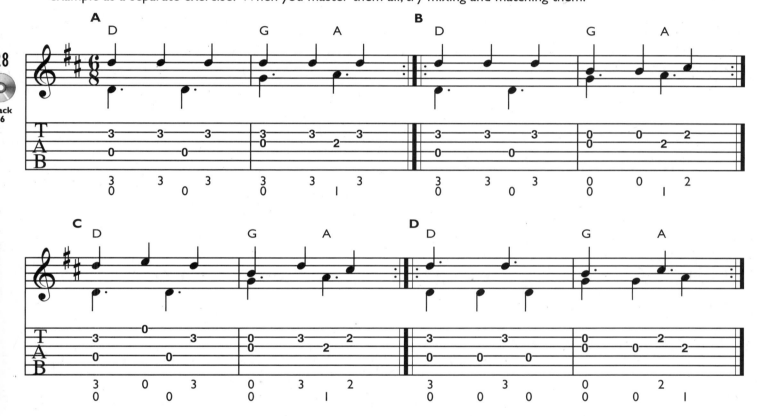

Example 29 shows a I-IV progression in the key of E using arpeggios in the bass. The last measure inverts the rhythm (turns it upside down). Take this one slowly, one measure at a time.

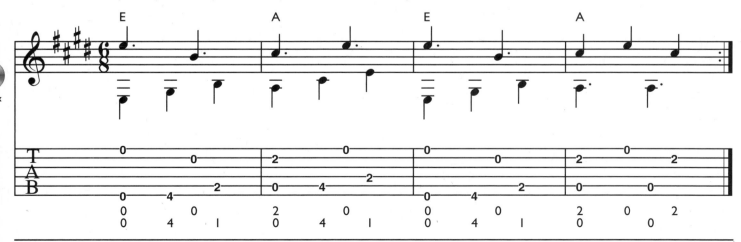

CHAPTER 4

Introducing the Modes

By performing a simple mathematical trick with the major scale, you can generate six more scales known as the *modes* of the major scale. Each of these scales has its own emotional quality, its own diatonic harmony and its own melodic sound.

The modes have Greek names that harken back to ancient music. They are heard in all styles of music, from folk and blues to jazz and rock.

This book will examine three of the most common modes in depth, but first here is a brief, whirlwind introduction to the modes.

LESSON 1: GENERATING THE MODES FROM A PARENT SCALE—THE RELATIVE VIEW

To generate the modes, follow these steps:
1. Write out the interval structure of a major scale using whole steps (W) and half steps (H). The major scale itself is also known as the first mode, *Ionian*. For now, let's work in C. We will generate other modes from this *parent scale*.

2. Think of the whole steps and half steps as a series. Rotate the first interval to the end of the series (move the first whole step to the end). This generates the second mode, *Dorian*.

3. Another rotation produces the third mode, *Phrygian*.

Below are the seven modes, shown with their interval structures and example scales using C as the parent scale. Try to memorize the names of the modes in order. You do not necessarily have to memorize the interval structures.

Mode #	Name	Structure	Example
·1	Ionian	W W H W W W H	C D E F G A B C
2	Dorian	W H W W W H W	D E F G A B C D
3	Phrygian	H W W W H W W	E F G A B C D E
4	Lydian	W W W H W W H	F G A B C D E F
5	Mixolydian	W W H W W H W	G A B C D E F G
6	Aeolian	W H W W H W W	A B C D E F G A
7	Locrian	H W W H W W W	B C D E F G A B

LESSON 2: THE PARALLEL VIEW

Another way to look at each mode is to compare it to the major scale in the same key as the mode. In other words, you would compare the mode to its *parallel major scale* and see which scale degrees stay the same and which change. For example, compare D Dorian and D Major.

D MAJOR (D IONIAN)

Notes:	D	E	F#	G	A	B	C#	D
Structure:	1	2	3	4	5	6	7	8

D DORIAN

Notes:	D	E	F♮	G	A	B	C♮	D
Structure:	1	2	♭3	4	5	6	♭7	8

Notice that in D Dorian the 3rd and 7th degrees are one half step lower than they were in D Major. They are referred to as ♭3 and ♭7 (flat three and flat seven). This is a useful way to look at the modes, because it helps you quickly identify what is different about the sound of the scale.

Here is a list of the modes with their scale degrees and example notes using C as note number 1. The list starts with Ionian and then shows the modes *in order of closest similarity*.

MODE	SCALE DEGREES							IN C						
Ionian	1	2	3	4	5	6	7	C	D	E	F	G	A	B
Mixolydian	1	2	3	4	5	6	♭7	C	D	E	F	G	A	B♭
Dorian	1	2	♭3	4	5	6	♭7	C	D	E♭	F	G	A	B♭
Aeolian	1	2	♭3	4	5	♭6	♭7	C	D	E♭	F	G	A♭	B♭
Phrygian	1	♭2	♭3	4	5	♭6	♭7	C	D♭	E♭	F	G	A♭	B♭
Locrian	1	♭2	♭3	4	♭5	♭6	♭7	C	D♭	E♭	F	G♭	A♭	B♭
Lydian	1	2	3	#4	5	6	7	C	D	E	F#	G	A	B

Notice that each scale differs from the previous one by only one note. Lydian is placed at the end because it is actually like Locrian with a ♭1 (flat one). Since it would be illogical and confusing to lower your tonal center by one half step, the flats in Lydian are all cancelled out, leaving you with a #4 (sharp four).

DO NOT PANIC!

If you find all of this a bit mind-blowing, don't worry. Just use this introduction as a reference while you work on the upcoming lessons.

The following lessons will cover only three of the modes. You are already familiar with Ionian as the major scale. You will now learn about Mixolydian, Dorian and Aeolian, which are much more common in modern acoustic music than any of the other modes.

To learn more about all of the modes, check out *The Guitar Mode Encyclopedia* by Jody Fisher, also published by The National Guitar Workshop and Alfred, and *The Ultimate Guitar Scale Bible* by Mark Dziuba, published by The National Guitar Workshop.

CHAPTER 5

The Mixolydian Mode

LESSON 1: THE TWO VIEWS

THE RELATIVE VIEW

As you learned in Chapter 5, the Mixolydian mode is the 5th mode of the major scale. Below is the relative view of E Mixolydian, which is the 5th mode of A Major. In other words, A Major (A Ionian) is the parent scale of E Mixolydian.

THE PARALLEL VIEW

Compare the E Mixolydian scale with its parallel major key, E Major (Ionian). The Mixolydian scale is distinguished by its 7th degree, which is one half step lower than it is in the major scale. This is referred to as ♭7 (flat seven).

Here is a comparison of E Major and E Mixolydian diatonic harmony. Use the triads shown, or any familiar fingerings of these chords to hear the sound.

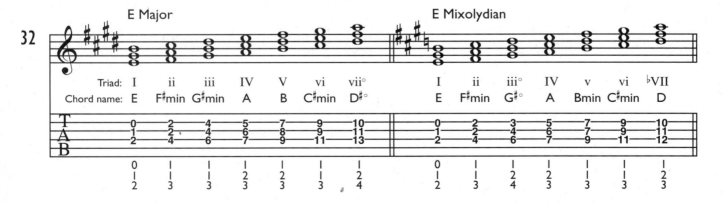

LESSON 2: DISTINGUISHING FEATURES OF THE MIXOLYDIAN MODE

As you now know, the Mixolydian mode is like a major scale with a ♭7. When you looked at the parallel view in Lesson 1, you observed a different harmonic character for the scale. The most noticeable feature is that the v (five) chord is *minor*! Compare the E Major and E Mixolydian I-IV-V progression.

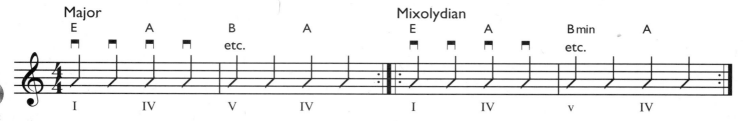

Another special feature of Mixolydian is the chord built on the ♭7. It is a major chord. Its root is one whole step below the *tonic* note (the 1st scale degree). Example 34 is a typical Mixolydian progression using the ♭VII chord. You may recognize it as being in the style of the classic rock song, *Gloria*.

EXPLORING THE MIXOLYDIAN SOUND

The Mixolydian mode and its harmonies have a very unique sound and emotional quality. Because of its ♭7 note, it has a darker, bluesier quality than the major (Ionian) scale. Once you have learned more Mixolydian songs and have become familiar with its sound, you will develop your own associations with the scale. *No Ex-Temptations* is another chord progression in E Mixolydian. It is in the style of The Rolling Stones' *No Expectations*. Note that the three chords used are I (E Major), IV (A Major) and ♭VII (D Major).

NO EX-TEMPTATIONS

Track 40

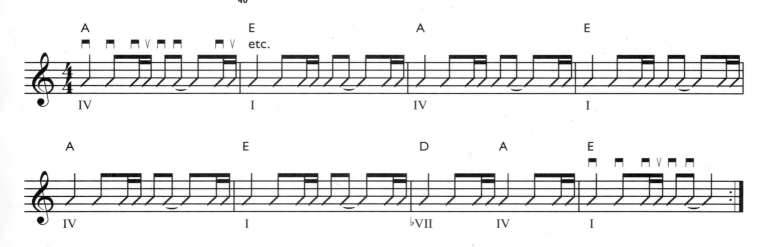

PART TWO—MODAL SOUNDS

Here is a more interesting version of *No Ex-Temptations* using triads up and down the neck with some hammer-ons and slides. Note that the ♭VII chord can always be found one whole step below the I chord.

Track
41

NO EX-TEMPTATIONS TRIAD SOLO

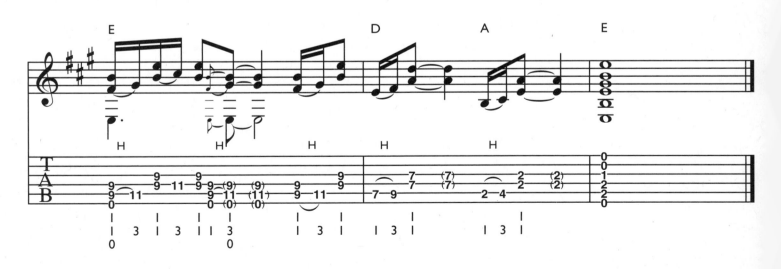

Over the Waterfall (below) is an example of the Mixolydian mode used in an old Appalachian fiddle tune. It is very common to mix modes in one song in all styles of music. For example, the verses of a song might be in Mixolydian, while the chorus is in Ionian.

In the case of *Over the Waterfall*, the A section is in D Mixolydian, using a C♯ (♭7) in the melody and a C Major chord (♭VII) in the harmony. The B section is in D Ionian, using a C♯ (7) in the melody and an A Major chord (V) in the harmony. Here are fingerings for D Ionian and D Mixolydian:

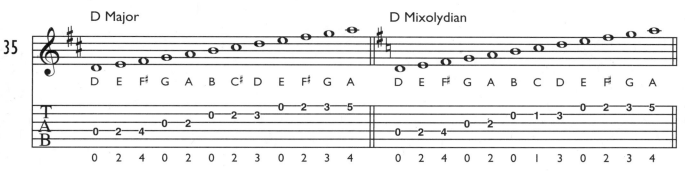

Now try *Over the Waterfall*. Note how the shift to Ionian in the B section "brightens-up" the bluesy quality established at the end of the A section. For the melody, make sure to use alternate picking. For the chords, use open chords with a country or bluegrass style strum.

 ## OVER THE WATERFALL

Track 42

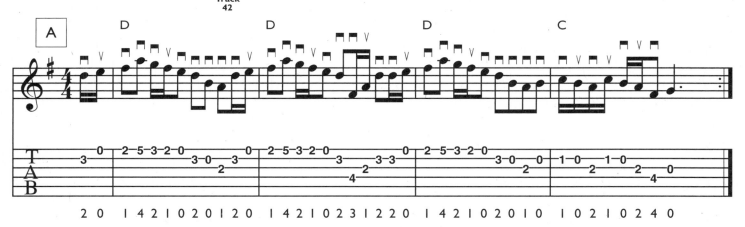

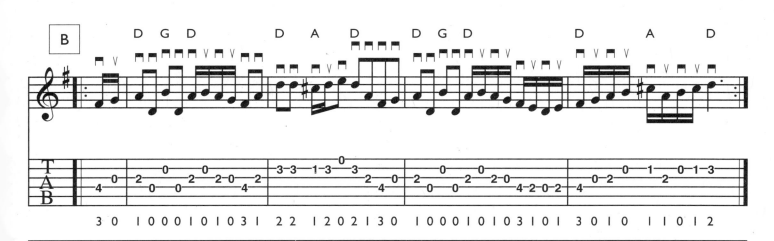

Part Two—Modal Sounds

LESSON 4: IMPROVISING IN THE MIXOLYDIAN MODE (THE JERRY GARCIA EFFECT)

The Mixolydian mode is a versatile and fun scale to use for improvisation. It is the natural choice to use with a Mixolydian progression. It can also be used over a major progression to add a touch of bluesy tension (the ♭7 of the Mixolydian against the ♭7 of the major scale). Jerry Garcia of The Grateful Dead made the Mixolydian mode a part of his signature sound, combining it with his fluid phrasing and melodic ideas borrowed from bluegrass banjo and guitar picking.

You have already learned that you can transform a major scale into Mixolydian by lowering the 7th scale degree. Another trick is to use your major pentatonic fingerings as a "skeleton" for building a Mixolydian scale that goes up and down the length of the neck.

Here is a fingering for the A Major Pentatonic scale, followed by A Mixolydian in the same position. The notes that are added to the major pentatonic scale to create the Mixolydian mode are highlighted.

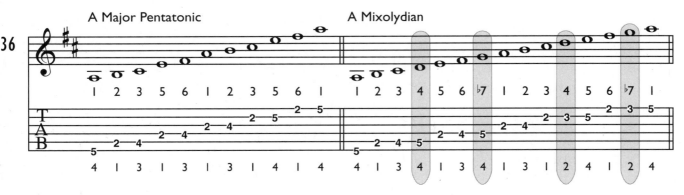

Remember that the major pentatonic scale is made up of scale degrees 1, 2, 3, 5 and 6. These scale degrees are common to both the major scale and the Mixolydian mode. This means that you can improvise over major and Mixolydian chord progressions using the major pentatonic scale.

However, to add the real color of the Mixolydian scale, you just need to add two notes, 4 and ♭7. Scale degree 4 can be found one half step above 3. The ♭7 note can be found one half step above 6 (one whole step below 1). Notice how these notes have been added in the fingering in example 37.

You can do this with all five positions of the major pentatonic scale(pages 174-176, *Intermediate Acoustic Guitar*), in any key! Below is an A Mixolydian scale that connects three positions of the A Major Pentatonic scale. Try playing this fingering forwards and backwards, and use it to improvise melodies.

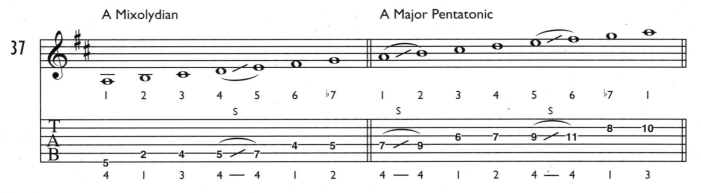

Franklin's Mower is a progression in A Mixolydian and is in the style of The Grateful Dead's *Franklin's Tower.*

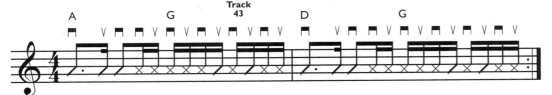

FRANKLIN'S MOWER

Track 43

Franklin's Mower Solo uses the A Mixolydian scale in the style of Jerry Garcia. It uses some of the same positions as the connected scale in example 37 on page 240. Garcia made great use of a device called *sequencing* in his solos. A *sequence* is a melodic figure that is repeated at different pitch levels. This can be seen in the first bar of the solo, where an ascending three-note pattern (A, B, C♯) is sequenced up the scale twice (B, C♯, D and C♯, D, E).

Garcia also used accented notes to emphasize certain pitches and rhythms in the solo. Try picking this solo in a flowing, connected style, using a stronger attack to make the accented notes "pop out" of the melody. Don't forget to make up your own Mixolydian improvisations using the scales and chord progressions in this lesson!

FRANKLIN'S MOWER SOLO

Track 44

Chapter 5—The Mixolydian Mode **241**

CHAPTER 6
The Dorian Mode

THE RELATIVE VIEW

Dorian is the second mode of the major scale. Example 38 shows the relative view of D Dorian, which is the second mode of C Major. In other words, C Major (C Ionian) is the parent scale of D Dorian.

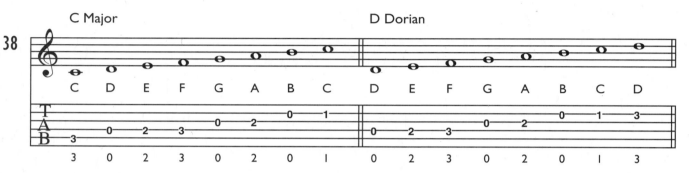

THE PARALLEL VIEW

Example 39 shows the D Dorian mode compared to its parallel major key, D Major. Note that Dorian is like Mixolydian in that it has a lowered 7th degree (♭7). Dorian also has a lowered 3rd (♭3). Any scale or chord with a lowered 3rd is designated *minor*. Therefore, Dorian is known as a *minor mode*. The notes that are changed to create the Dorian mode are highlighted.

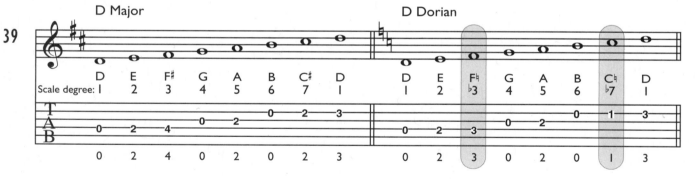

Example 40 compares the diatonic harmonies of D Major and D Dorian. Use the triads shown, or any familiar fingerings for these chords.

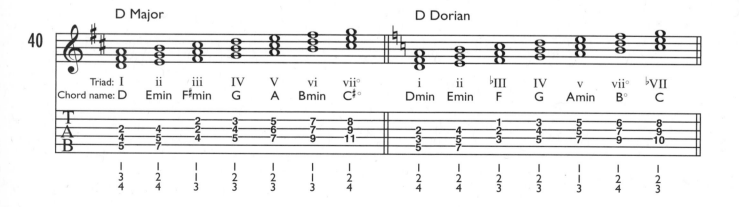

PART TWO—MODAL SOUNDS

LESSON 2: DISTINGUISHING FEATURES OF THE DORIAN MODE

Dorian is a minor mode. Its ♭3 note creates a minor i (one) chord. As with Mixolydian, the v (five) chord is minor, and the ♭VII (seven) chord is major. Because they have so much in common, Dorian can be thought of as the minor cousin of Mixolydian.

The major IV chord is an integral part of the Dorian sound. You can hear it as the G chord in *Walk, Don't Drive*, which is a D Dorian progression in the style of the acoustic rock song, *Drive* by R.E.M.

WALK, DON'T DRIVE

Track 45

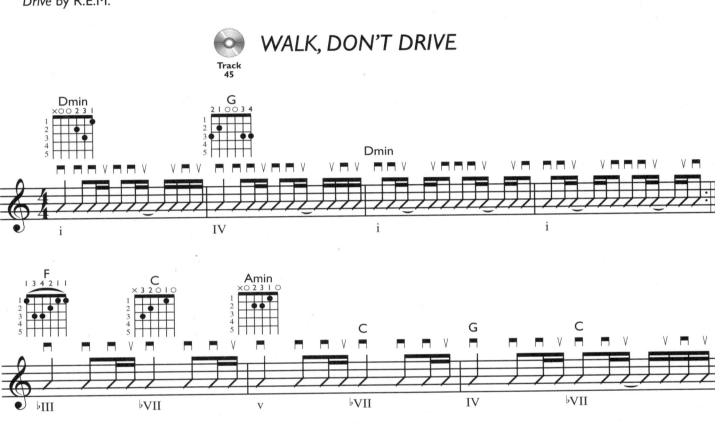

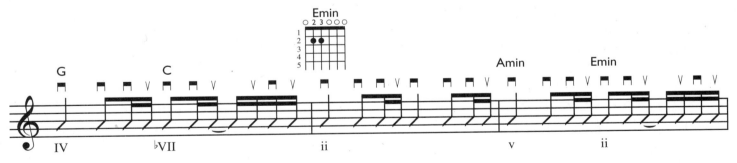

PART TWO—MODAL SOUNDS

Dorian is very closely related to the minor pentatonic scale, since they both contain ♭3 and ♭7 scale degrees. This makes Dorian an excellent choice for soloing over a blues progression. You can also play Dorian over a Mixolydian progression. The ♭3 in Dorian gives it a darker emotional quality that sometimes brings out the bluesy quality of a Mixolydian song.

The Dorian mode also works great with Dorian progressions! As you have seen, the Dorian sound is typified by a minor i chord, a major IV chord, and a minor v chord. Many improvisational songs and jams are based on the simplest Dorian progression: minor i to major IV.

Here it is in A Dorian:

This kind of repeated, simple progression is known as a *vamp*. You can also add 7ths or 9ths to the chords to create more harmonic density. In Dorian, i is a minor 7 (or minor 9) chord, IV is a dominant 7 (or dominant 9) chord.

Como Va-Va Vamp is a Dorian vamp shown with minor7 and minor9 chords. This vamp is in the style of Santana's *Oye Como Va*.

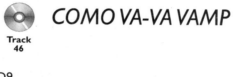

COMO VA-VA VAMP

Track 46

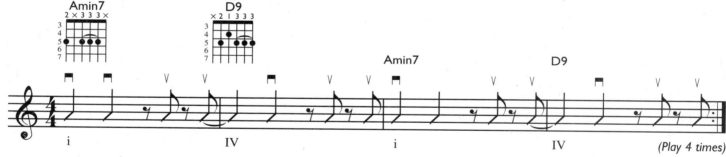

(Play 4 times)

Carlos Santana's big career breakthrough was his performance at Woodstock in 1969. His re-emergence as a major force in the music industry came with his 1999 landmark album "Supernatural," which spawned the hit Smooth with vocalist Rob Thomas of Matchbox 20.

PART TWO—MODAL SOUNDS

In the Lesson 2, you saw that the major pentatonic scale shares notes with the Mixolydian mode. In the same way, you can use the minor pentatonic scale as a *skeleton* for the Dorian mode. The minor pentatonic scale contains the scale degrees 1, ♭3, 4, 5 and ♭7. Just add in a 2 (one whole step above 1, one half step below ♭3) and a 6 (one whole step above five, one half step below ♭7) to make the Dorian mode.

Here is the most common fingering for A Minor Pentatonic, followed by A Dorian:
Try this solo on *Como Va-Va Vamp* using the A Dorian scale.

 COMO VA-VA VAMP SOLO

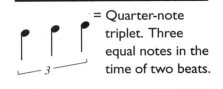

Track 47

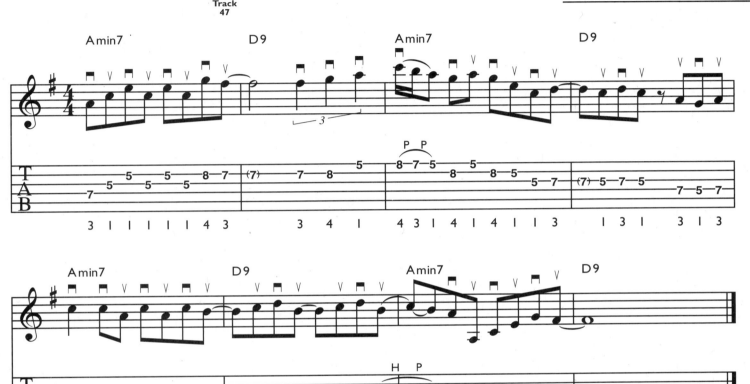

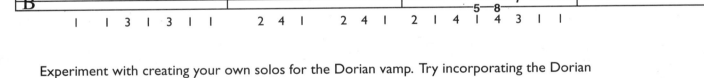

Experiment with creating your own solos for the Dorian vamp. Try incorporating the Dorian notes into all of the minor pentatonic positions you have learned!

SECRETS OF THE MASTERS

It is very important to understand that A Dorian is its own tonality, just like A Major and A Mixolydian. It has its own harmonic rules, such as the minor i chord, the major IV, the minor v and the major ♭VII.

As you learn more about the modes, go back and analyze songs you know or are learning. Evaluate which chords are the s, IV and V chords. Are they major or minor? Are any other chords used, such as ii, iii, vi or vii? Do any of these fit the "profile" of one of the modes you have learned?

It is very common for modes to change in different sections of a song, and sometimes within a phrase. The more familiar you become with the modes, the more you will be able to make the most of the progressions in your playing!

Dorian is one of the most common modal scales heard in Irish and Appalachian old-time fiddle music. In old-time music, many fiddle tunes that are referred to by the generic term "modal" are actually in the Dorian mode. In this lesson, you will learn a traditional Irish jig called *Scatter the Mud*. It is in A Dorian and is easily played in the second position, so it will be helpful to review fingerings for A Minor Pentatonic and A Dorian in that position.

Here is the A Minor Pentatonic fingering in the second position, followed by the A Dorian mode:

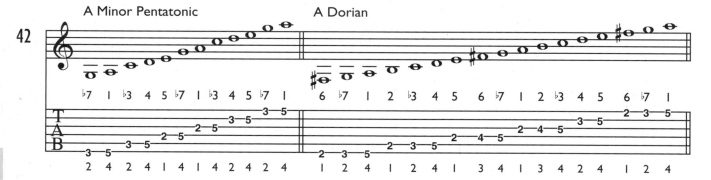

IRISH ORNAMENTS

A cool feature of Irish style playing on the guitar is the use of *ornaments*. These are tiny melodic figures such as *trills*, *turns* and *grace notes* that add a bit of decoration and rhythmic zing to the basic melody. Example 43 shows a few ornaments to try.

Use these examples as models to create your own ornament ideas. You can incorporate these into your own improvisations in any key.

PART TWO—MODAL SOUNDS

PLAYING A JIG

Irish jigs are set in $\frac{6}{8}$ time. A measure of $\frac{6}{8}$ is divided into two beats, with three eighth notes in each beat. This can be a challenge to your alternate picking, because the second three-note group begins with an upstroke.

Try this counting and picking exercise using the open 1st string:

44

Now try playing the jig, ornaments and all! For an accompaniment, the chords can be played with simple downstrokes, or you can use one of the $\frac{6}{8}$ strum patterns found on pages 136 and 137.

SCATTER THE MUD

Track 49

CHAPTER 7

The Aeolian Mode
LESSON 1: THE TWO VIEWS

THE RELATIVE VIEW

The *Aeolian* (pronounced ay-OH-lee-un) mode is the 6th mode of the major scale. Example 45 shows the relative view of A Aeolian, which is the 6th mode of C Major (C Ionian).

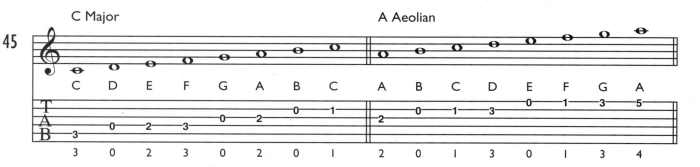

RELATIVE MINOR/NATURAL MINOR

Every major key has a *relative minor key*, whose tonic is found on the 6th degree of the major scale. The *natural minor* scale is the scale of the relative minor key. If you play a scale starting on the 6th degree of a major scale, you get a natural minor scale. The Aeolian mode is exactly the same as the natural minor scale. For example, the A Aeolian mode can also be called the A Natural Minor scale. The key of A Aeolian, or A Minor, is the relative minor key of C Major.

The Aeolian mode shares a strong bond to the parent major scale. It is very common for a piece of music to shift emphasis between the relative major key and its relative minor key. For example, a song in C Major may have passages that emphasize A Minor.

HOW TO FIND THE RELATIVE MAJOR/MINOR KEY

Remember, Aeolian is the 6th mode. This means that the 6th note of any major key is the tonal center of the relative minor. Likewise, the third note of any Aeolian scale is the tonal center of its relative major. Practice calculating relative majors and minors by filling in these keys. The correct answers are given at the bottom of the page.

RELATIVE MAJOR	RELATIVE MINOR
C	A
D	B
F	_____
B♭	_____
A♭	_____

Answers:
F Major/D Minor, B♭ Major/G Minor, A♭ Major/F Minor

THE PARALLEL VIEW

Example 46 shows A Aeolian as compared to A Major (A Ionian). Notice that the Aeolian mode has a ♭7 and ♭3 just like Dorian, but it also has a ♭6. The notes that are changed to create the Aeolian mode are highlighted.

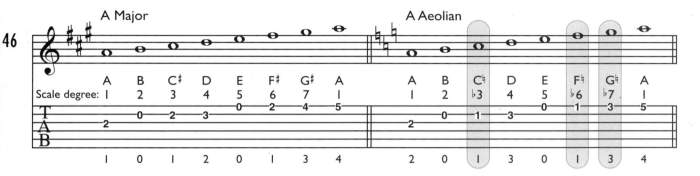

Here is a comparison of A Ionian and A Aeolian harmonies:

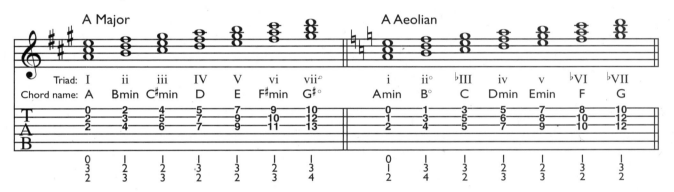

LESSON 2: DISTINGUISHING FEATURES OF THE AEOLIAN MODE

Like Dorian, Aeolian is a minor mode. Its i chord is minor, as is its v chord. It also has a major ♭VII (flat seven) chord just like Dorian and Mixolydian. The iv chord is also minor, which is the feature that most clearly distinguishes it from the Dorian mode.

Here are two typical Aeolian progressions:

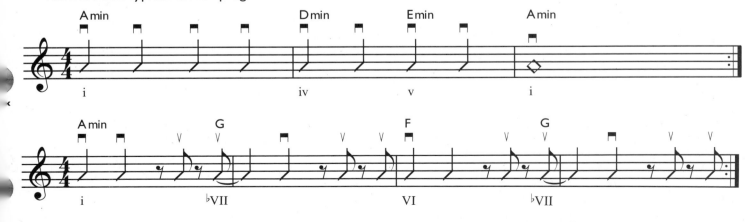

Down on my knees is a D Aeolian vamp in the style of Eric Clapton's *Layla*.

DOWN ON MY KNEES

Track 52

Of course, Aeolian sounds best over progressions that use Aeolian harmony. However, the ♭6 note in the Aeolian scale can sometimes sound interesting in a Dorian or blues progression, giving them a slightly exotic sound. To improvise on this progression, use the D Minor Pentatonic scale and add note scale degrees 2 and ♭6 to create the Aeolian. Here are two fingerings to get you started. The notes that are added to the minor pentatonic scale to create the Aeolian mode are highlighted.

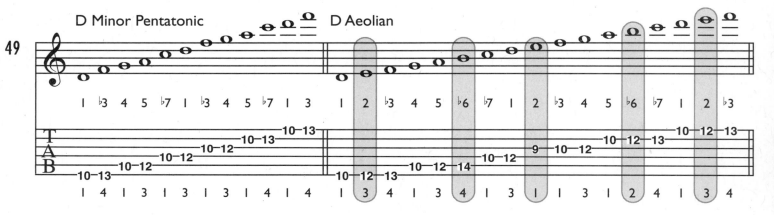

Here is a brief example of some soloing over the *Down on My Knees* progression:

DOWN ON MY KNEES SOLO

Track 53

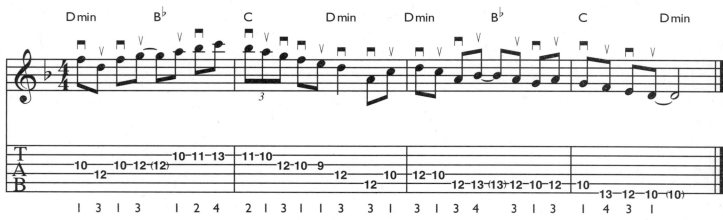

LESSON 4: IMPROVISING IN A RELATIVE MAJOR/MINOR CONTEXT

Paradox Found is a progression that moves between B Minor and its relative major key, D Major. It is in the style of Sarah McLachlan's *Building a Mystery*.

PARADOX FOUND

Track 54

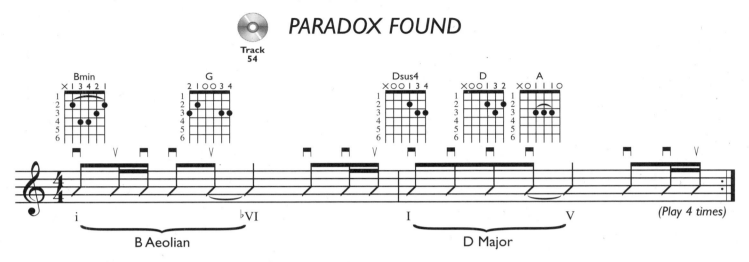

Notice that this progression has a very cyclical, unending quality to it. It constantly propels itself back to the B Minor chord at the beginning. The tonal center of the progression is somewhat ambiguous. It pulls equally towards B Minor and D Major. Fortunately, these two keys are relatives. Their scales, B Aeolian (B Natural Minor) and D Major (D Ionian), have identical notes.

Here are fingerings for B Aeolian and D Major in the 7th position:

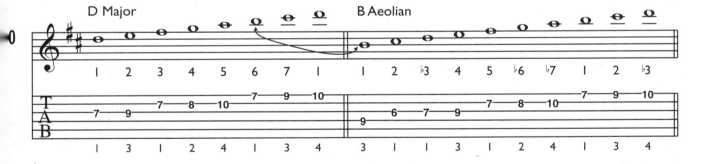

Try improvising over *Paradox Found* using the scales in example 50. Here is an example solo to get you started:

PARADOX FOUND SOLO

Track 55

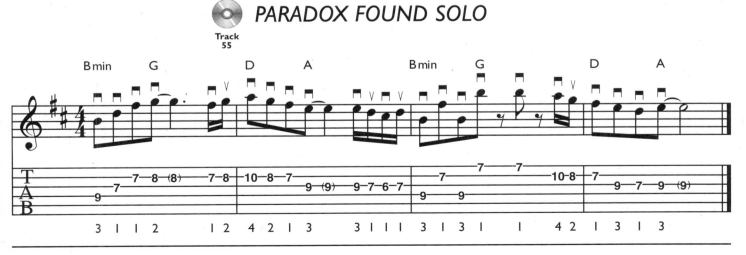

From the Horse's Mouth is another song that utilizes both the relative minor and relative major tonal centers. In this case, the verses of the song are in E Minor (E Aeolian), while the chorus is strongly in G Major (G Ionian). The chord progression is in the style of Neil Young's *Rockin' In The Free World*.

FROM THE HORSE'S MOUTH

Track 56

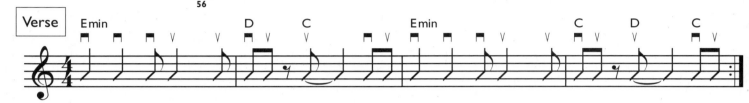

Example 51 below shows two scale fingerings that you can use to improvise on *From the Horse's Mouth*. The first is an E Aeolian scale that connects several positions. The second is a G Major (Ionian) scale in similar positions. Use the E Aeolian for the verses and the G Ionian for the chorus.

Notice that the "tag" chord at the end of the chorus is A Major. In the key of E Minor, this would be a major IV (four) chord. You could, therefore, play some E Dorian material over those two bars before switching back to Aeolian. This is because Dorian has a major IV chord. To find an E Dorian mode, simply play the E Aeolian fingering and raise the ♭6 up one half step to the ♮6. Here are the scales for improvising over *From the Horse's Mouth*.

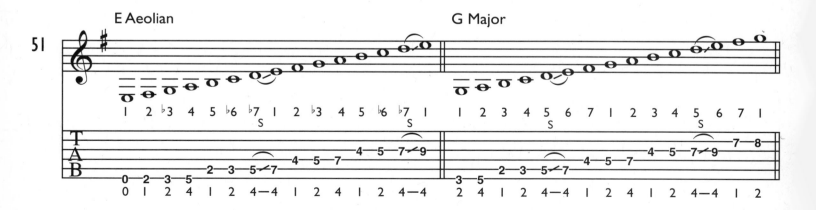

Below is a sample solo for *From the Horse's Mouth*. Note the use of E Aeolian in the verse, G Major in the chorus and E Dorian over the A chord.

FROM THE HORSE'S MOUTH SOLO

LESSON 5: VARIATIONS ON THE AEOLIAN MODE— THE HARMONIC MINOR SCALE

Centuries ago, composers writing in minor keys wanted to be able to use a major V chord to create a stronger harmonic resolution to the i chord. To do this, they simply raised the 3rd of the v chord to make it major (V). The 3rd of the V chord is scale degree 7 in the scale, which in Aeolian is normally ♭7. By raising ♭7 up to ♮7, they created what we now call the *harmonic minor scale*. Its name is derived from its function in adjusting the harmony of the key, making the minor v chord into major V.

Here is a B Aeolian scale compared to B Harmonic Minor:

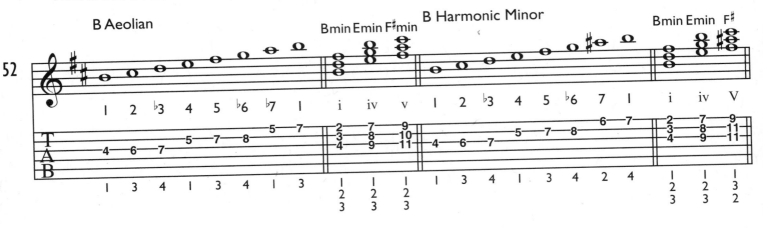

Harmonic minor is often heard as a temporary sound in a piece that is mostly Aeolian. However, the harmonic minor scale has an interesting sound all its own. This is due to the large interval between the ♭6 and ♮7. This interval, a distance of three half steps, is called an *augmented 2nd*. The augmented 2nd gives the harmonic minor scale an exotic quality reminiscent of Gypsy and Middle Eastern scales. *Soup du Jour Stomp* is a Gypsy-swing style progression in B Harmonic Minor.

SOUP DU JOUR STOMP

Track 58

You can use the harmonic minor scale to improvise whenever you are in a passage of music involving a minor iv chord and a major V chord. You can also use it when you want to add the exotic flavor of the augmented 2nd. Example 53 shows a fingering for B Harmonic Minor based on the B Minor Pentatonic scale at the 4th position. Note the ♭6 (one half step above 5) and ♮7 (one half step below 1).

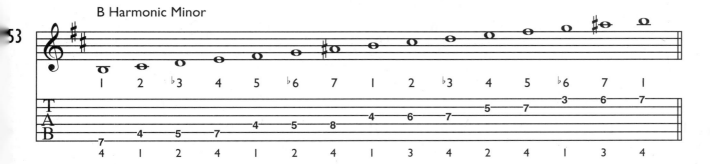

Try improvising on *Soup du Jour Stomp* with the B Harmonic Minor scale. Here is a sample solo:

Track
59

SOUP DU JOUR STOMP SOLO

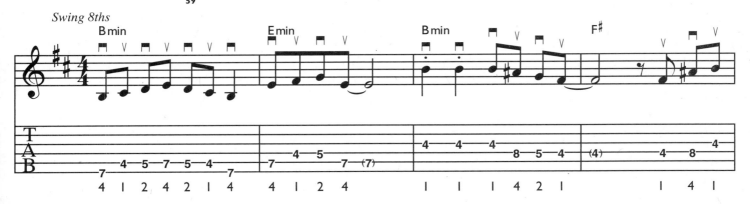

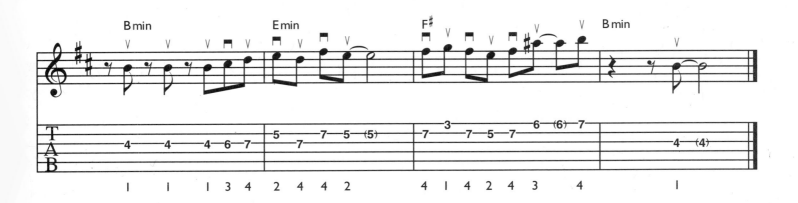

The influence of jazz and "world" sounds on modern music has made harmonic minor an accepted and interesting sound. However, the composers of centuries past found the augmented second a bit jarring, especially for vocal melodies. In order to straighten out passages that used the ♮7 in a minor key, the composers also would raise the ♭6 to ♮6. This formed what we now call the *melodic minor scale,* creating a major IV chord to go with the major V.

Example 54 compares the harmonic and melodic minor scales. Note that, in the melodic minor scale, the ♭6 has been raised to ♮6. This makes the top four notes (the upper *tetrachord*) of the melodic minor scale exactly the same as that of the major scale. The note that is changed to create the melodic minor is highlighted.

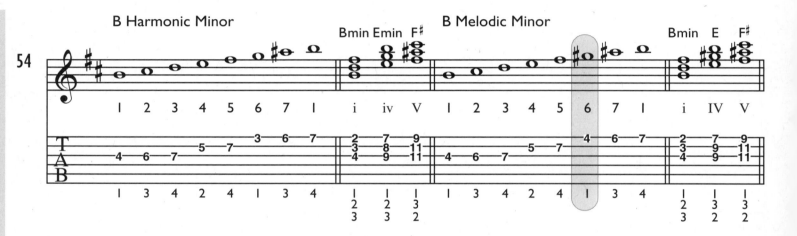

As with the harmonic minor, melodic minor was usually only used in a small passage of a piece when the melody was ascending through the 6th and 7th scale degrees to the tonic (1). Classical musicians understand this scale as descending differently than it ascends—the ♮6 and ♮7 are returned to ♭6 and ♭7, respectively, for the descent. Jazz musicians and modern composers have employed the ascending melodic minor as a unique sound in itself. For that reason, it is often called *jazz minor.* Its defining features are the minor i, the major IV and the major V. Here is a funk progression in B Melodic Minor:

MINOR FUNK B MELODIC

Track 60

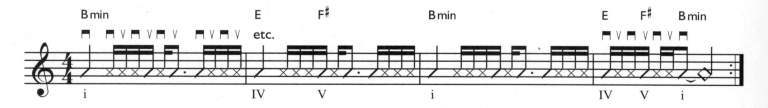

Example 55 shows a fingering for B Melodic Minor in the same position as the B Harmonic Minor fingering shown in example 53 on page 255.

55

B Melodic Minor

Here is a brief example of improvisation in the melodic minor. Try constructing other melodic minor fingerings on the neck and improvising with them!

Track
61

MINOR FUNK B MELODIC SOLO

SECRETS OF THE MASTERS

By now, you should be able to identify scale degrees you use in your improvisations. For example, you should know which note in your scale fingering is 2, or ♭6, or ♮7. Knowing this allows you to keep track of the scales in your memory, and recall them to use as you like.

If you are having trouble with this, or if you feel that you are restricted to fingerings you have learned in this book, go back and experiment with the major scale and the Mixolydian and Dorian modes.

1. Try them in every fingering you can think of, even on one string at a time.

2. Improvise on lots of different types of songs, and experiment with scales that may not even go with the harmony.

3. Become familiar with the scale degrees, and how they are raised or lowered to make new scales. Learning the fingerboard well takes time, so don't rush through the steps!

PART TWO—MODAL SOUNDS

CHAPTER 8

New Tunings and Techniques

LESSON 1: CROSS-STRING SCALES IN OPEN G

This lesson will use the open G tuning introduced on page 188. Here is a review of the open-string notes, as well as matching frets (shown in grey) on adjacent strings for tuning.

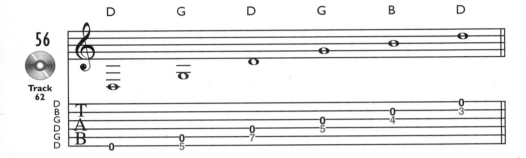

56 Track 62

CROSS-STRING SCALES

Cross-string scales are scales that place each consecutive note on a different string from the previous note. This allows consecutive scale notes to ring through each other, resulting in a harp-like "bleed" of one melody note into the next. This is a fun technique that looks good, feels cool and sounds great!

Here are the G Major and G Mixolydian scales in cross-string fingerings:

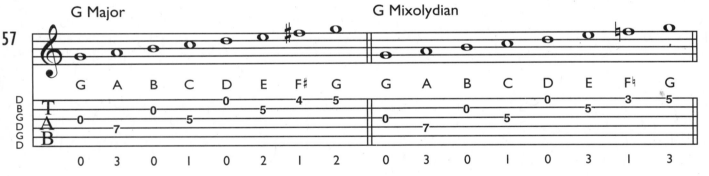

Following are some exercises to help you learn the technique. Repeat each one several times, slowly and patiently, before moving on to the next. It can take some time to get used to playing a higher note on a lower string. Try to hold your fingers down as long as possible, allowing the notes to sustain and ring into each other.

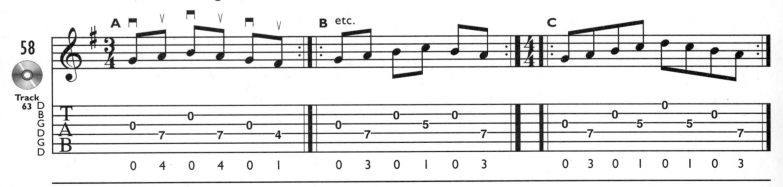

58 Track 63

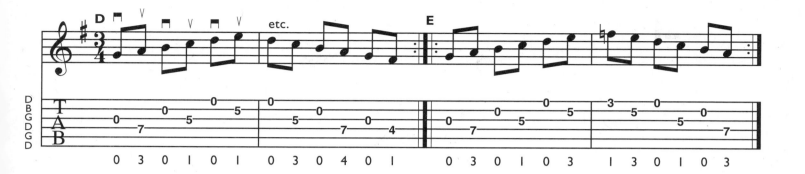

This is the famous Shaker folk melody, *Simple Gifts,* in cross-string fingering. Try to sustain each note as long as possible to get the harp effect. Bass notes are included to imply the chord changes, so use a combination of pick and right-hand fingers, or fingerpick the whole thing.

 SIMPLE GIFTS

Track 64

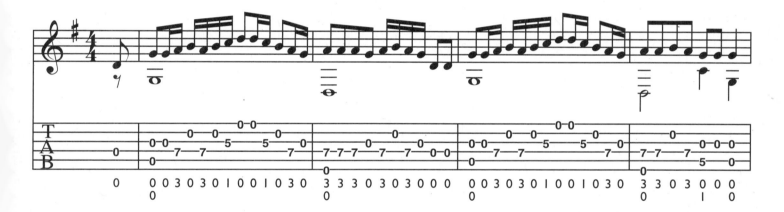

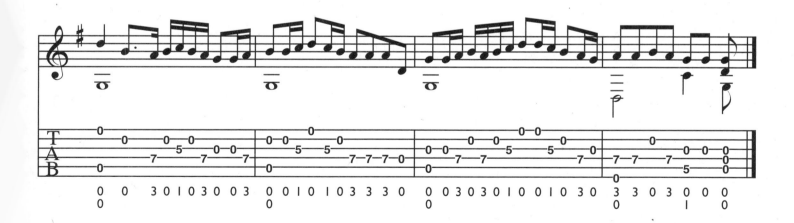

D Minor tuning is a variation on open D tuning (page 190). From Open D tuning (D-A-D-F♯-A-D), the 3rd string is tuned from F♯, which is the major 3rd of a D Major chord, to F♮, which is the minor 3rd (♭3) of a D Minor chord. This tuning also has a close cousin one whole step higher, E Minor tuning (E-B-E-G-B-E).

Here are the open-string notes and matching frets on adjacent strings for D Minor tuning:

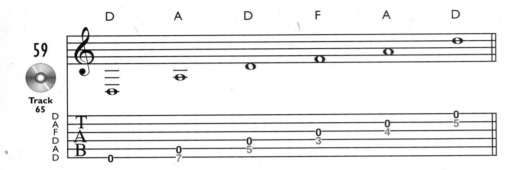

D Minor tuning is heard in the music of Delta blues and slide players, and is a popular variation on open D. Here are some of the chords available in open D:

Here are some power chords and movable voicings:

SPECIAL FEATURE: USING D MINOR TUNING TO PLAY IN D MAJOR

One of the most intriguing features of D Minor tuning is that the interval relationships between the 1st, 2nd and 3rd strings are the same as in standard tuning. In other words, the top three strings of D Minor tuning are the same as standard tuning dropped one whole step. The lower strings are the same as they were in open D or drop-D tunings.

The Delta blues guitarist, Bukka White, used D Minor tuning extensively. He often played in the key of D Major using D Minor tuning. To do this, you can use blues licks usually played on the top three strings in standard tuning (like the Delta blues licks you learned on page 146). Using exactly the same fingerings (but now in D Minor tuning), combine them with a drone chord on the lower strings.

You can also use the triad shapes you learned in standard tuning on the first three strings. They will sound a whole step lower due to the lower tuning of D Minor, but the shapes are the same.

Try *Going Back to Aberdeen* on page 261. The first measure is in the style of Bukka White's *Aberdeen Mississippi Blues*. The other measures incorporate blues licks normally played in standard tuning in the key of E (which are now in D due to the lower tuning) and some other chords and licks common in D Minor tuning.

GOING BACK TO ABERDEEN

Chapter 8—New Tunings and Techniques   **261**

By tuning the 6th string of the guitar down to C, you greatly expand the range of the instrument. C tunings bring out the "baritone" register of the guitar by emphasizing the lower pitches and harmonies. Some guitarists have tuned the 6th string to B, A or even low G, but this can result in too little string-tension, causing poor intonation and tone. To compensate, players will occasionally use a heavier gauge 6th string. C tunings work just fine without any string alterations, however, and still provide the depth of a low bass.

Open C tuning uses the notes of a C Major triad: C, E and G. Here are the open-string notes and matching frets (shown in grey) on adjacent strings for open C:

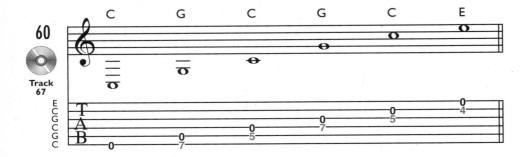

Track 67

Here are some forms for open-position chords in open C:

Here are some power chords and movable forms in open C:

SPECIAL FEATURE: TRIADS ON THE FIRST THREE STRINGS

In your mental organizer of alternate tunings, file open C next to open G and open D. They are all closely related. The interval relationships between the top three strings in open C (G,C and E), are mathematically identical to that of strings 2, 3 and 4 in open G, and strings 3, 4 and 5 in open D. (This does not mean they are tuned to the same pitches. It means the distances between the notes are the same.)

You may recall from *Intermediate Acoustic Guitar* that you could play triads and scales on strings 2, 3 and 4 in open G tuning just as you would in standard. In open D tuning, these triad shapes were moved one string lower, to strings 3, 4 and 5. In open C tuning, they are moved to strings 1, 2 and 3.

Here is a C Major scale harmonized in triads on the first three strings in Open C:

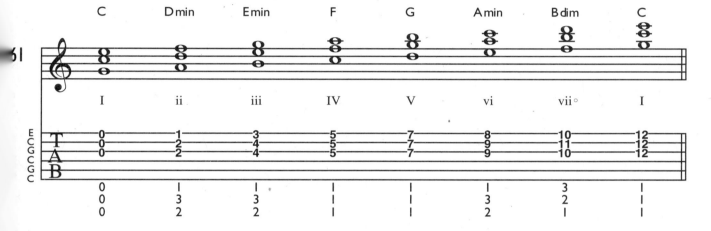

SPECIAL FEATURE: OCTAVES

In open C tuning, you have three C strings, two G strings and one E string. The C's and G's are great for playing parallel octaves (as you did in the open G tuning lesson on page 189). In addition, any lick or run you play on strings 5 and 6 can be played an octave higher at the same frets on strings 3 and 4. Here is an example:

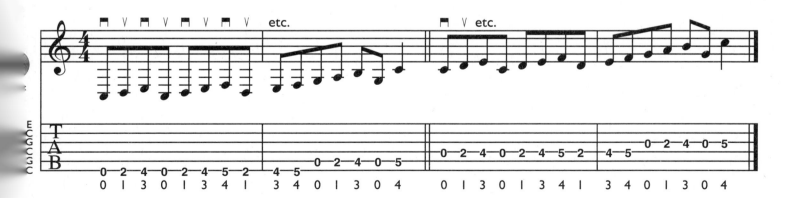

This arrangement of the traditional tune, *John Henry*, uses bluegrass-style picking to exploit the possibilities of open C tuning. The first verse of the tune uses the lower and middle octave of the tuning, starting out on strings 5 and 6 and then moving to strings 3 and 4. The second verse uses triads, pedal tones, harmonics and bluegrass licks on the first three strings.

JOHN HENRY

Track 69

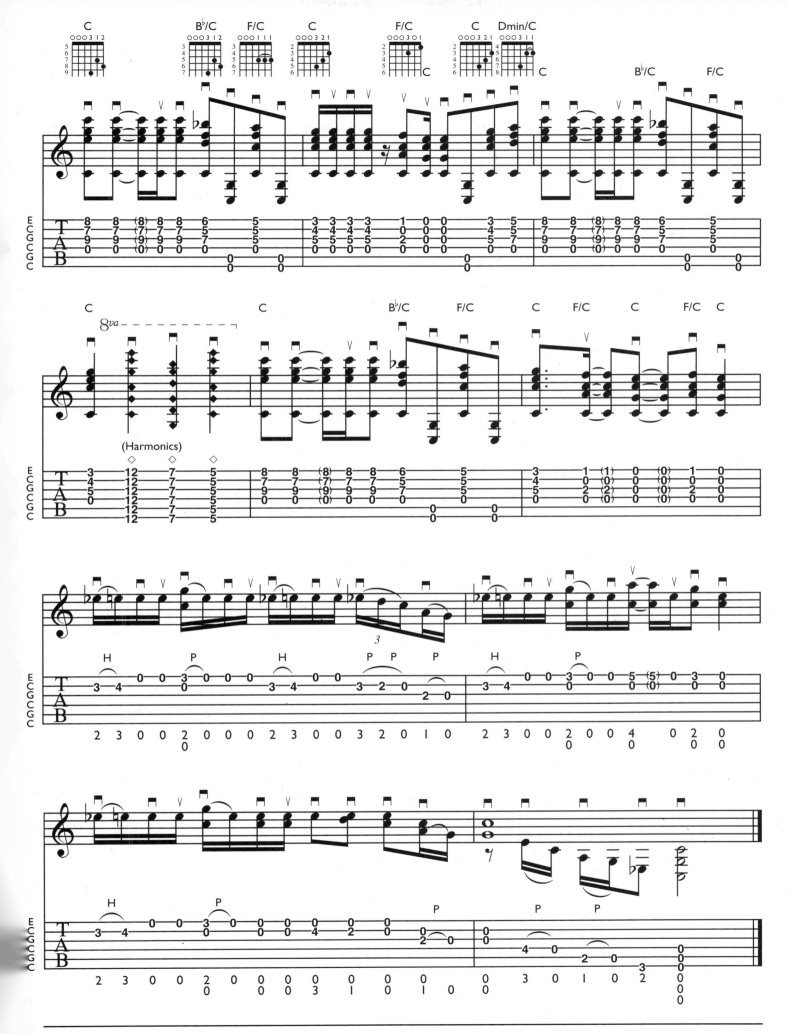

CHAPTER 9

Sus4 Tunings

Not all alternate tunings form an open major or minor chord. One of the most versatile alternate types of tuning is *suspended tuning*. In suspended tunings, the strings are tuned to a chord in which the 3rd has been replaced by the 2nd (*sus2*) or the 4th (*sus4*). Of all the suspended tunings, DADGAD is the most often used. The notes of the tuning form a Dsus4 chord.

Here are the open strings and matching notes (shown in grey) on adjacent strings for DADGAD:

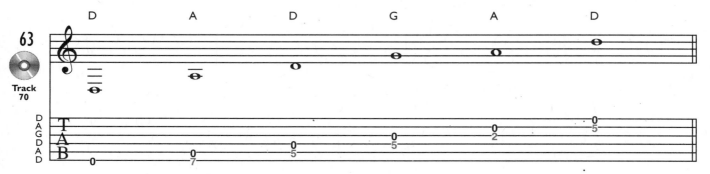

DADGAD has such a unique sound and interval structure that players such as Pierre Bensusan and some Irish guitarists have made it their standard tuning. DADGAD is a staple tuning in many other players' repertoire as well, including Michael Hedges, Leo Kottke, Joni Mitchell, John Renbourn, Richard Thompson and even Jimmy Page of Led Zeppelin fame (really quite a good acoustic guitarist).

Here are some chord voicings for open chords in DADGAD:

Here are some movable voicings:

SPECIAL FEATURE #1: THE DULCIMER EFFECT

Notice that in DADGAD, the 2nd and 3rd strings (A and G) are only a whole step apart. This makes it very easy to play a doubled unison note on two strings. This is an integral part of the music of the Appalachian Mountain dulcimer, which uses two unison melody strings played against two drone strings. With DADGAD, you get a six-string dulcimer!

Here is an example of a D Mixolydian scale played in doubled unison notes:

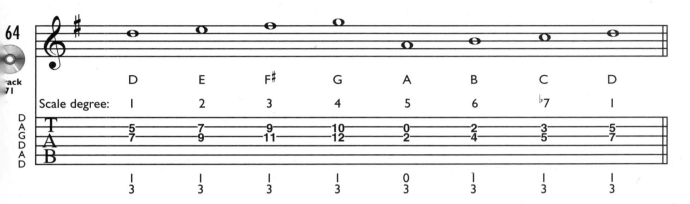

Example 65 is a D Mixolydian melody played dulcimer-style. The standard music notation shows only the melody notes. Play these on the 2nd and 3rd strings simultaneously; moving up and down the neck, while strumming all six strings, as shown in the diagrams above the music. Try creating your own melodies and improvisations using this technique. Also try other D scales, such as D Ionian, D Dorian and D Aeolian.

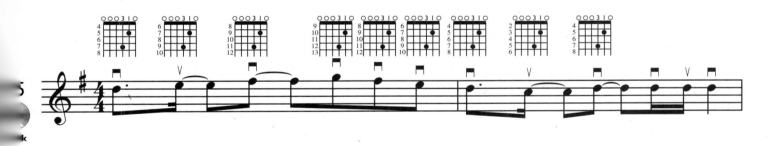

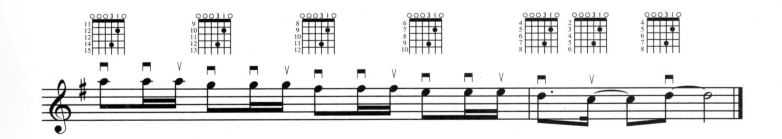

SPECIAL FEATURE #2: CROSS-STRING SCALES

Like open G, DADGAD is a great tuning for cross-string scale passages (see page 266). The whole step between the open 2nd and 3rd strings helps eliminate some of the jumps and stretches required in other tunings. The following example is an arrangement of the traditional fiddle tune, *Bonaparte's Retreat*. You will use a combination of cross-string fingerings, hammer-ons and pull-offs. Remember to keep the notes ringing into each other as long as possible!

Track 73

BONAPARTE'S RETREAT

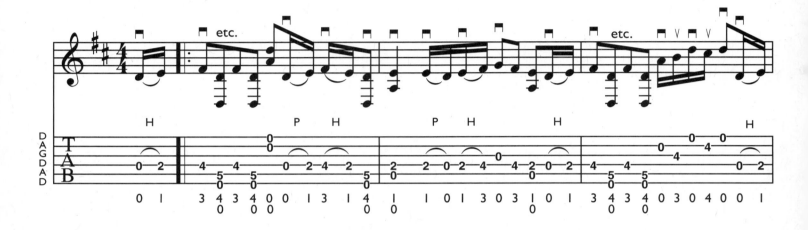

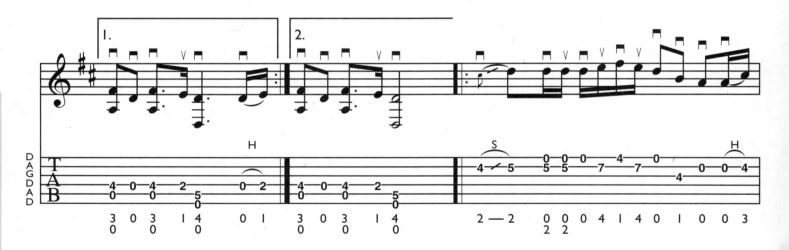

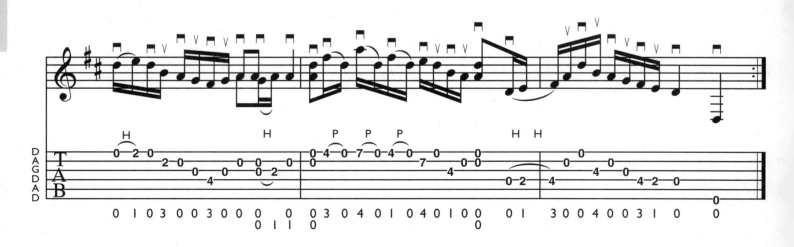

SPECIAL FEATURE #3: 3RDS, 6THS AND 10THS

DADGAD tuning is especially accommodating to melodies harmonized in 3rds, 6ths or 10ths. In *Intermediate Acoustic Guitar*, you learned that a melody can be harmonized in major and minor 3rds or 6ths going up the neck on two strings. The 10th interval is the same as a 3rd plus one octave.

By placing a melody or scale passage on the 3rd string, you can harmonize it on either the 6th, 4th or 1st strings. All three of these strings are tuned to the same note (D). This makes it especially easy to create a variety of chord voicings using the same combinations of pitches.

Here are a few scale passages harmonized in 3rds, 6ths and 10ths in DADGAD:

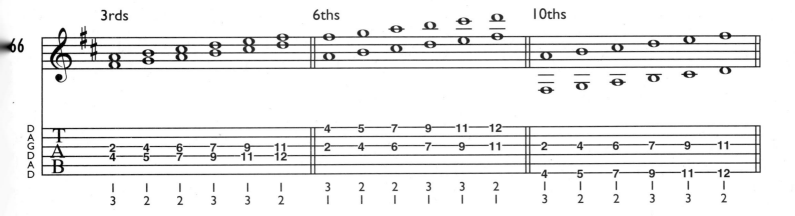

When you combine a harmonized melody with open strings, you get a unique texture that sounds like melody, chords and pedal tones all at once. This texture can be used to give a sense of melodic motion to a basic chord progression. The tensions and doublings created by the open strings add a jangling, ringing effect. Example 67 shows a progression with basic chords, then example 68 shows it again using 10ths and drone strings.

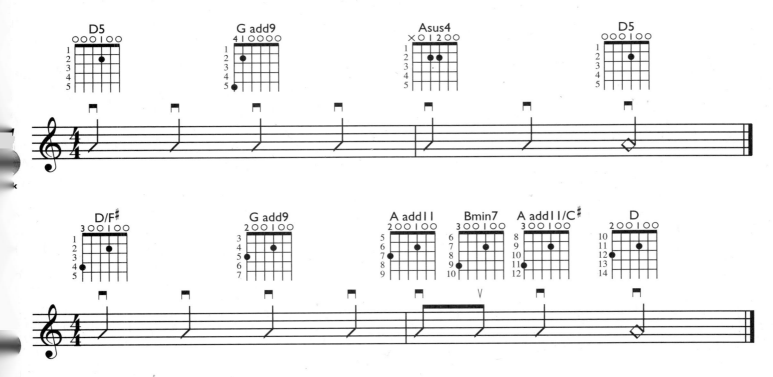

The next tune brings together the various features of DADGAD tuning discussed in this lesson:

- The opening progression (A section) is inspired by Joni Mitchell's style of combining simple, one- or two-finger chord voicings with open pedal tones.

- The B section is based on Michael Hedges' use of power chords in the bass register, plus hammer-ons and cross-string fingerings.

- The C section is inspired by Pierre Bensusan's use of 3rds and 10ths to harmonize a melody.

- The *coda* (ending section) incorporates the dulcimer effect as well as open-string harmonics at the 12th, 5th and 7th frets.

Track 76

ROAD MUSIC FOR TIME TRAVELERS

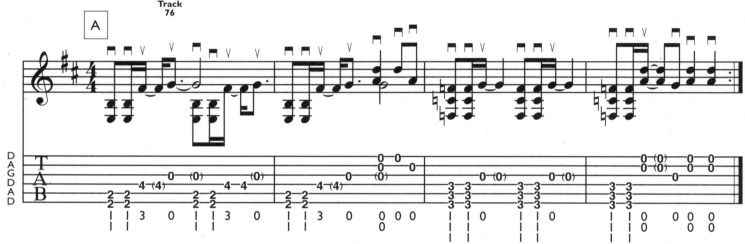

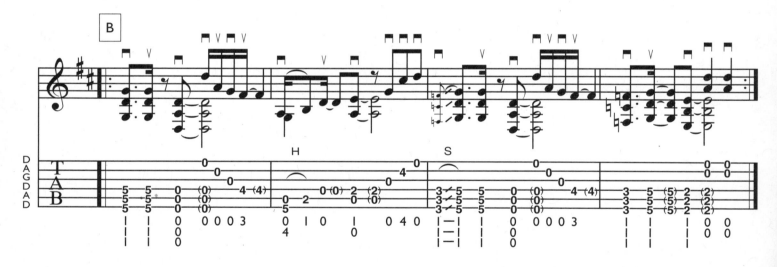

To Coda

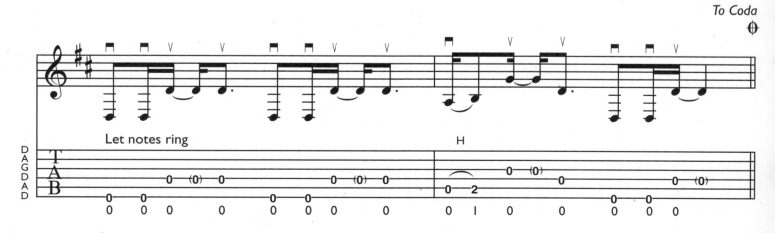

An unusual but fun tuning to try is D-G-D-G-C-D. Traditional Appalachian banjo players use this tuning. The tuning has several nicknames (and variations) such as "sawmill tuning," "modal tuning" and "mountain minor tuning." The open strings form the notes of a Gsus4 chord.

Here are the open strings and matching notes on adjacent strings for sawmill tuning:

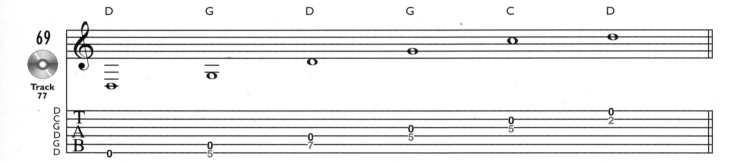

The interval structure of sawmill tuning is identical to DADGAD, but moved one string higher. In other words, any chord shapes you played in DADGAD on the 2nd, 3rd, 4th, 5th and 6th strings can now be played on the first five strings in sawmill tuning (1st, 2nd, 3rd, 4th and 5th).

Here are some open-position chords in the key of G for sawmill tuning:

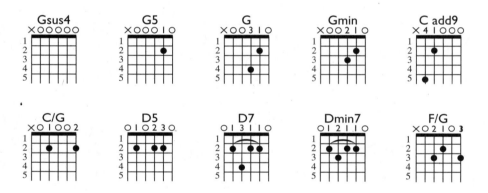

Here are some power chords and movable chords for sawmill tuning:

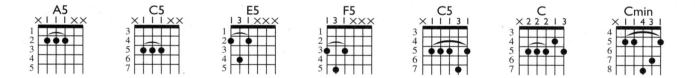

Sawmill tuning is great for playing modal fiddle tunes and banjo tunes. The term "modal" in this case refers to fiddle tunes in the Mixolydian, Dorian and Aeolian modes, all of which work very well in this tuning. The melodies can be played with just a few notes, while the open strings act as drones and chord tones.

Pretty Polly is a traditional banjo tune that is well known in old-time and bluegrass circles. Many of the fingerings and riffs in this example are the same as those used in *clawhammer* or *frailing* (a technique involving strumming down with the backs of the fingernails) banjo players. The following shuffle rhythm is built into the rhythm of the clawhammer banjo style:

You can throw in the shuffle to "keep time" whenever the melody reaches a long note. Try *Pretty Polly* slowly at first. If you keep your wrist loose and use lots of "snap" when you strum, you should be able to build up the speed to a brisk pace.

PRETTY POLLY

Track 78

Part Three—Alternate Tunings

CHAPTER 10

Radical Alternate Tunings

LESSON 1: HYBRID TUNINGS

Many players in every style of acoustic music use the tunings you have learned so far. Some players prefer to go even farther out on the limb and create their own tunings. Ani DiFranco, Michael Hedges, David Wilcox and Thurston Moore of Sonic Youth are among the most prominent users of "radical" alternate tunings.

One type of radical alternate tuning is the *hybrid tuning*. These tunings do not necessarily form open chords. Instead, they combine aspects of two or more other tunings to facilitate the goals of the player. For example, you might tune your guitar to open G, then drop the 6th string down to C so that your C chords have a very low bass note.

One fun and unusual example of a hybrid tuning is C-G-D-G-B-E. This is standard tuning with the 5th and 6th strings dropped to G and C, respectively, creating a C Major 9 chord. Richard Thompson uses this tuning (and a capo) in his song *1952 Vincent Black Lightning*.

Here are the open strings and matching frets for adjacent strings for this tuning:

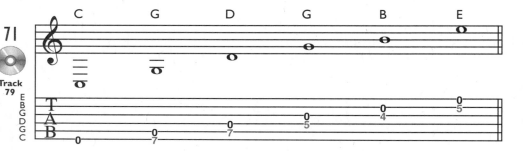

On the surface, this may look like a good tuning for the key of C, which is true. However, you can also play bluegrass and Cajun-style licks in the key of G in this tuning, using the 5th string as an open bass note. Then, when you want a C chord, you get a super-low bass note on the 6th string. Try this example in the Cajun style:

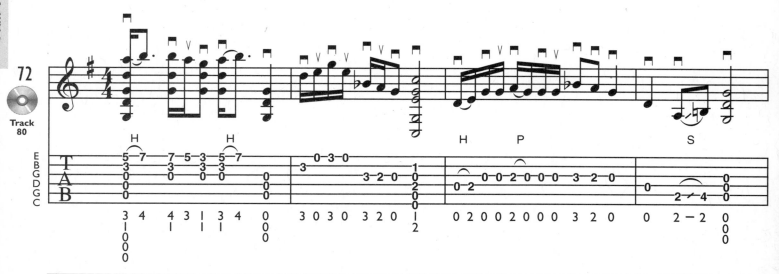

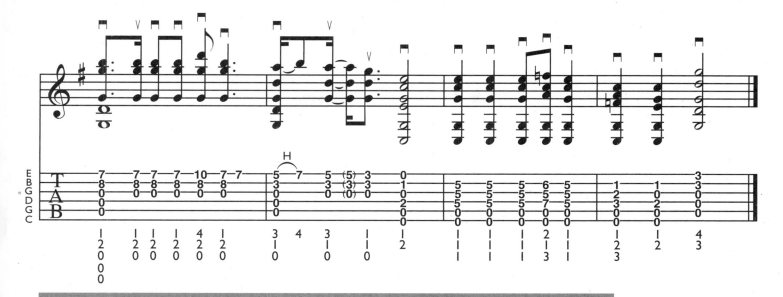

LESSON 2: UNISON TUNINGS

In *unison tunings*, two or more strings are tuned to the same pitch. This creates a droning, ringing, dulcimer-like effect. The trick is to choose unison notes that don't put too much strain on one string (by tuning it too high), or too little tension on another (by tuning it too low). Ani DiFranco and Michael Hedges have both used unison tunings extensively. In her song *Out of Range*, Ani DiFranco uses this tuning: G-G-C-G-C-D. From standard tuning, tune your 6th string up to G and your 5th string down to G. The rest is identical to the sawmill banjo tuning (page 272).

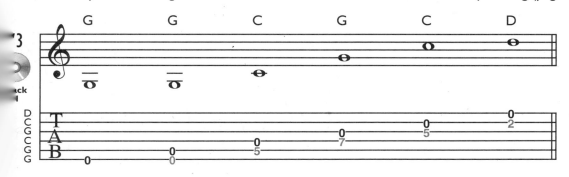

Keep Drivin' is in the style of Ani DiFranco's *Out of Range*.

KEEP DRIVIN'

Track 82

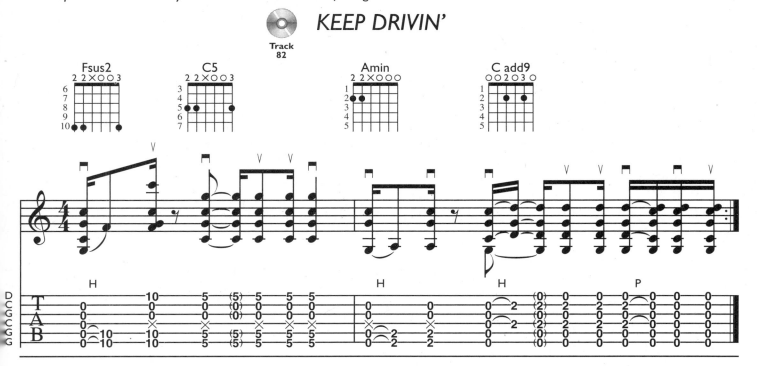

Here is another unison tuning, used by Michael Hedges in his arrangement of Bob Dylan's *All Along the Watchtower*: D-A-E-E-A-A. This tuning uses two sets of unisons. From standard tuning, tune the 6th string down to D, the 4th string up to E, the 3rd string down to E, the 2nd string down to A and the 1st string *way* down to A.

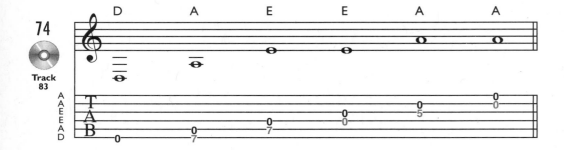

The *Rock'n'Roll Tree Elf* is in the style of some of Michael Hedges' licks in *All Along the Watchtower* and uses D-A-E-E-A-A tuning.

THE ROCK'N'ROLL TREE ELF

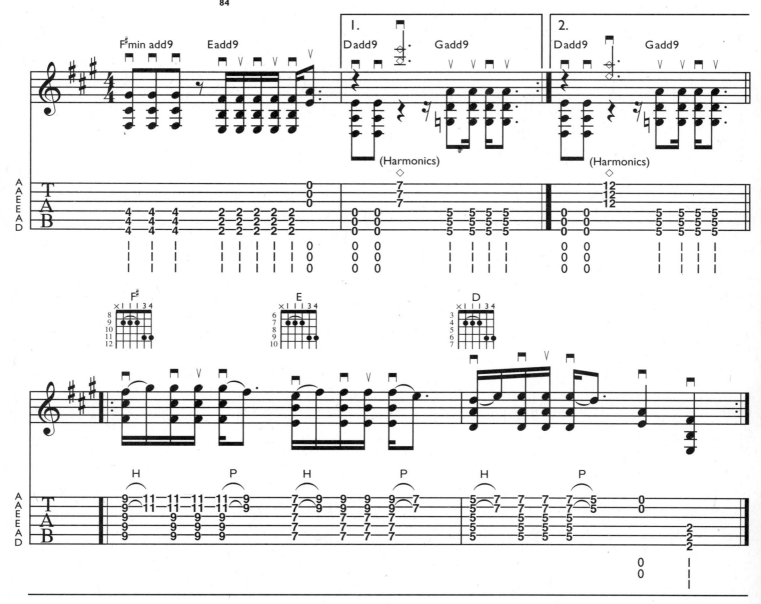

A GREAT BIG LIST OF ALTERNATE TUNINGS

Here is a list of many alternate tunings, grouped by similarities. If you are interested in alternate tunings, try as many as you can think of (and keep an extra few sets of strings handy!). A slight variation of a tuning you already know can open up a world of new possibilities for chord voicings, scale fingerings and sounds.

The strings in each tuning are listed from low to high, with common nicknames or chord equivalents shown in parentheses.

STANDARD TUNING

E-A-D-G-B-E

VARIATIONS OF STANDARD TUNING

D-A-D-G-B-E (Drop D)

D-A-D-G-B-D (Double drop D)

MAJOR TRIAD OPEN TUNINGS

D-G-D-G-B-D (Open G)

E-A-E-A-C♯-E (Open A)

D-A-D-F♯-A-D (Open D)

E-B-E-G♯-B-E (Open E)

C-G-C-G-C-E (Open C)

MINOR TRIAD OPEN TUNINGS

D-G-D-G-B♭-D (G Minor)

E-A-E-A-C-E (A Minor)

D-A-D-F-A-D (D Minor)

E-B-E-G-B-E (E Minor)

C-G-C-G-B-E♭ (C Minor)

SUS 2 TUNINGS

D-A-D-E-A-D (Dsus2)

E-B-E-F♯-B-E (Esus2)

D-G-D-G-A-D (Gsus2)

C-G-C-G-C-D (Csus2)

SUS 4 TUNINGS

D-A-D-G-A-D (Dsus4)

D-G-D-G-C-D (Sawmill Banjo Tuning – Gsus4)

7/9 CHORD TUNINGS

C-G-C-G-B-E (C Major 7)

C-G-D-G-B-C (C Major 9)

C-G-C-G-B♭-E (C7)

C-G-C-G-B♭-D (C9)

D-A-D-F♯-A-C (D7)

D-A-D-F-A- C (D Minor 7)

HYBRID TUNINGS

C-G-D-G-B-E (Also a C Major 9 chord – standard tuning with low C and G)

C-G-D-G-B-D (Open G with low C)

D-A-D-G-A- E (Dsus4 add 9)

D-A-C-G-A-D (D7sus4)

E-A-D-G-B-D (Standard with high drop D)

E-B-D-G-A-D (Like DADGAD with low E and B)

UNISON TUNINGS

A-A-D-G-A-D

G-G-C-G-C-D

D-A-E-E-A-A

C-G-D-D-A-E

CHAPTER 11

Building a Piece

IMAGINE THE POSSIBILITIES

All of the techniques and music theory you have learned are tools you can use to make your own compositions or arrangements of other pieces of music. Creating your own music is exciting and fun. There are so many possibilities that sometimes it can be difficult to know where to begin. This chapter will take you through the development of a few ideas into a full-blown musical arrangement. Each step along the way will point to the next step, but will also suggest other directions as well. To master an instrument is to understand that each new skill or technique opens a world of possibilities!

SECRETS OF THE MASTERS

You have been exposed to many textures, special effects and complicated techniques. It is tempting to cram everything you know into every piece of music you play, but sometimes a musical idea is best communicated in its simplest form. A passage that is easy to play physically may also carry a great depth of emotion.

As you go through the process of composing or arranging your music, be sure to stop along the way and evaluate whether each step is adding to the music, or covering up the beauty it may have had in a simpler form.

LESSON 1: GETTING YOUR MATERIALS TOGETHER

YOU HAVE TO START SOMEWHERE

Composition may start with a melody, a chord progression, a rhythm, a tuning or even a vague mood. The piece you will work with in this chapter will begin as a simple melody in the key of D Major. It is harmonized using the I, IV and V chords of D Major, which are D, G and A respectively. Play this passage at a moderate tempo, using a simple folk strum for the accompaniment.

OHIO NIGHTS (VERSE)

Track 85

UNITY AND CONTRAST

These are the two prime forces that drive the decisions you will make as a composer and arranger. *Unity* describes the elements of the piece that relate to each other because of what they have in common. This can mean a repeated section, a sequenced phrase—even a pedal tone. *Contrast* describes elements that add variety and differences between sections. This can mean a chord change, a key change, a change in mood or texture or any other change. Music tends to seek a balance of these prime forces.

Ohio Nights (Verse) on page 278 employs both unity and contrast in a single phrase. Notice how the ascending figure in the first measure is used to start the two following measures, while the last measure contrasts by having the melody descend.

Here is another passage of music that could go with the first melody. It preserves a similar mood, but begins with the V chord, A, to contrast from the first melody.

OHIO NIGHTS (CHORUS)

Track 86

FORM

Now that you have two ideas to work with, you can begin to think about choosing a form for the piece. Some examples of form include the *twelve-bar blues*, the *thirty-two-bar song form*, *fiddle tune form* and classical forms such as *sonatas* and *fugues* (get out your music dictionary). The two sections you have learned fit well in a "verse-chorus" relationship, as found in many contemporary rock, folk and country songs. The first melody is the verse, and the second melody is the chorus.

LESSON 2: FLESHING OUT THE FORM—ADDING CONTRASTING ELEMENTS

TAKE ME TO THE BRIDGE

Though countless folk songs have only two sections that alternate, many contemporary songs have one or more sections that contrast with the verse and chorus. A *bridge* is a section of a song that introduces new musical material after the verse and chorus have been well established through repetition.

The verse and chorus we have so far are both set in D Major. They use simple primary chords (I, IV and V). A common technique used for writing the bridge is to give the impression of a key change. This can be done through a jump to another key (*modulation*), a change of mode in the main key or a switch to the relative minor (page 248). The relative minor of D Major is B Minor (B Aeolian). It is the key of the vi chord, which is B Minor.

Here is a possible bridge for *Ohio Nights*. The melody indicated uses long tones to follow the direction of the chord progression.

OHIO NIGHTS (BRIDGE)

Track 87

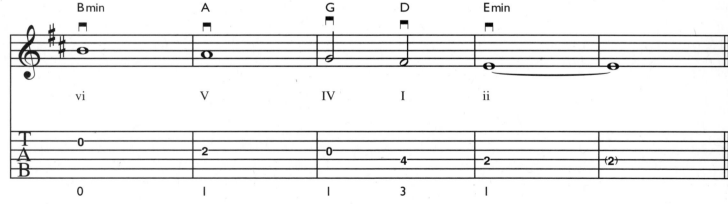

THE SEARCH FOR THE ELUSIVE HOOK

Another way to add contrast to the verse-chorus form is to add a short riff or chord passage that can be repeated between sections of the song. This can be referred to as a *vamp*, a *tag* or an *instrumental hook*. While this piece has no words, you may find yourself working with vocal material. In that case, a short instrumental figure can provide a break for the singer, as well as add a "hook" that is memorable and catches the ear of the listener.

An example of an instrumental hook would be the guitar riffs heard in songs such as the Beatles' *Day Tripper*, or the fiddle and saxophone hook in Dave Matthews Band's *Ants Marching*. Roger McGuinn of the Byrds was famous for creating instrumental hooks using his electric twelve-string guitar. These can be heard in the Byrds' arrangements of *Mr. Tambourine Man* and *Turn! Turn! Turn!*

In the case of *Ohio Nights*, a good way to make a hook might be to change modes. Since the verse and chorus are in major, and the bridge is in the relative minor, a little dash of Mixolydian might be just the thing for this piece! Here is a short figure in D Mixolydian you can use as an instrumental hook for the song.

OHIO NIGHTS (INSTRUMENTAL HOOK)

Track 88

Now that you have all the elements of a song worked out, you must decide how you want to present them on the guitar. Here are some possibilities:

1. Sing the melody (or get another player to perform it) while you play the chords.
2. Work up a fingerstyle arrangement that incorporates the melody and the harmony.
3. Experiment with other grooves, styles or tunings for the song.

Suppose you wanted to present *Ohio Nights* using an alternate tuning. Since it is set in D Major, one of the D tunings would be first choice. These include drop D, double drop D, open D and DADGAD (as well as countless variations of them all).

The ascending figure in the verse would fit very well in DADGAD, since three of the four notes can be found on open strings. Here are the first two bars shown in DADGAD tuning:

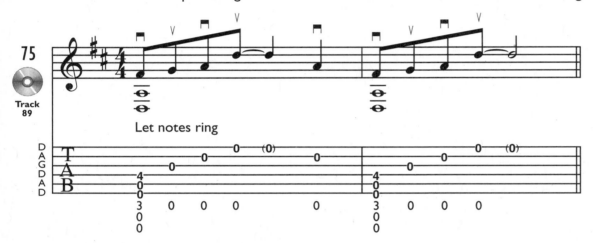

SELECTING VOICINGS AND HARMONY

Selecting chord voicings and harmonies requires careful consideration of both musical and technical factors. What chord tones do you want to emphasize? What open-string notes do you want to leave ringing? What is the easiest position on the neck to use for this passage?

The chorus of *Ohio Nights* begins with an A chord. Example 76 shows the first two bars of the chorus in two different fingerings. The first is in open position, the second uses cross-string fingerings to help the melody and the chords come out more comfortably. The second example flows better than the first, and provides a fuller sound.

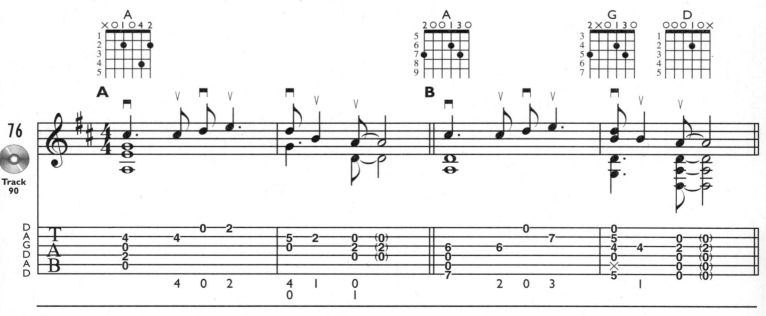

SELECTING TEXTURES

It is a good idea to try using different textures for different sections of a song. This helps them stand out as new sections, and allows you to create transitions between texture changes. Here are some examples of different textures to use in a song.

1. The verses use an open texture of melody and bass line, while the chorus uses full chords.
2. The verse and chorus are played in the lower register of the instrument while the hook is played in a higher register.
3. The verse and chorus use a gentle, sustained texture while the bridge uses a more rhythmic, percussive sound.

Ohio Nights is developing so that the verses use melodies with bass lines, while the chorus uses full chords. Both the verse and chorus use a fairly slow, gentle rhythm. The bridge is an opportunity to incorporate some new textures, such as arpeggios and slightly more percussive chords. Example 77 shows the first line of the bridge with some arpeggios and power chords. Notice the descending power chords in bar 3 that "walk" the G chord down to the D chord in bars 3 and 4.

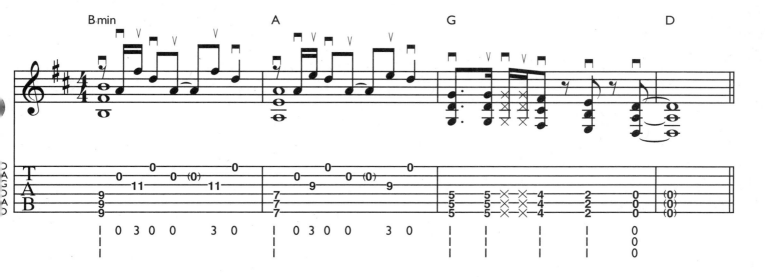

SECRETS OF THE MASTERS

As you develop your own arrangements, resist the temptation to focus on one section of the song to the exclusion of the others. You may develop a really cool arrangement for the bridge, for example, but it may no longer relate to the other sections of the song. This can create a sudden, jarring change in the music that may damage the flow of the song. (On the other hand, sometimes a sudden, jarring change can be exciting!)

SPECIAL EFFECTS

Once you get the basic pieces of your arrangement together and have made some decisions regarding setting and texture, start playing the piece in a fairly simple form. Listen for spots that might benefit from special effects such as harmonics, hammer-ons, pull-offs and scale passages. Remember that not every space in the music cries out to be filled! But sometimes special effects can provide just the right amount of excitement and flavor, especially in transitions from one idea to the next.

Below are a couple of examples from *Ohio Nights* where effects might work well. The first example is the last two bars of the verse, where you could add a short melodic figure in the bass. The second example is the end of the bridge, where a slap harmonic would sound great with the E Minor chord.

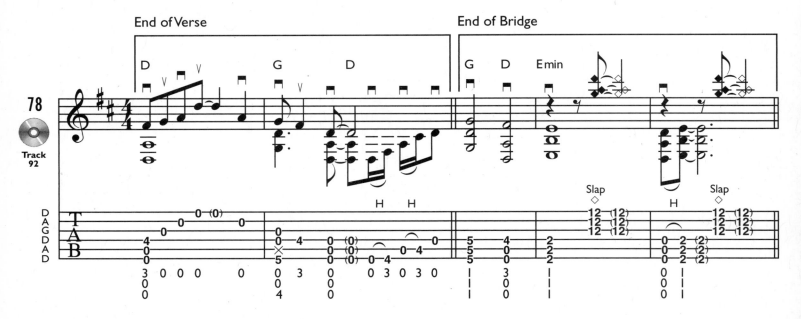

FINAL ASSEMBLY: INTRO AND CODA

The final step in polishing up an arrangement is to decide if you want to add any introductory material (an *intro*) or extra material at the end (a *coda*). These are not always necessary, but they can be a fun way to set the mood of a piece, or to provide some space for improvisation without interrupting the flow of the song.

On the following pages is a complete arrangement of *Ohio Nights* in DADGAD tuning. All the elements you have examined are present in this arrangement, including melody, harmony, form, texture and special effects. Here is a brief outline of the final form of the song:

1. Intro
2. Verse 1
3. Chorus 1
4. Instrumental hook
5. Verse 2 (incorporating variations of rhythm and special effects)
6. Chorus 2 (also incorporating some special effects)
7. Bridge
8. Repeat Instrumental hook
9. Repeat Verse 2
10. Repeat Chorus 2
11. Coda

> This piece has D.S. 𝄋 al Coda ⊕ (see page 287). This means to go back to the 𝄋 sign and play up to the ⊕ (to Coda). Then skip to the coda section at the end to finish the tune.

Congratulations on having completed *The Complete Acoustic Guitar Method*. Your education is just beginning. Seek information and inspiration wherever you can. Becoming the best player you can be is a life-long process. Happy learning!

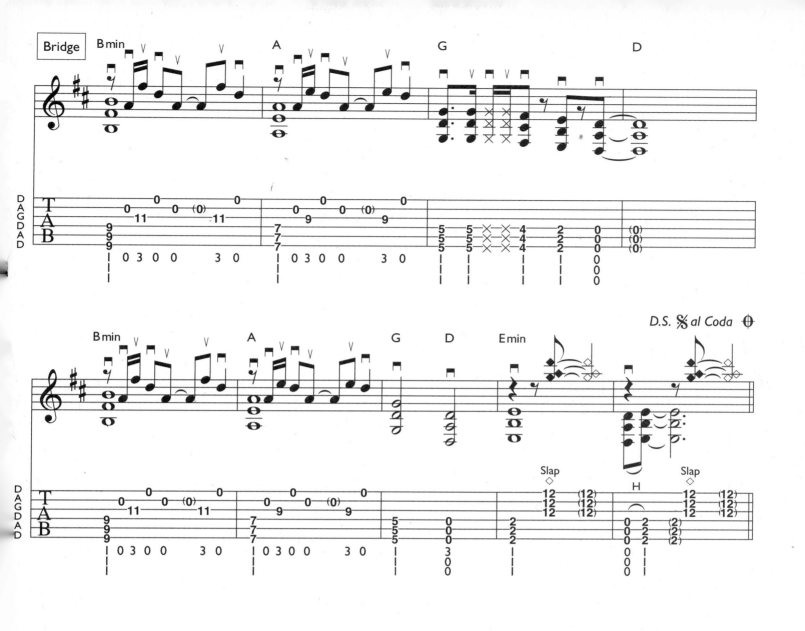

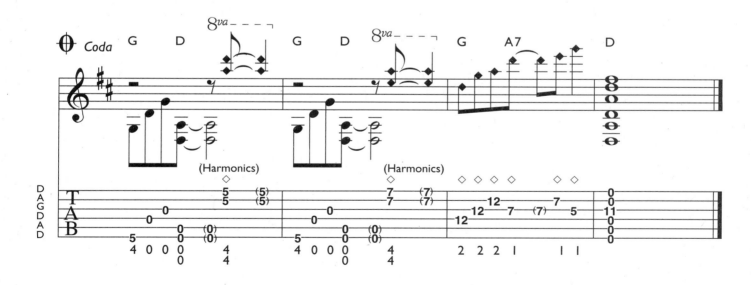